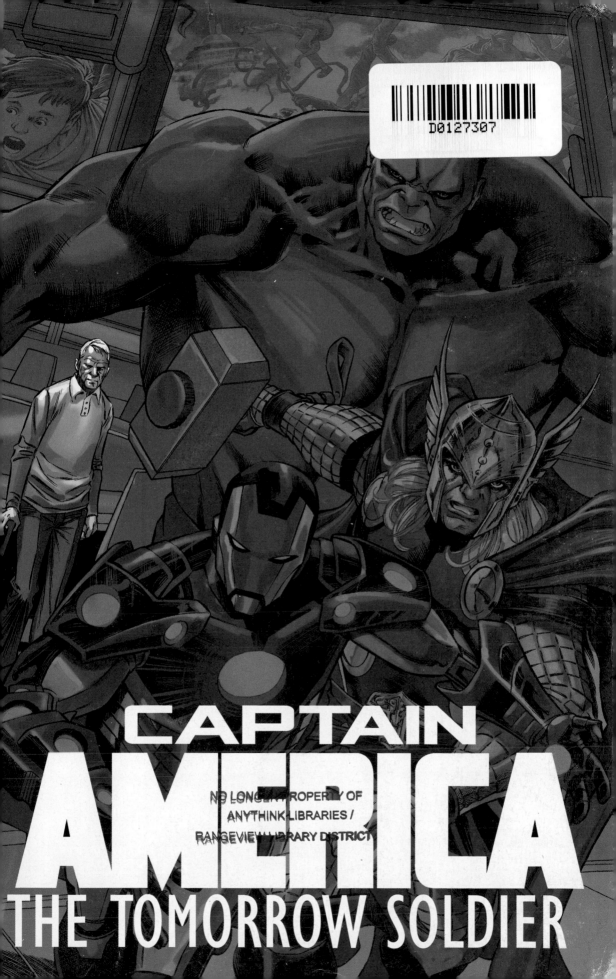

# CAPTAIN AMERICA

## THE TOMORROW SOLDIER

# THE TOMORROW SOLDIER

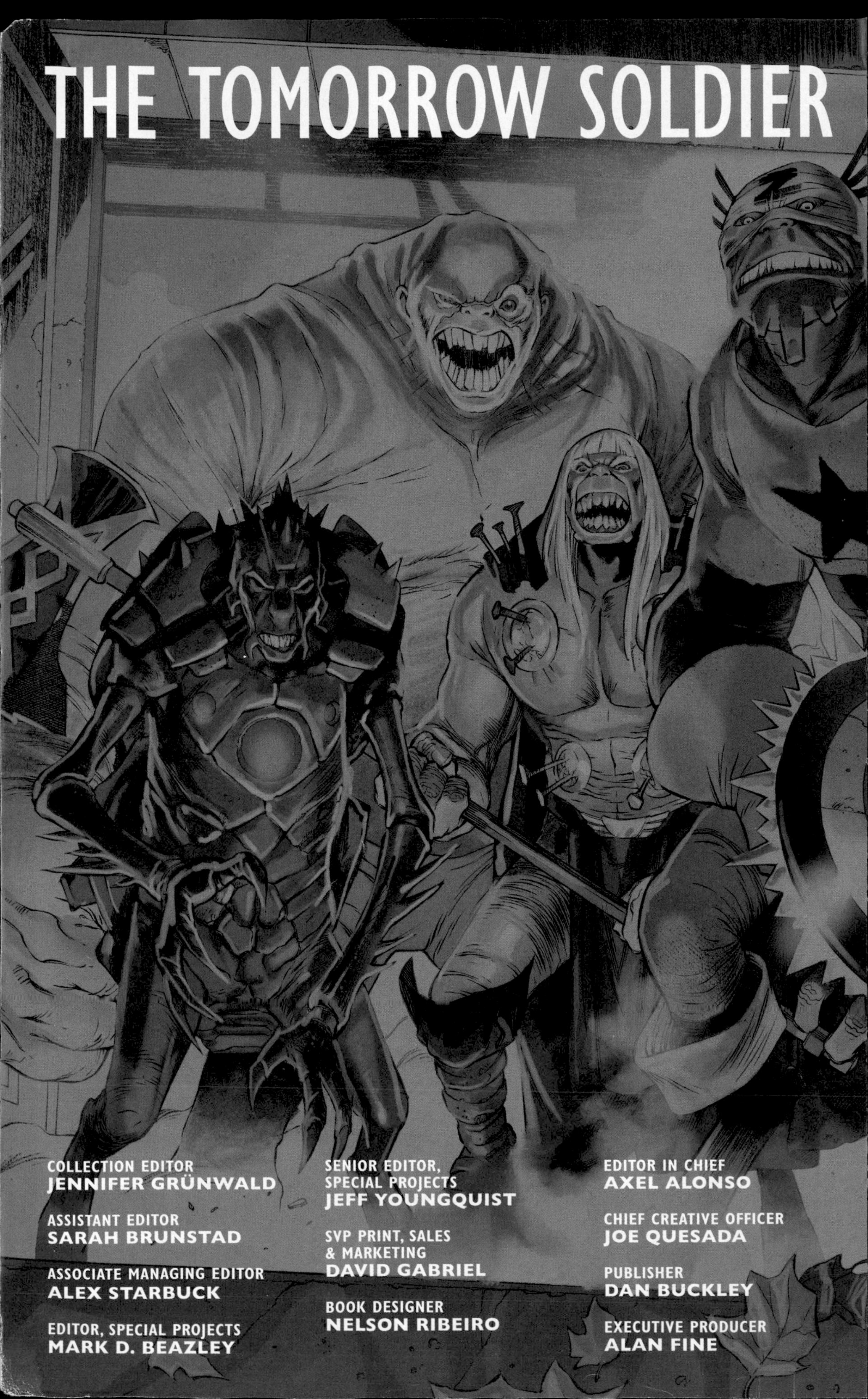


COLLECTION EDITOR
**JENNIFER GRÜNWALD**

ASSISTANT EDITOR
**SARAH BRUNSTAD**

ASSOCIATE MANAGING EDITOR
**ALEX STARBUCK**

EDITOR, SPECIAL PROJECTS
**MARK D. BEAZLEY**

SENIOR EDITOR, SPECIAL PROJECTS
**JEFF YOUNGQUIST**

SVP PRINT, SALES & MARKETING
**DAVID GABRIEL**

BOOK DESIGNER
**NELSON RIBEIRO**

EDITOR IN CHIEF
**AXEL ALONSO**

CHIEF CREATIVE OFFICER
**JOE QUESADA**

PUBLISHER
**DAN BUCKLEY**

EXECUTIVE PRODUCER
**ALAN FINE**

WRITER
# RICK REMENDER

PENCILERS
# CARLOS PACHECO
WITH **PAUL RENAUD** (#24)
& **STUART IMMONEN** (#25)

INKERS
# MARIANO TAIBO
WITH **PAUL RENAUD** (#24)
& **WADE VON GRAWBADGER** (#25)

COLORISTS
# DEAN WHITE
WITH **LEE LOUGHRIDGE** (#22),
**SONIA OBACK** (#24),
**VERONICA GANDINI** (#25)
& **MARTE GRACIA** (#25)

LETTERER
# VC'S JOE CARAMAGNA

COVER ART
# CARLOS PACHECO & DEAN WHITE (#22-24)
AND **STUART IMMONEN,**
**WADE VON GRAWBADGER**
& **MARTE GRACIA** (#25)

ASSISTANT EDITOR
# JAKE THOMAS

EDITOR
# TOM BREVOORT

CAPTAIN AMERICA CREATED BY **JOE SIMON** & **JACK KIRBY**

CAPTAIN AMERICA VOL. 5: THE TOMORROW SOLDIER. Contains material originally published in magazine form as CAPTAIN AMERICA #22-25 and MARVEL 75TH ANNIVERSARY CELEBRATION #1. First printing 2015. ISBN# 978-0-7851-8956-5. Published by MARVEL WORLDWIDE, INC., a subsidiary of MARVEL ENTERTAINMENT, LLC. OFFICE OF PUBLICATION: 135 West 50th Street, New York, NY 10020. Copyright © 2015 MARVEL No similarity between any of the names, characters, persons, and/or institutions in this magazine with those of any living or dead person or institution is intended, and any such similarity which may exist is purely coincidental. **Printed in the U.S.A.** ALAN FINE, President, Marvel Entertainment; DAN BUCKLEY, President, TV, Publishing and Brand Management; JOE QUESADA, Chief Creative Officer; TOM BREVOORT, SVP of Publishing; DAVID BOGART, SVP of Operations & Procurement, Publishing; C.B. CEBULSKI, VP of International Development & Brand Management; DAVID GABRIEL, SVP Print, Sales & Marketing; JIM O'KEEFE, VP of Operations & Logistics; DAN CARR, Executive Director of Publishing Technology; SUSAN CRESPI, Editorial Operations Manager; ALEX MORALES, Publishing Operations Manager; STAN LEE, Chairman Emeritus. For information regarding advertising in Marvel Comics or on Marvel.com, please contact Jonathan Rheingold, VP of Custom Solutions & Ad Sales, at jrheingold@marvel.com. For Marvel subscription inquiries, please call 800-217-9158. **Manufactured between 6/26/2015 and 8/3/2015** by R.R. DONNELLEY, INC., SALEM, VA, USA.
10 9 8 7 6 5 4 3 2 1

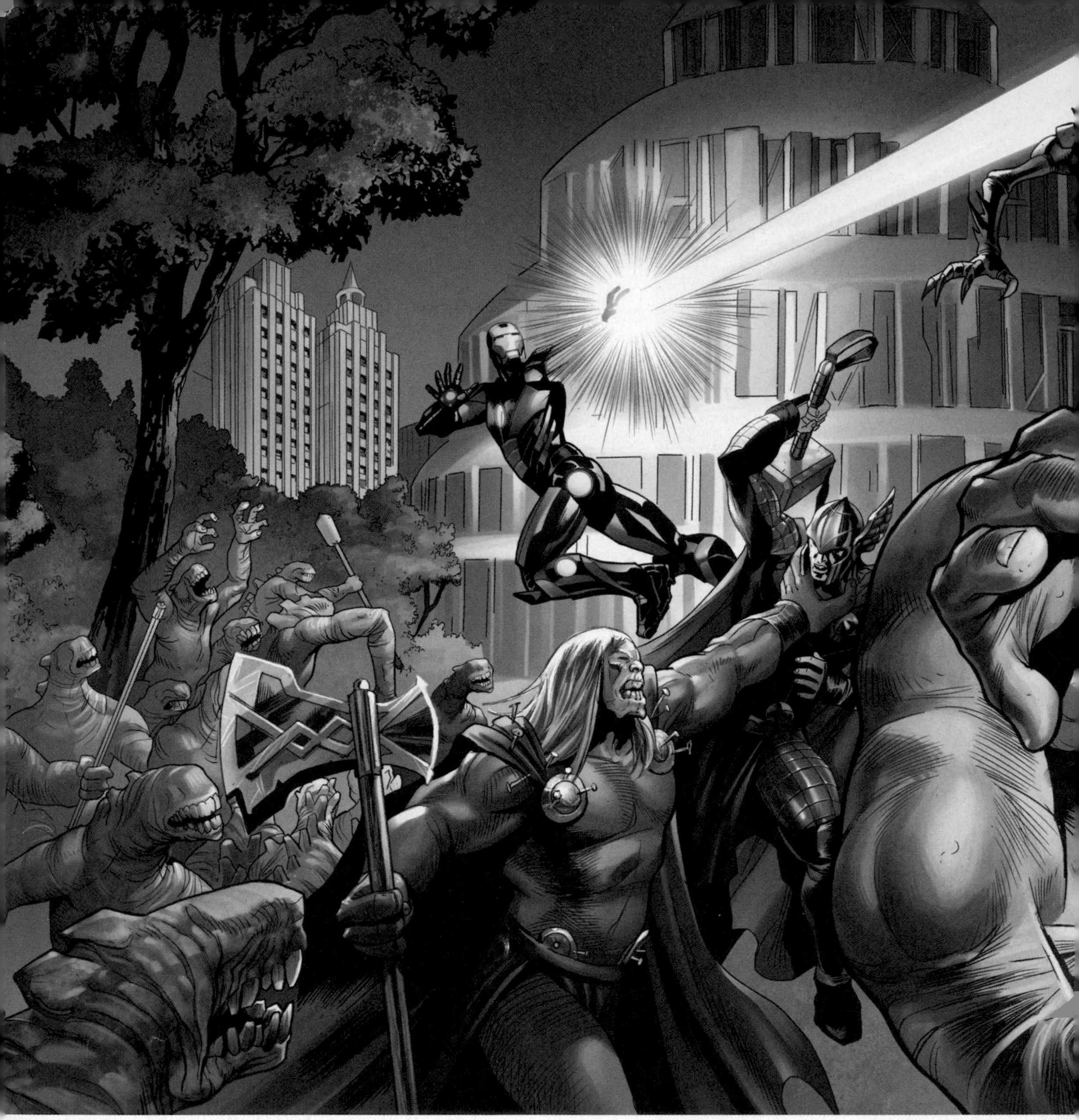

During WWII a secret military experiment turned scrawny Steve Rogers into America's first super-soldier, Captain America. Near the end of the war Rogers was presumed dead in an explosion over the English Channel.

Decades later Captain America was found frozen in ice and revived. Steve Rogers awakened to a world he never imagined, a man out of time. He again took up the mantle of Captain America, defending the U.S. and the world from threats of all kinds.

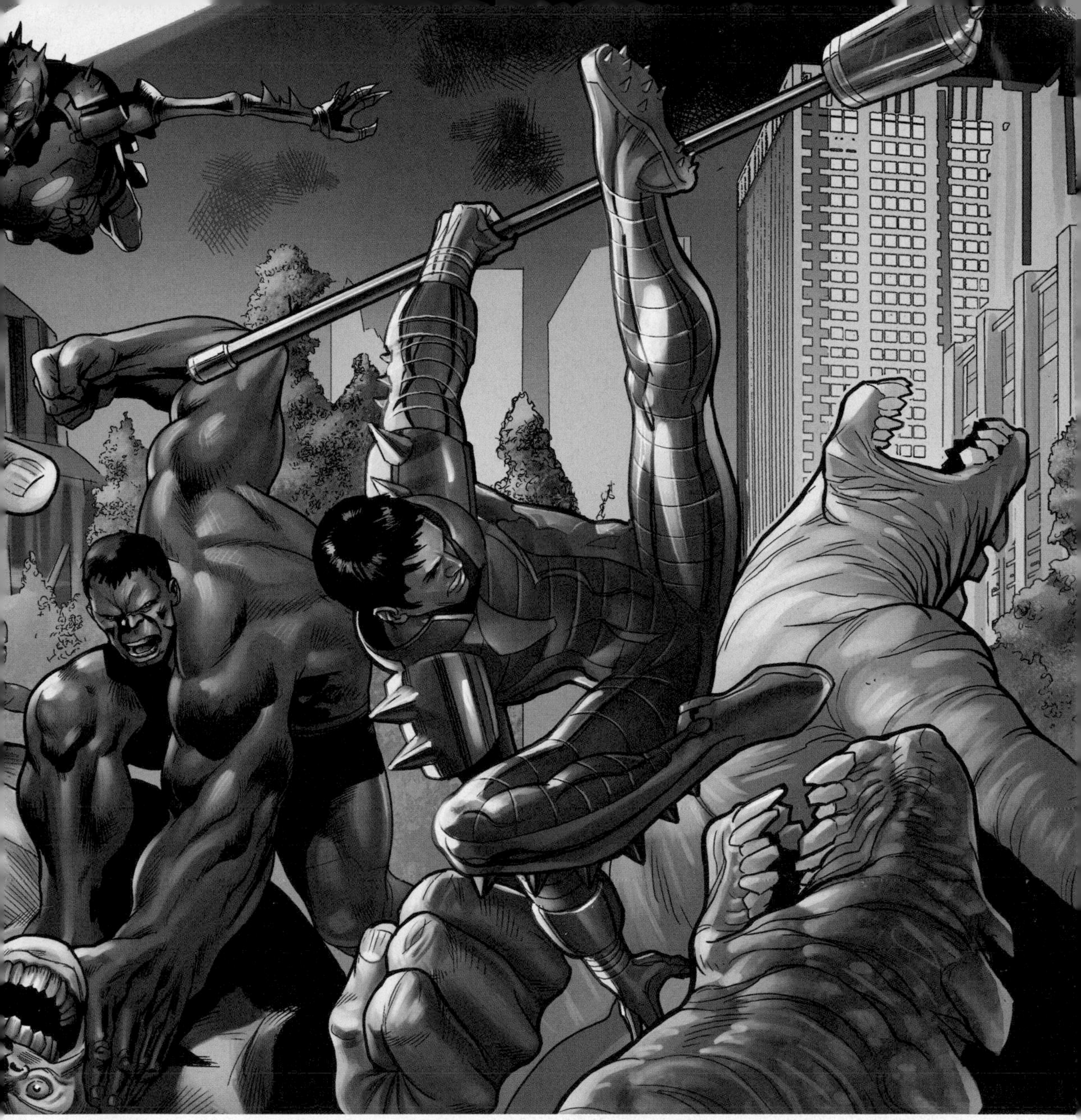

**PREVIOUSLY...**

Captain America was kidnapped by Arnim Zola and brought to Dimension Z, where Zola ruled as a harsh dictator. Zola wanted to use the Super-Soldier Serum in Cap's genetic code to make his own race of super-beings, but Cap broke free before he could finish his experiments, taking Zola's infant child Ian with him. After spending ten years in Dimension Z raising Ian as his own, Cap defeated Zola and escaped with Jet Black, Zola's daughter, but lost both lost both his lover Sharon Carter and Ian.

Upon his return Cap, with the help of Sam WIlson, a.k.a. the Falcon, worked to train Jet Black to be a hero. In a battle with the Iron Nail, a former S.H.I.E.L.D. agent who attempted to overthrow the powerhouses of the West, the Super-Soldier Serum within Captain America was neutralized, causing him to age rapidly into an old man!

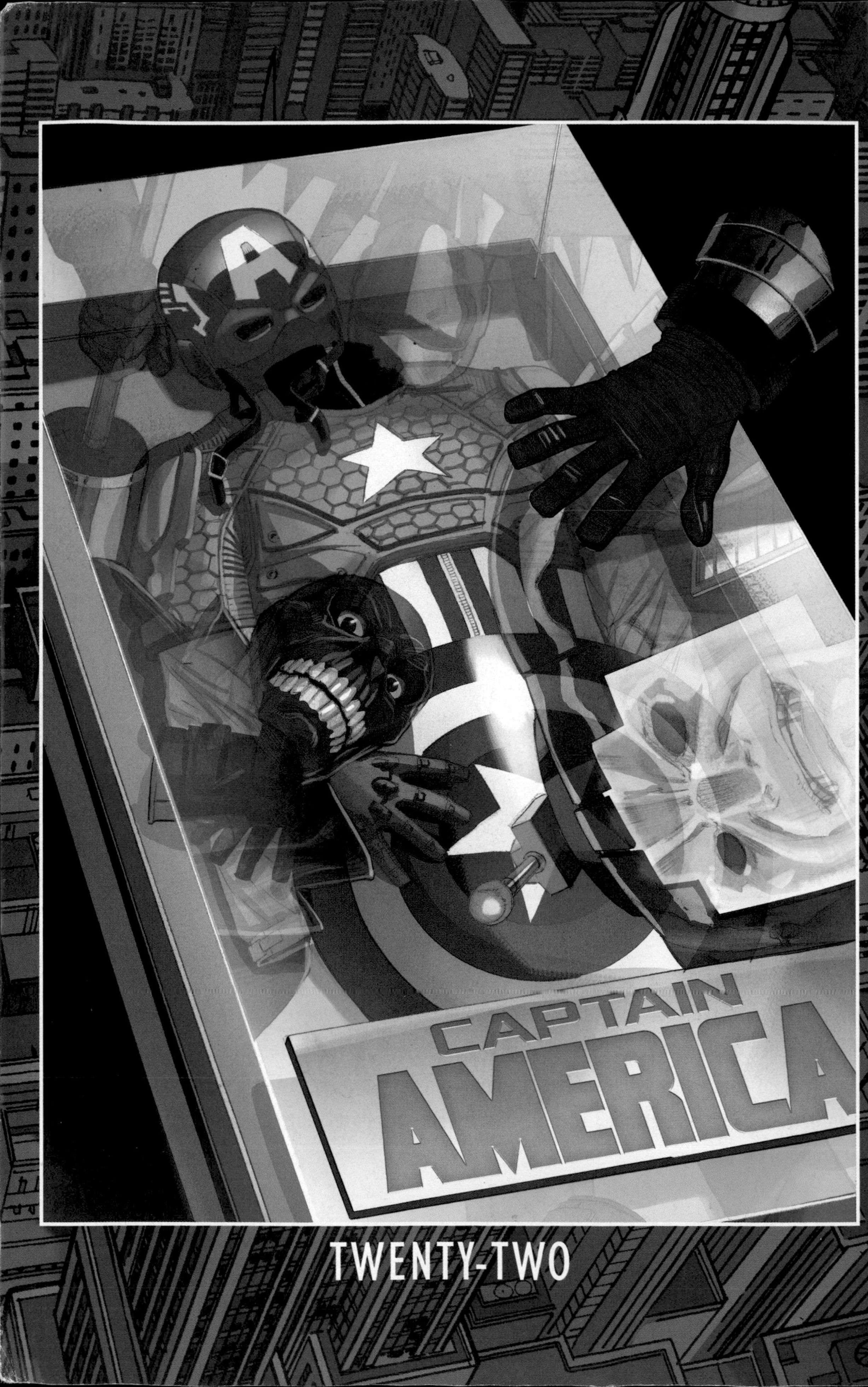
CAPTAIN
AMERICA

# TWENTY-TWO

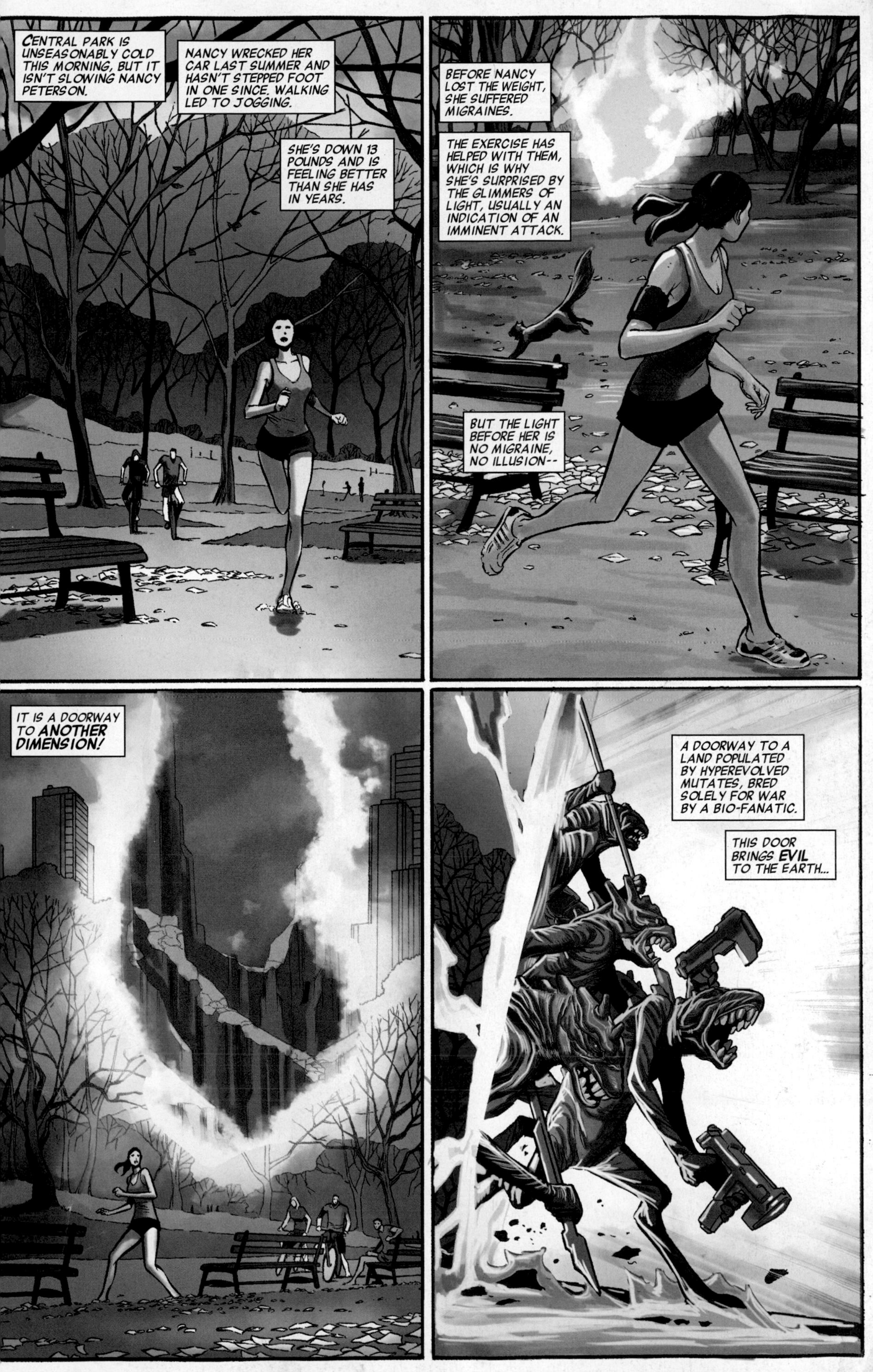
CENTRAL PARK IS UNSEASONABLY COLD THIS MORNING, BUT IT ISN'T SLOWING NANCY PETERSON.
NANCY WRECKED HER CAR LAST SUMMER AND HASN'T STEPPED FOOT IN ONE SINCE. WALKING LED TO JOGGING.
SHE'S DOWN 13 POUNDS AND IS FEELING BETTER THAN SHE HAS IN YEARS.
BEFORE NANCY LOST THE WEIGHT, SHE SUFFERED MIGRAINES.
THE EXERCISE HAS HELPED WITH THEM, WHICH IS WHY SHE'S SURPRISED BY THE GLIMMERS OF LIGHT, USUALLY AN INDICATION OF AN IMMINENT ATTACK.
BUT THE LIGHT BEFORE HER IS NO MIGRAINE, NO ILLUSION--
IT IS A DOORWAY TO ANOTHER DIMENSION!
A DOORWAY TO A LAND POPULATED BY HYPEREVOLVED MUTATES, BRED SOLELY FOR WAR BY A BIO-FANATIC.
THIS DOOR BRINGS EVIL TO THE EARTH...

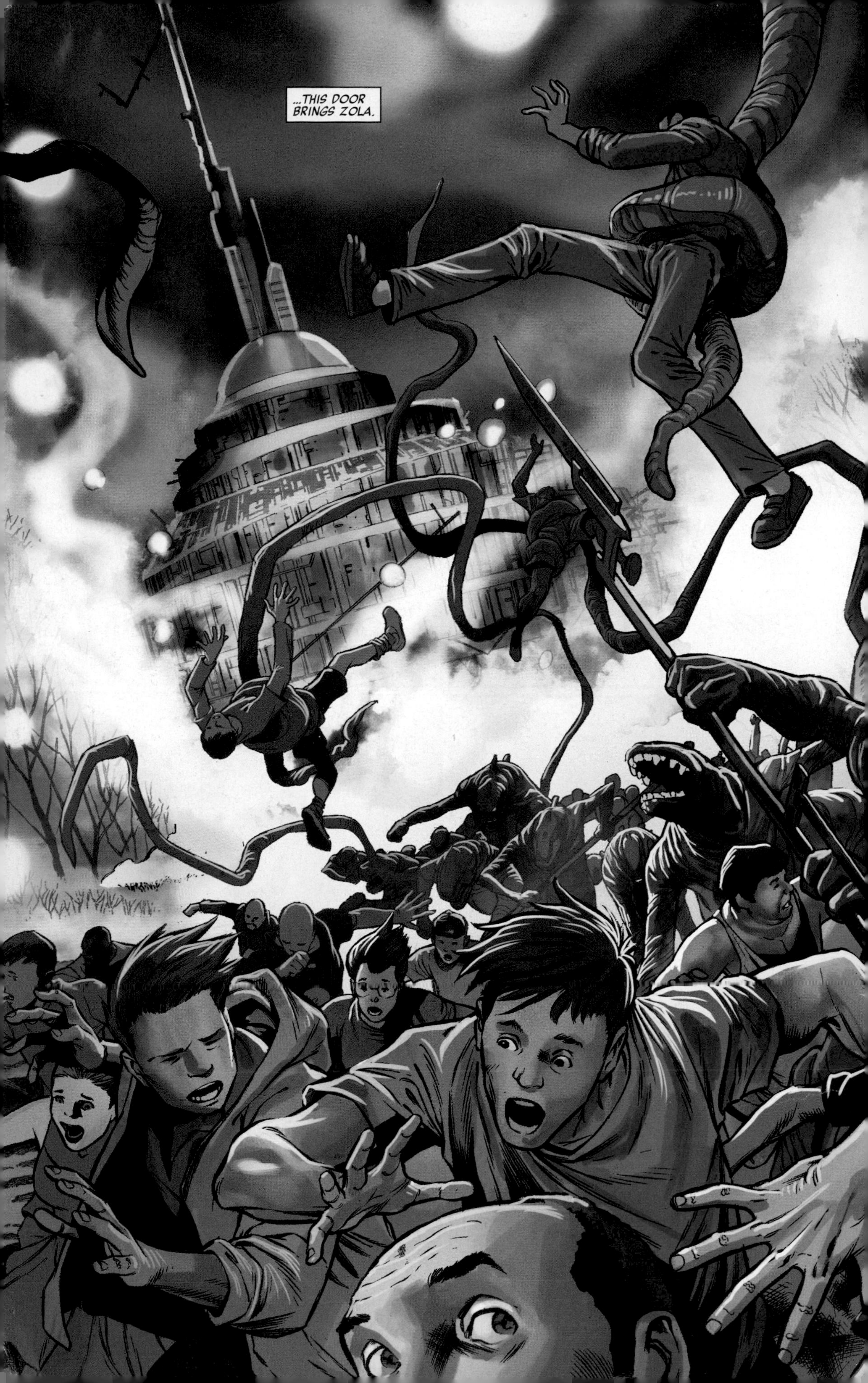
...THIS DOOR BRINGS ZOLA.

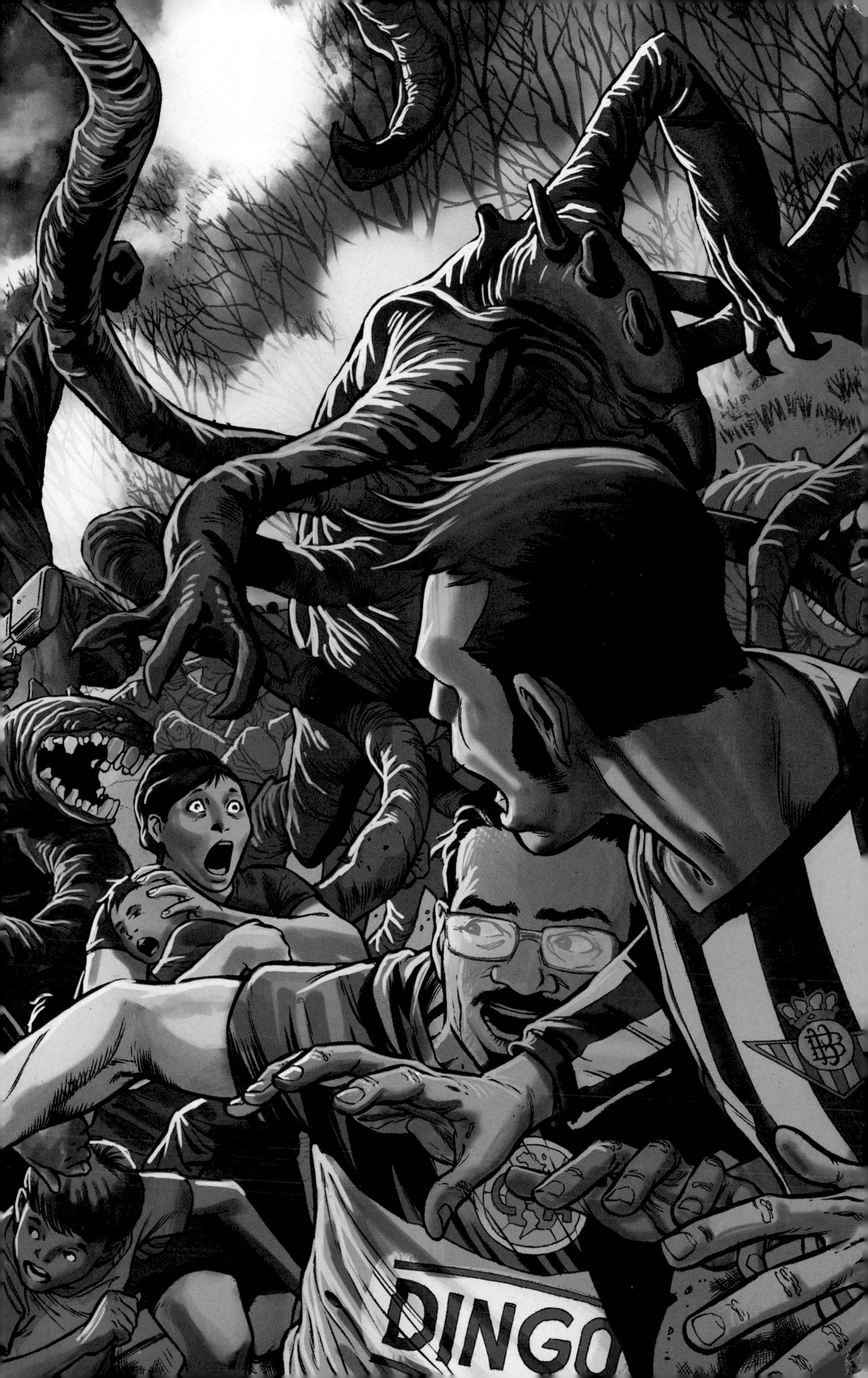
DINGO

A LONE FIGURE EMERGES, SURVEYING THIS ALIEN LANDSCAPE.

A COMPUTER WHIRRS FOR A MOMENT BEFORE INDICATING THE LOCATION OF HIS TARGET.

HE HAS BEEN WAITING YEARS FOR THIS MOMENT.

TRAINED ALL HIS LIFE FOR IT.

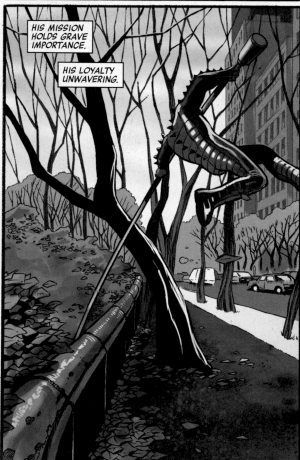

HIS MISSION HOLDS GRAVE IMPORTANCE.

HIS LOYALTY UNWAVERING.

HE WILL NOT FAIL.

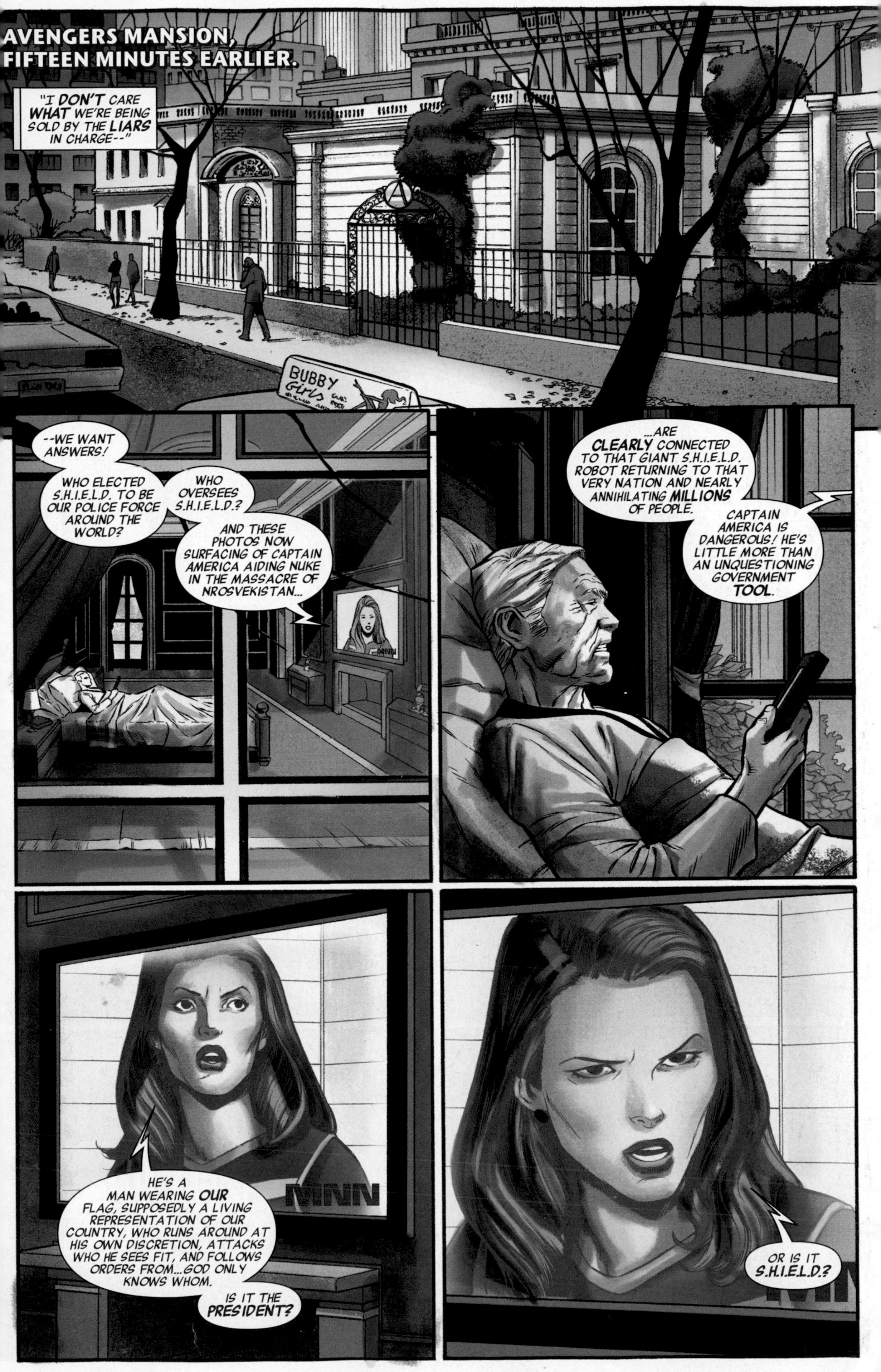
AVENGERS MANSION, FIFTEEN MINUTES EARLIER.
"I DON'T CARE WHAT WE'RE BEING SOLD BY THE LIARS IN CHARGE--"
BUBBY Girls
--WE WANT ANSWERS!
WHO ELECTED S.H.I.E.L.D. TO BE OUR POLICE FORCE AROUND THE WORLD?
WHO OVERSEES S.H.I.E.L.D.?
AND THESE PHOTOS NOW SURFACING OF CAPTAIN AMERICA AIDING NUKE IN THE MASSACRE OF NROSVEKISTAN...
...ARE CLEARLY CONNECTED TO THAT GIANT S.H.I.E.L.D. ROBOT RETURNING TO THAT VERY NATION AND NEARLY ANNIHILATING MILLIONS OF PEOPLE.
CAPTAIN AMERICA IS DANGEROUS! HE'S LITTLE MORE THAN AN UNQUESTIONING GOVERNMENT TOOL.
MNN
HE'S A MAN WEARING OUR FLAG, SUPPOSEDLY A LIVING REPRESENTATION OF OUR COUNTRY, WHO RUNS AROUND AT HIS OWN DISCRETION, ATTACKS WHO HE SEES FIT, AND FOLLOWS ORDERS FROM...GOD ONLY KNOWS WHOM.
IS IT THE PRESIDENT?
OR IS IT S.H.I.E.L.D.?

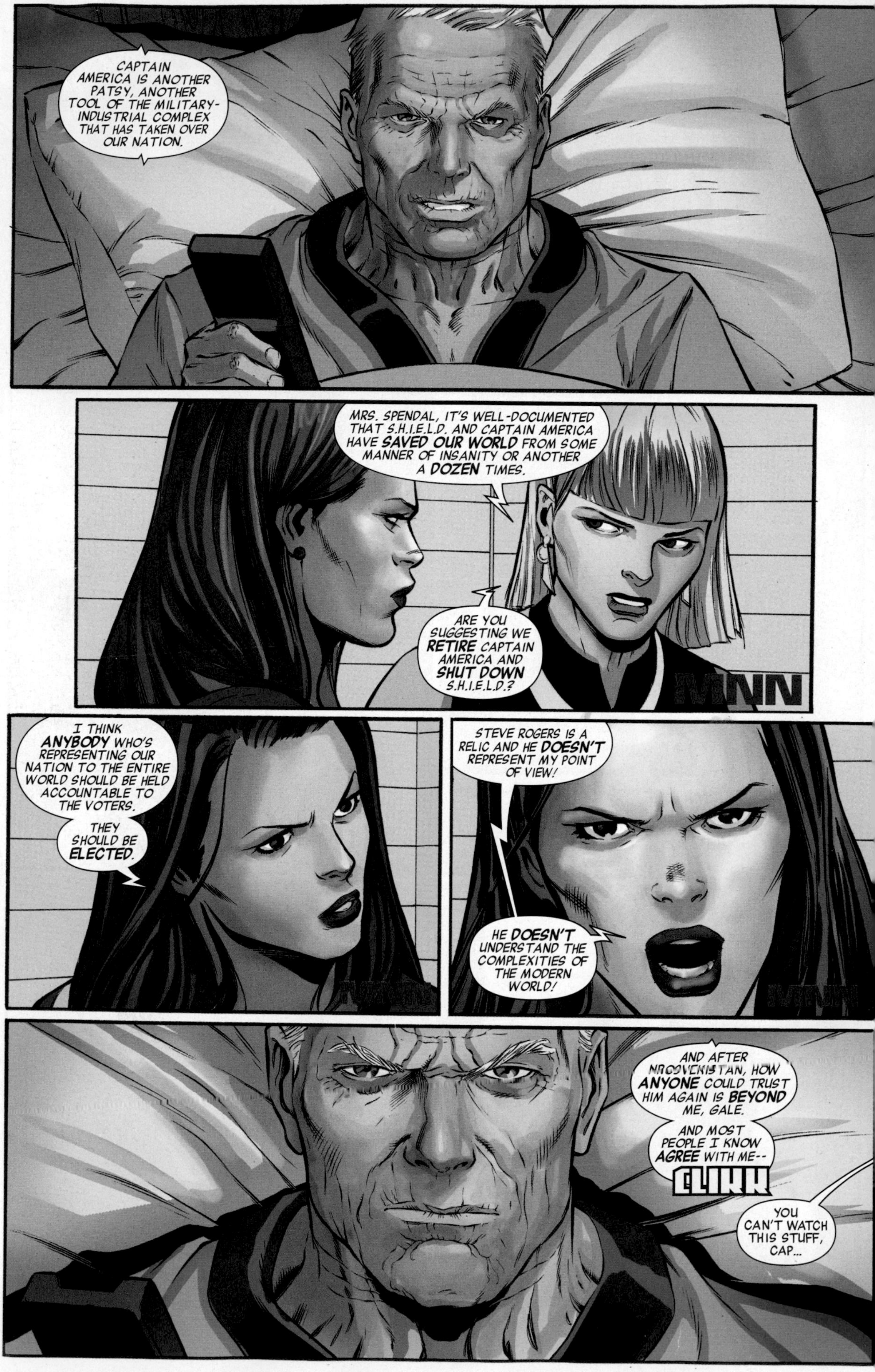
CAPTAIN AMERICA IS ANOTHER PATSY, ANOTHER TOOL OF THE MILITARY-INDUSTRIAL COMPLEX THAT HAS TAKEN OVER OUR NATION.
MRS. SPENDAL, IT'S WELL-DOCUMENTED THAT S.H.I.E.L.D. AND CAPTAIN AMERICA HAVE SAVED OUR WORLD FROM SOME MANNER OF INSANITY OR ANOTHER A DOZEN TIMES.
ARE YOU SUGGESTING WE RETIRE CAPTAIN AMERICA AND SHUT DOWN S.H.I.E.L.D.?
I THINK ANYBODY WHO'S REPRESENTING OUR NATION TO THE ENTIRE WORLD SHOULD BE HELD ACCOUNTABLE TO THE VOTERS.
THEY SHOULD BE ELECTED.
STEVE ROGERS IS A RELIC AND HE DOESN'T REPRESENT MY POINT OF VIEW!
HE DOESN'T UNDERSTAND THE COMPLEXITIES OF THE MODERN WORLD!
AND AFTER NROSVEKISTAN, HOW ANYONE COULD TRUST HIM AGAIN IS BEYOND ME, GALE.
AND MOST PEOPLE I KNOW AGREE WITH ME--
CLIKK
YOU CAN'T WATCH THIS STUFF, CAP...

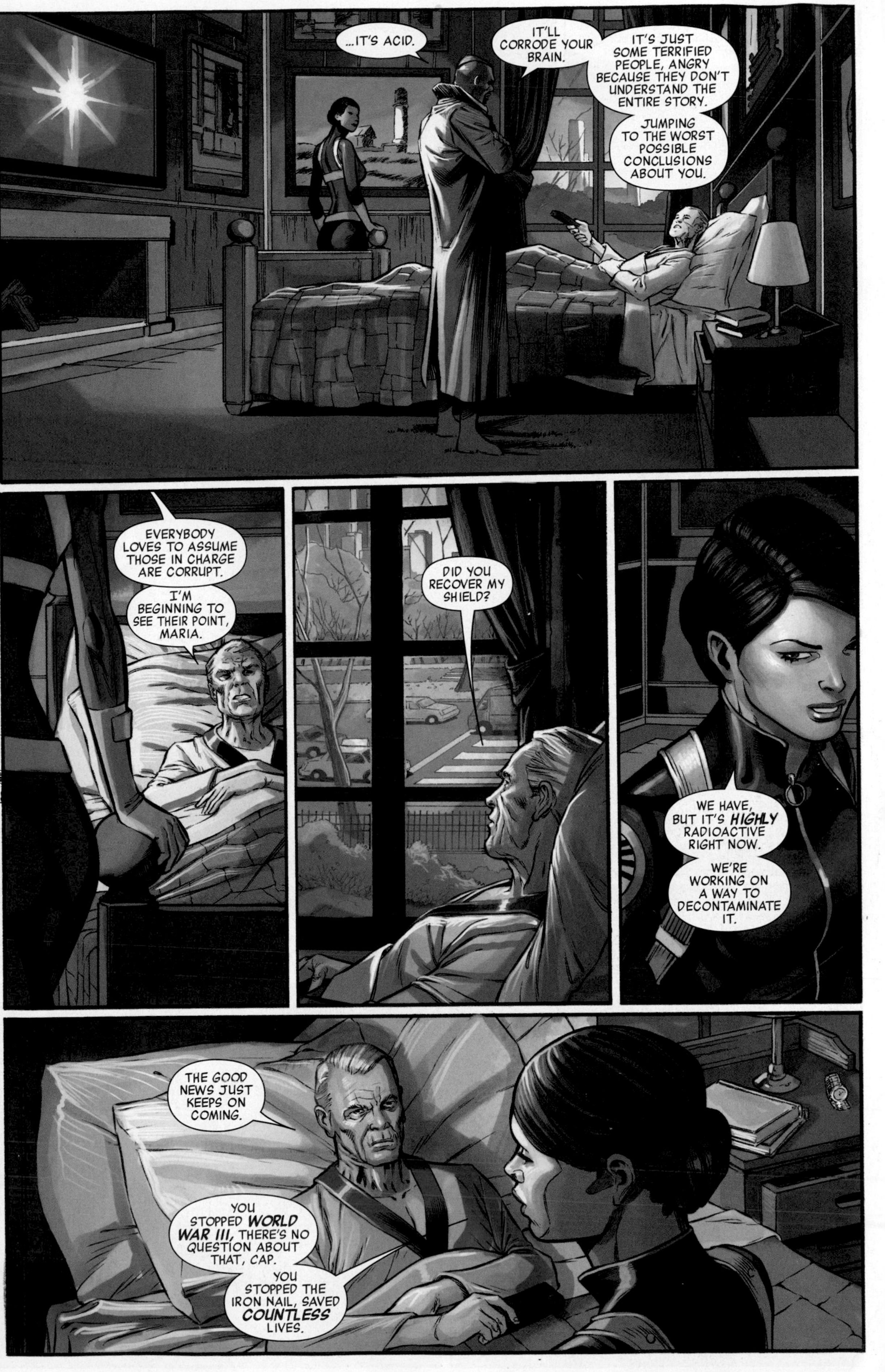
...IT'S ACID.
IT'LL CORRODE YOUR BRAIN.
IT'S JUST SOME TERRIFIED PEOPLE, ANGRY BECAUSE THEY DON'T UNDERSTAND THE ENTIRE STORY.
JUMPING TO THE WORST POSSIBLE CONCLUSIONS ABOUT YOU.
EVERYBODY LOVES TO ASSUME THOSE IN CHARGE ARE CORRUPT.
I'M BEGINNING TO SEE THEIR POINT, MARIA.
DID YOU RECOVER MY SHIELD?
WE HAVE, BUT IT'S HIGHLY RADIOACTIVE RIGHT NOW.
WE'RE WORKING ON A WAY TO DECONTAMINATE IT.
THE GOOD NEWS JUST KEEPS ON COMING.
YOU STOPPED WORLD WAR III, THERE'S NO QUESTION ABOUT THAT, CAP.
YOU STOPPED THE IRON NAIL, SAVED COUNTLESS LIVES.

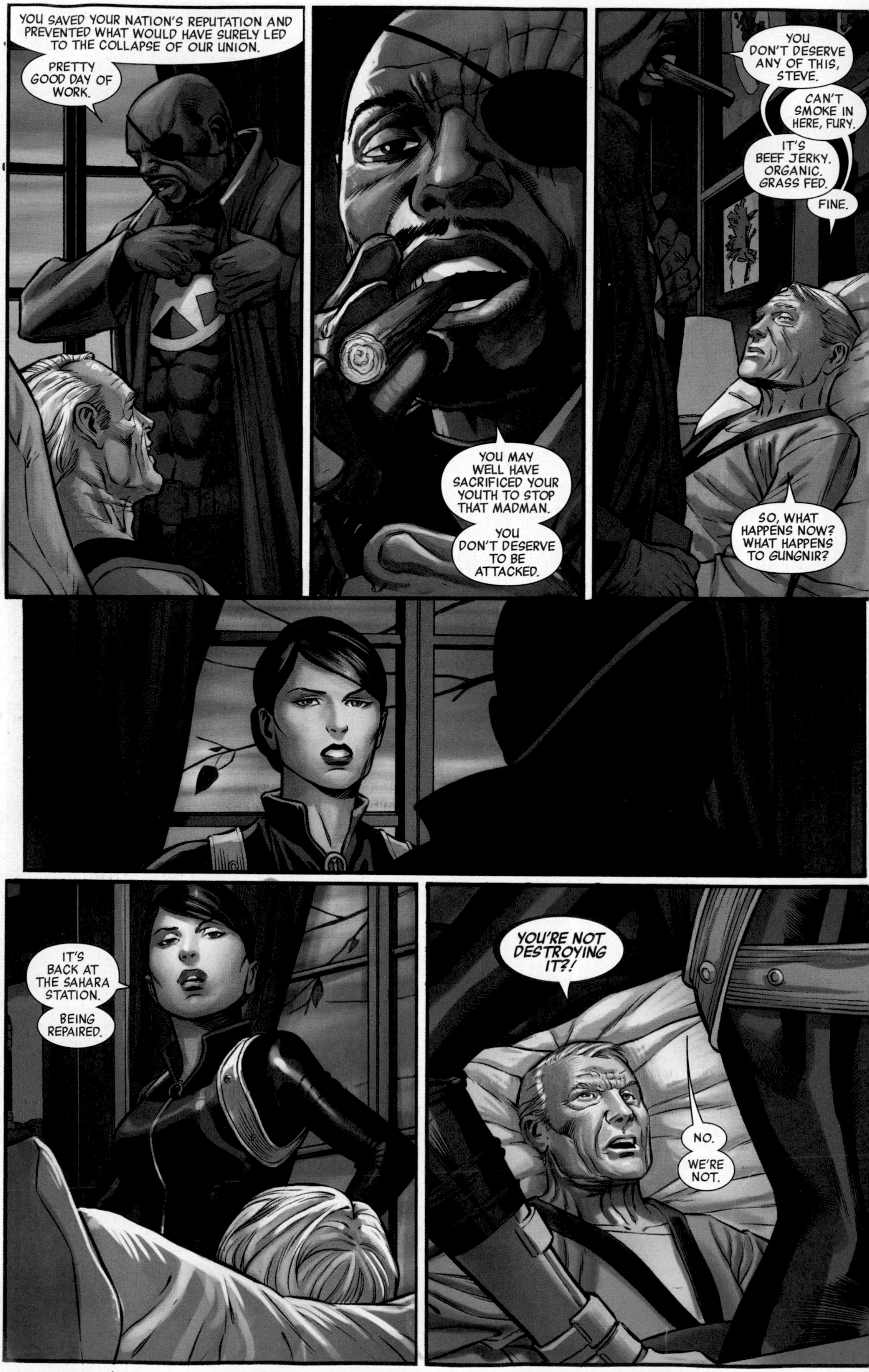
YOU SAVED YOUR NATION'S REPUTATION AND PREVENTED WHAT WOULD HAVE SURELY LED TO THE COLLAPSE OF OUR UNION.
PRETTY GOOD DAY OF WORK.
YOU MAY WELL HAVE SACRIFICED YOUR YOUTH TO STOP THAT MADMAN.
YOU DON'T DESERVE TO BE ATTACKED.
YOU DON'T DESERVE ANY OF THIS, STEVE.
CAN'T SMOKE IN HERE, FURY.
IT'S BEEF JERKY. ORGANIC. GRASS FED.
FINE.
SO, WHAT HAPPENS NOW? WHAT HAPPENS TO GUNGNIR?
IT'S BACK AT THE SAHARA STATION.
BEING REPAIRED.
YOU'RE NOT DESTROYING IT?!
NO.
WE'RE NOT.

MAYBE RAN SHEN WAS *RIGHT* ABOUT S.H.I.E.L.D.!

MAYBE YOU *HAVE* GROWN TOO POWERFUL FOR YOUR OWN GOOD.

THIS IS *INSANE!*

HOW INSANE IS IT?

HOW INSANE IS IT TO BUILD SOMETHING THAT WE CAN USE TO *PROTECT OURSELVES* THE NEXT TIME A *CELESTIAL EXECUTIONER* SHOWS UP?

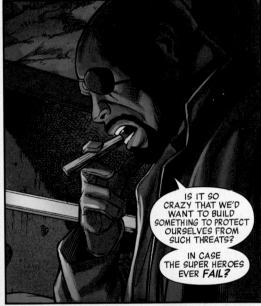

IS IT SO CRAZY THAT WE'D WANT TO BUILD SOMETHING TO PROTECT OURSELVES FROM SUCH THREATS?

IN CASE THE SUPER HEROES EVER *FAIL?*

SOME PEOPLE IN S.H.I.E.L.D. THINK IT'S CRAZY FOR HUMANITY TO PUT ALL OF ITS FAITH IN A SELF-APPOINTED BAND OF COSTUMED ADVENTURERS.

ALL RESPECT, CAPTAIN, YOU THINK S.H.I.E.L.D. GOT TOO BIG AND OVERREACHED?

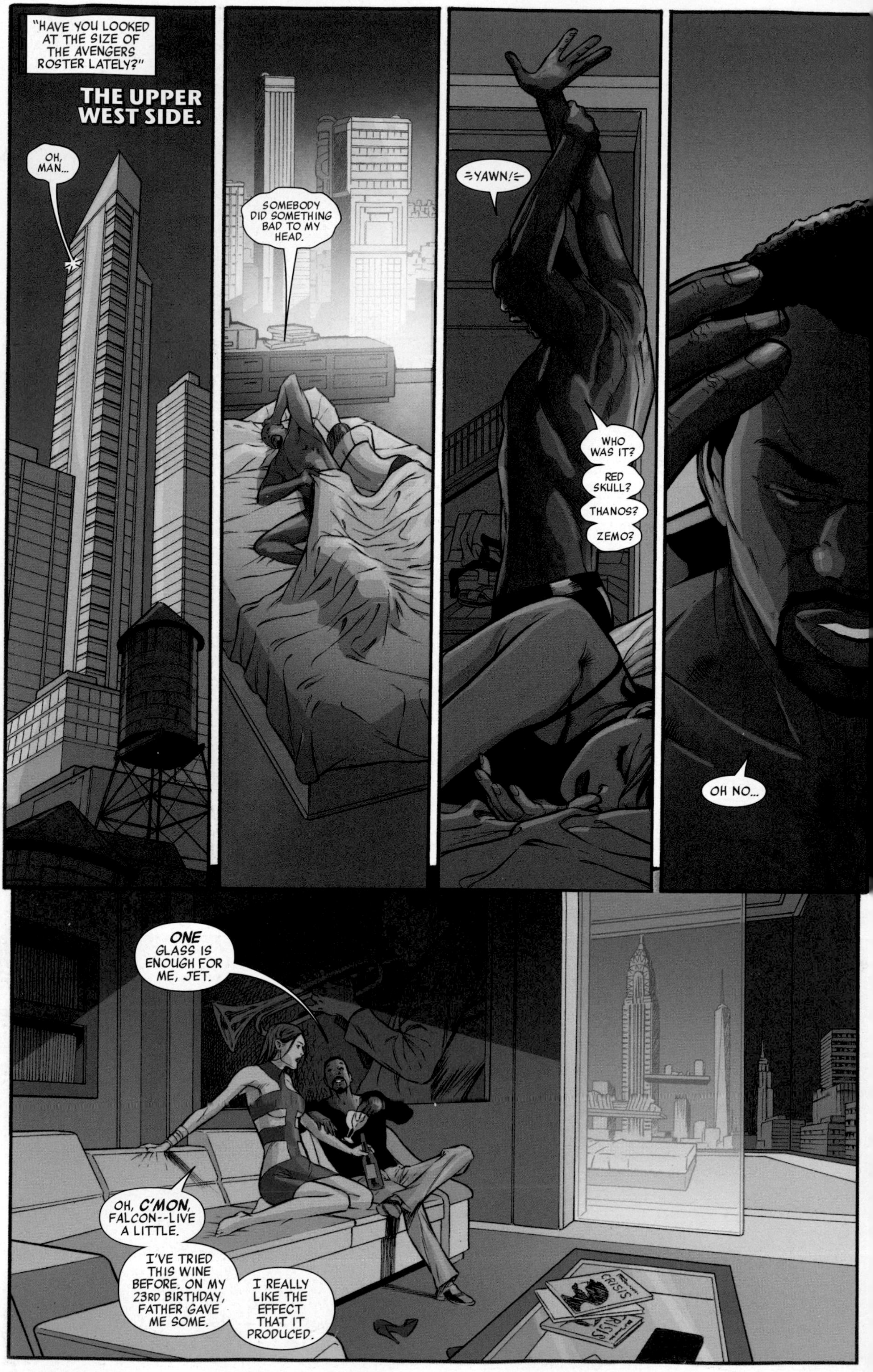
"HAVE YOU LOOKED AT THE SIZE OF THE AVENGERS ROSTER LATELY?"
THE UPPER WEST SIDE.
OH, MAN...
SOMEBODY DID SOMETHING BAD TO MY HEAD.
=YAWN!=
WHO WAS IT?
RED SKULL?
THANOS?
ZEMO?
OH NO...
ONE GLASS IS ENOUGH FOR ME, JET.
OH, C'MON, FALCON--LIVE A LITTLE.
I'VE TRIED THIS WINE BEFORE. ON MY 23RD BIRTHDAY, FATHER GAVE ME SOME.
I REALLY LIKE THE EFFECT THAT IT PRODUCED.
CRISIS
CRISIS

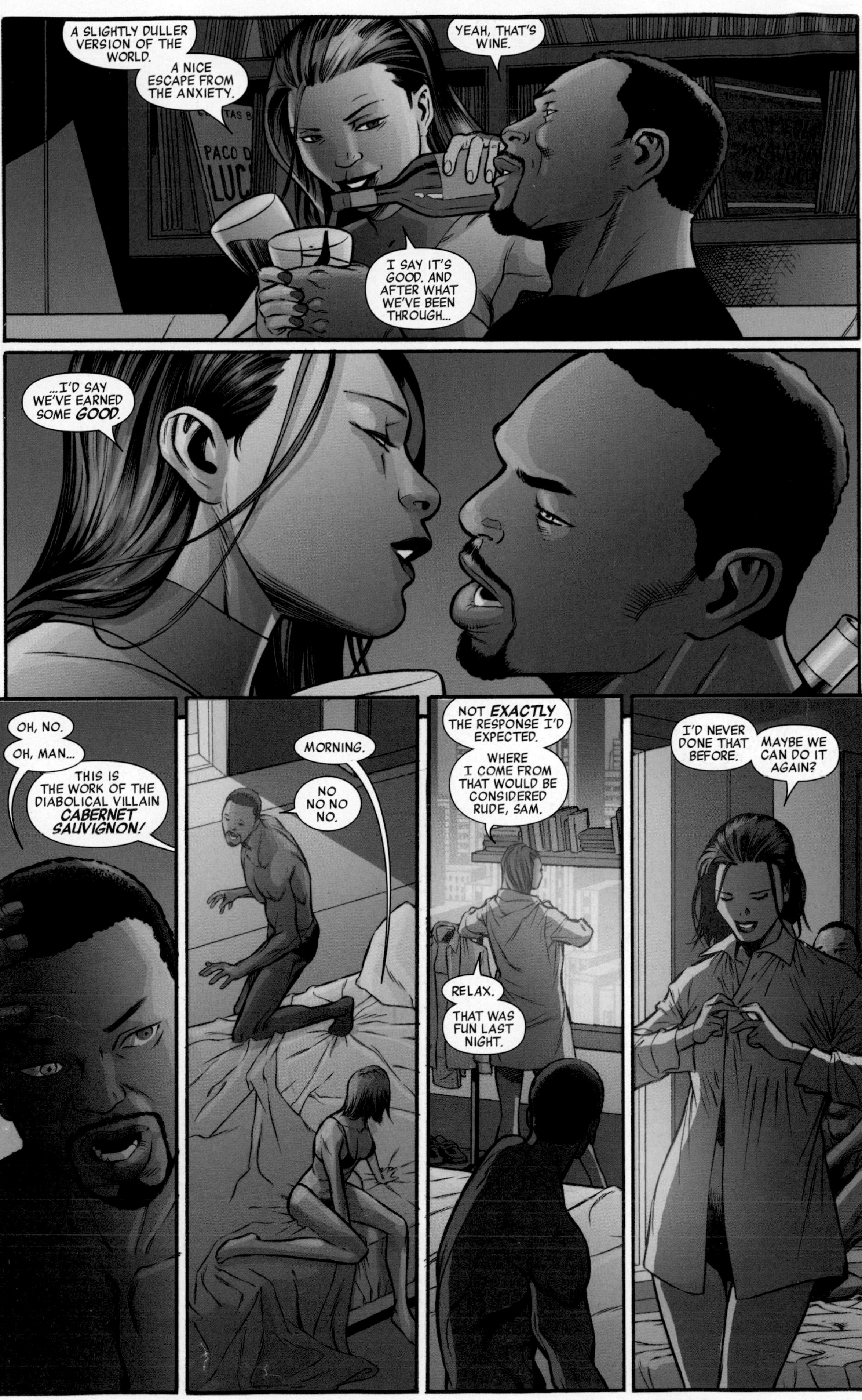
A SLIGHTLY DULLER VERSION OF THE WORLD.
A NICE ESCAPE FROM THE ANXIETY.
YEAH, THAT'S WINE.
I SAY IT'S GOOD. AND AFTER WHAT WE'VE BEEN THROUGH...
...I'D SAY WE'VE EARNED SOME GOOD.
OH, NO.
OH, MAN...
THIS IS THE WORK OF THE DIABOLICAL VILLAIN CABERNET SAUVIGNON!
MORNING.
NO NO NO NO.
NOT EXACTLY THE RESPONSE I'D EXPECTED.
WHERE I COME FROM THAT WOULD BE CONSIDERED RUDE, SAM.
RELAX.
THAT WAS FUN LAST NIGHT.
I'D NEVER DONE THAT BEFORE.
MAYBE WE CAN DO IT AGAIN?

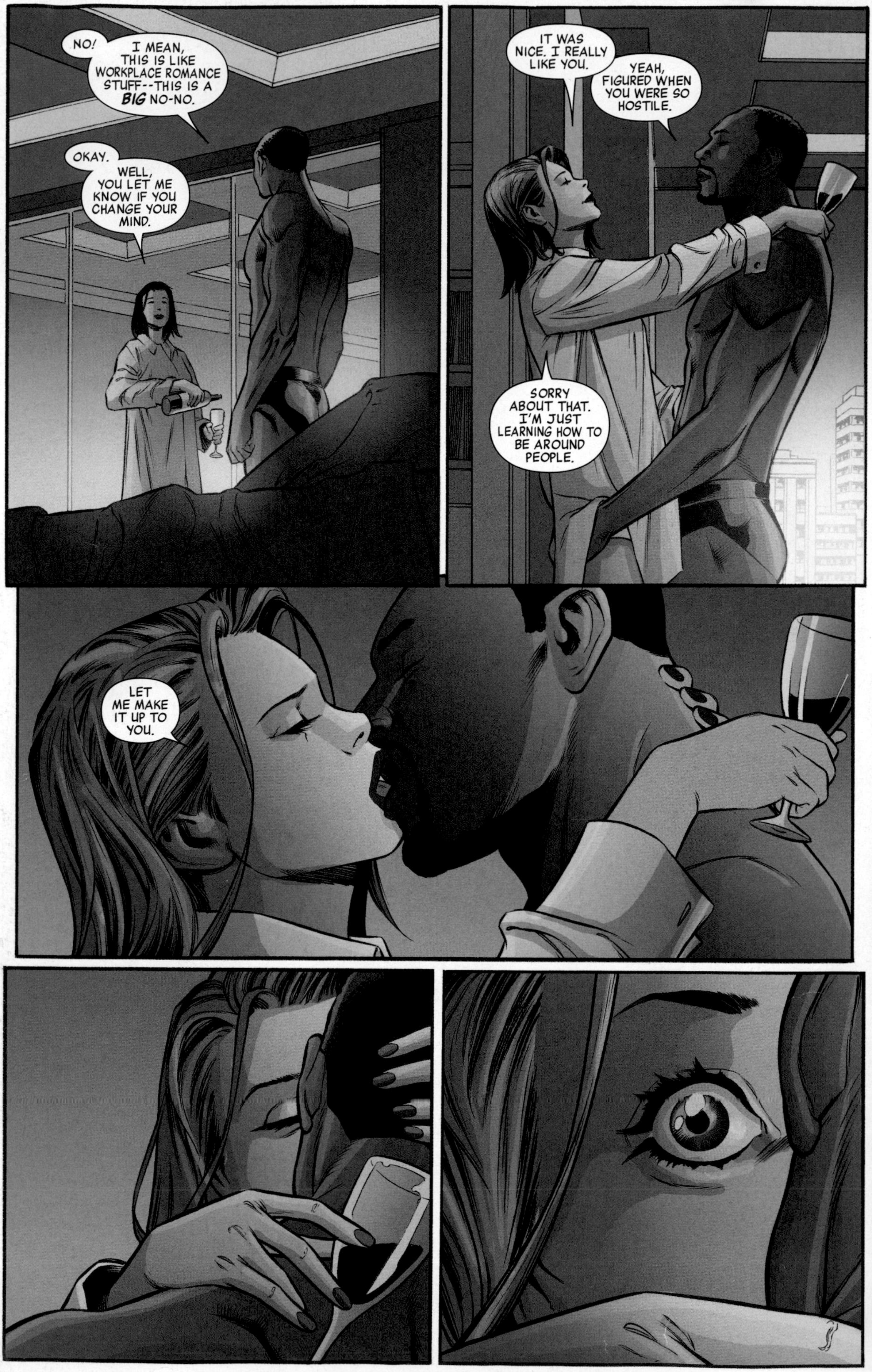
NO!
I MEAN, THIS IS LIKE WORKPLACE ROMANCE STUFF--THIS IS A BIG NO-NO.
OKAY.
WELL, YOU LET ME KNOW IF YOU CHANGE YOUR MIND.
IT WAS NICE. I REALLY LIKE YOU.
YEAH, FIGURED WHEN YOU WERE SO HOSTILE.
SORRY ABOUT THAT. I'M JUST LEARNING HOW TO BE AROUND PEOPLE.
LET ME MAKE IT UP TO YOU.

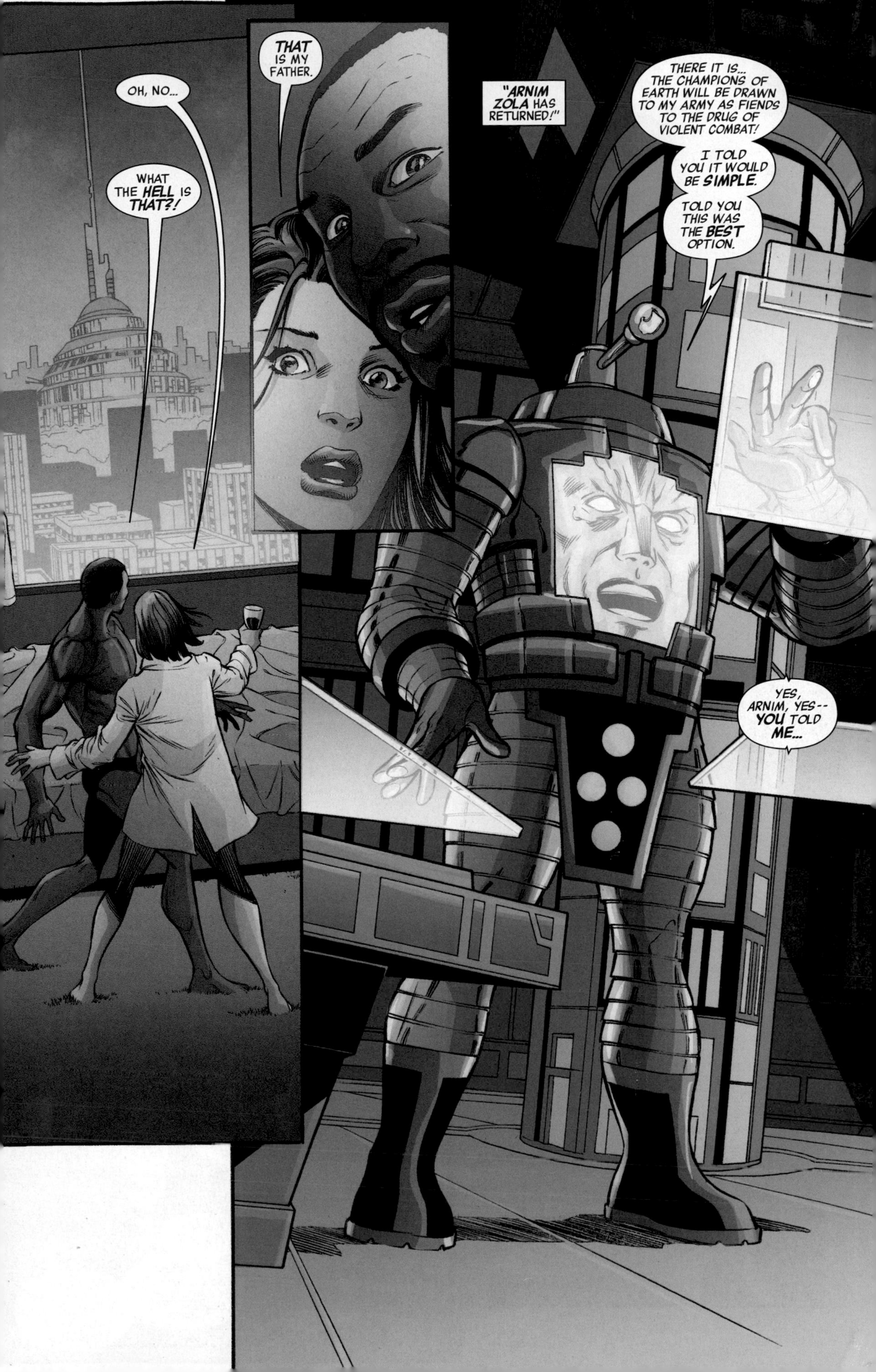
OH, NO...
WHAT THE HELL IS THAT?!
THAT IS MY FATHER.
"ARNIM ZOLA HAS RETURNED!"
THERE IT IS... THE CHAMPIONS OF EARTH WILL BE DRAWN TO MY ARMY AS FIENDS TO THE DRUG OF VIOLENT COMBAT!
I TOLD YOU IT WOULD BE SIMPLE.
TOLD YOU THIS WAS THE BEST OPTION.
YES, ARNIM, YES-- YOU TOLD ME...

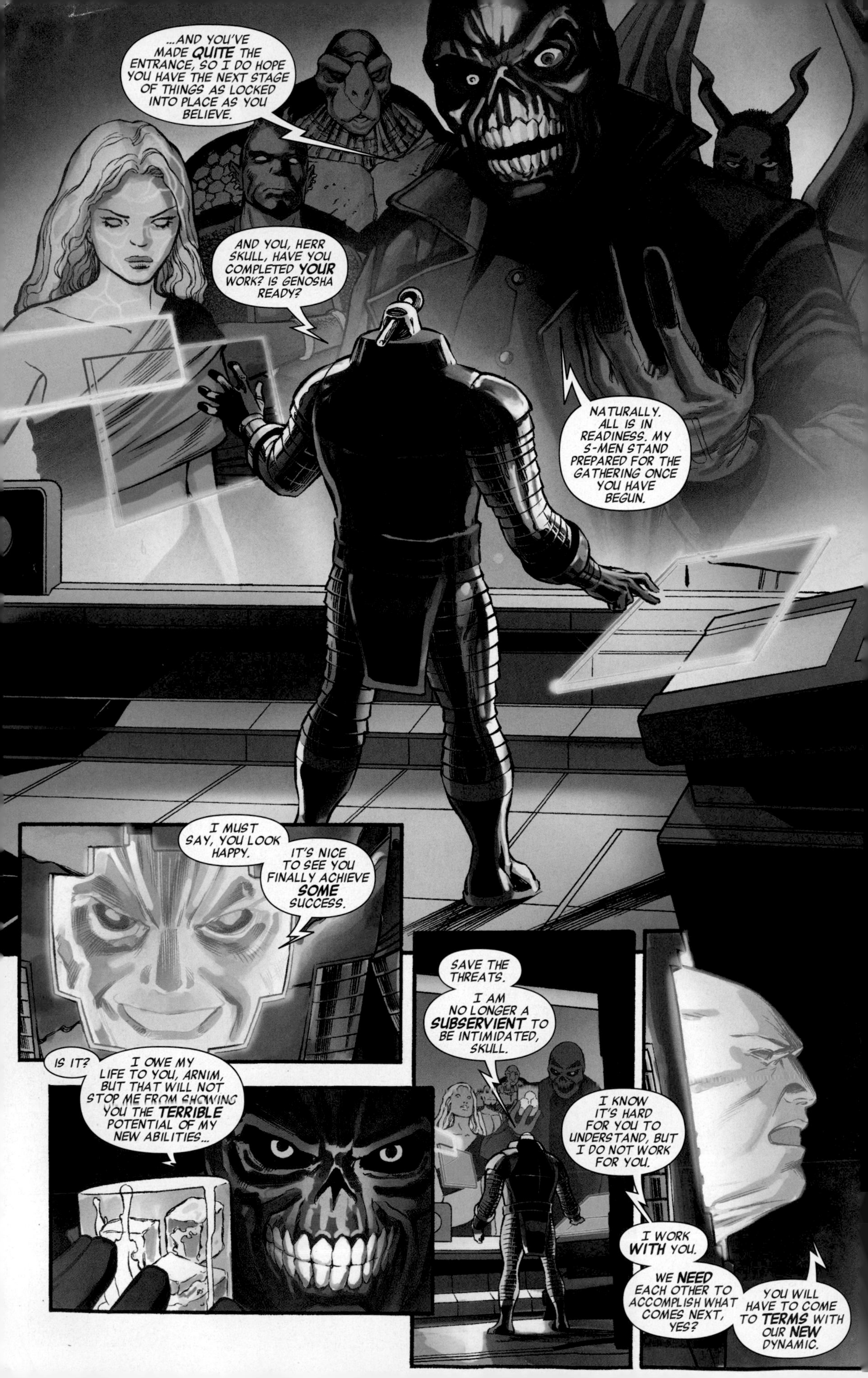
...AND YOU'VE MADE QUITE THE ENTRANCE, SO I DO HOPE YOU HAVE THE NEXT STAGE OF THINGS AS LOCKED INTO PLACE AS YOU BELIEVE.
AND YOU, HERR SKULL, HAVE YOU COMPLETED YOUR WORK? IS GENOSHA READY?
NATURALLY. ALL IS IN READINESS. MY S-MEN STAND PREPARED FOR THE GATHERING ONCE YOU HAVE BEGUN.
I MUST SAY, YOU LOOK HAPPY.
IT'S NICE TO SEE YOU FINALLY ACHIEVE SOME SUCCESS.
IS IT?
I OWE MY LIFE TO YOU, ARNIM, BUT THAT WILL NOT STOP ME FROM SHOWING YOU THE TERRIBLE POTENTIAL OF MY NEW ABILITIES...
SAVE THE THREATS.
I AM NO LONGER A SUBSERVIENT TO BE INTIMIDATED, SKULL.
I KNOW IT'S HARD FOR YOU TO UNDERSTAND, BUT I DO NOT WORK FOR YOU.
I WORK WITH YOU.
WE NEED EACH OTHER TO ACCOMPLISH WHAT COMES NEXT, YES?
YOU WILL HAVE TO COME TO TERMS WITH OUR NEW DYNAMIC.

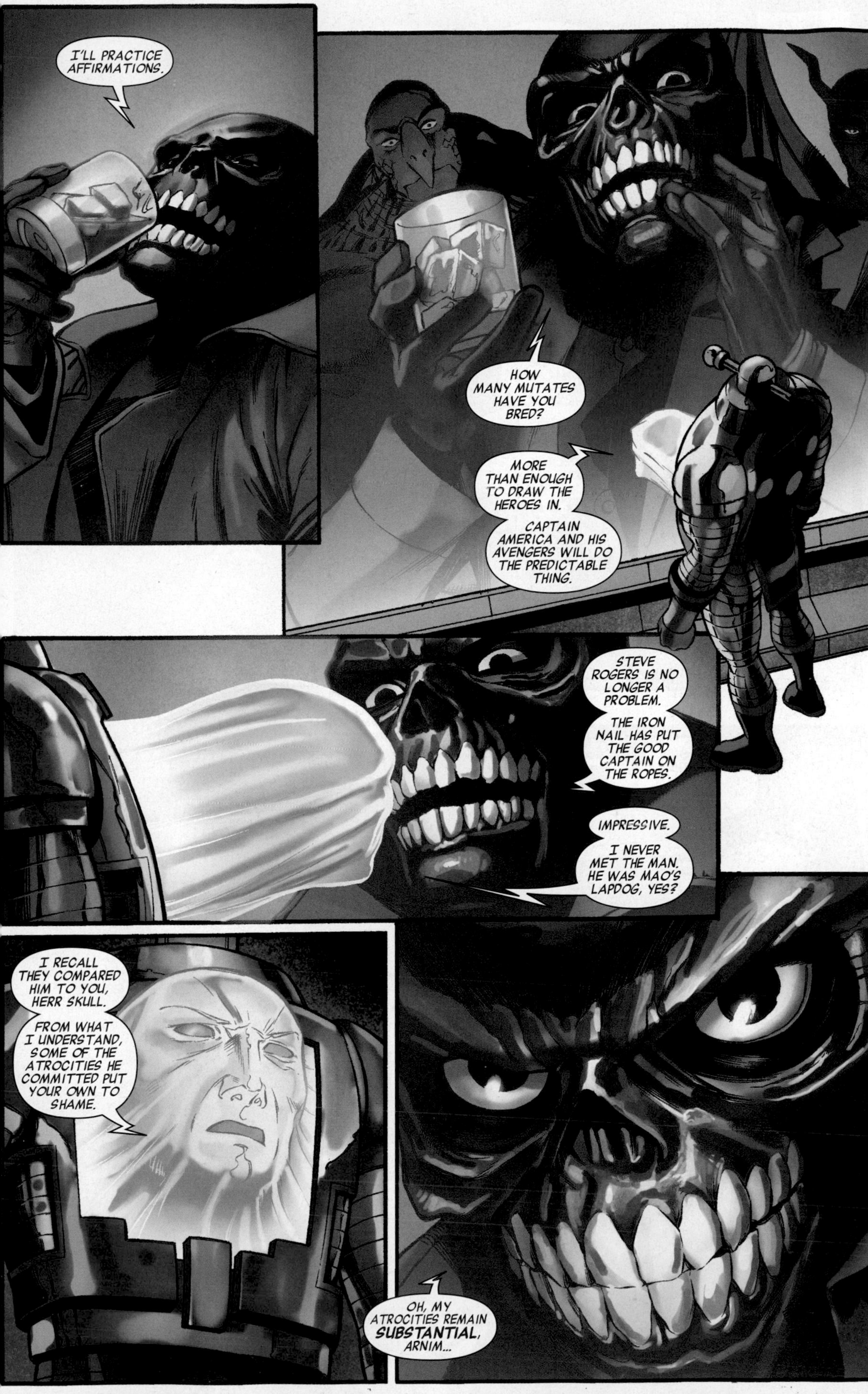
I'LL PRACTICE AFFIRMATIONS.
HOW MANY MUTATES HAVE YOU BRED?
MORE THAN ENOUGH TO DRAW THE HEROES IN.
CAPTAIN AMERICA AND HIS AVENGERS WILL DO THE PREDICTABLE THING.
STEVE ROGERS IS NO LONGER A PROBLEM.
THE IRON NAIL HAS PUT THE GOOD CAPTAIN ON THE ROPES.
IMPRESSIVE.
I NEVER MET THE MAN. HE WAS MAO'S LAPDOG, YES?
I RECALL THEY COMPARED HIM TO YOU, HERR SKULL.
FROM WHAT I UNDERSTAND, SOME OF THE ATROCITIES HE COMMITTED PUT YOUR OWN TO SHAME.
OH, MY ATROCITIES REMAIN SUBSTANTIAL, ARNIM...

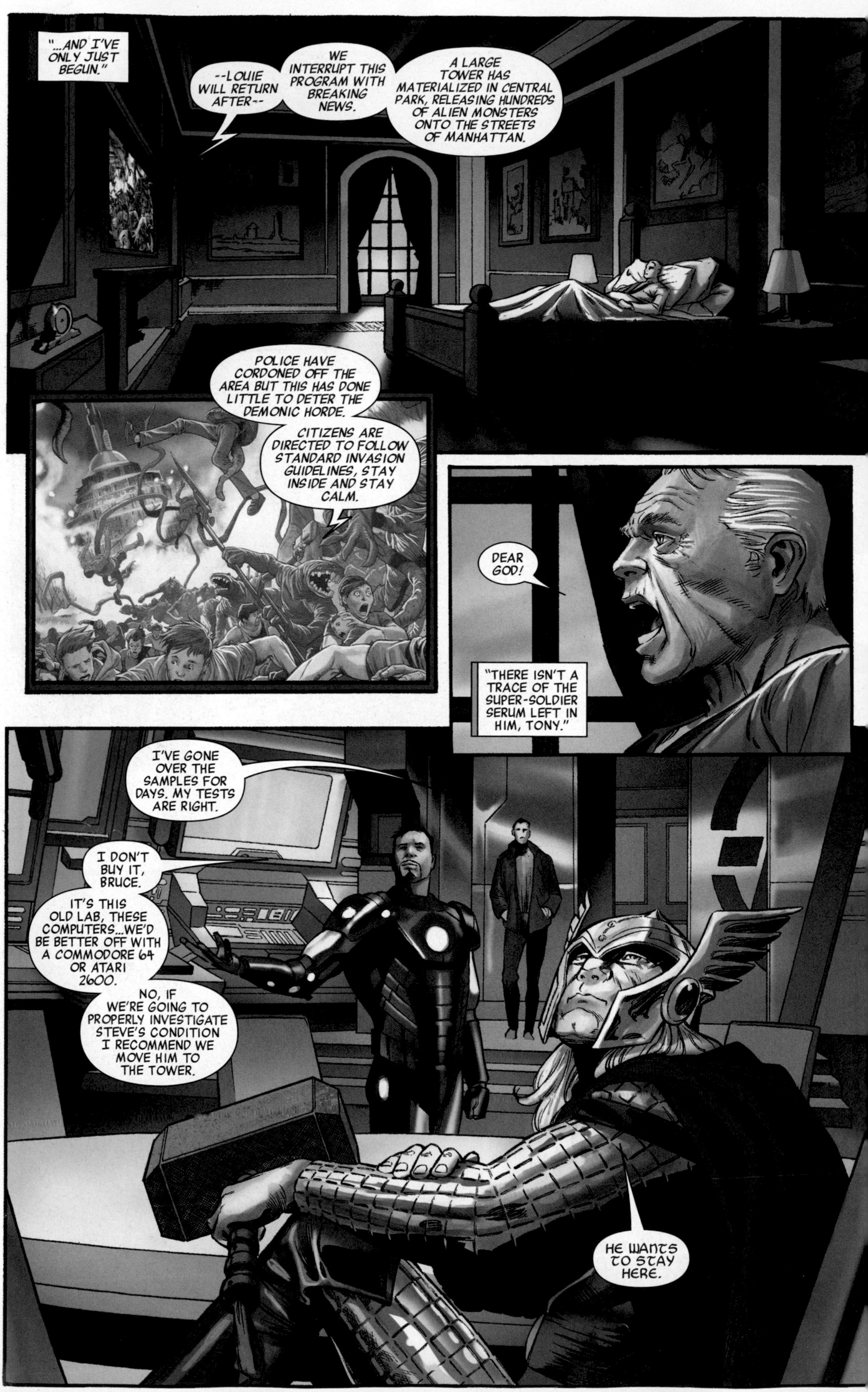
"...AND I'VE ONLY JUST BEGUN."
--LOUIE WILL RETURN AFTER--
WE INTERRUPT THIS PROGRAM WITH BREAKING NEWS.
A LARGE TOWER HAS MATERIALIZED IN CENTRAL PARK, RELEASING HUNDREDS OF ALIEN MONSTERS ONTO THE STREETS OF MANHATTAN.
POLICE HAVE CORDONED OFF THE AREA BUT THIS HAS DONE LITTLE TO DETER THE DEMONIC HORDE.
CITIZENS ARE DIRECTED TO FOLLOW STANDARD INVASION GUIDELINES, STAY INSIDE AND STAY CALM.
DEAR GOD!
"THERE ISN'T A TRACE OF THE SUPER-SOLDIER SERUM LEFT IN HIM, TONY."
I'VE GONE OVER THE SAMPLES FOR DAYS. MY TESTS ARE RIGHT.
I DON'T BUY IT, BRUCE.
IT'S THIS OLD LAB, THESE COMPUTERS...WE'D BE BETTER OFF WITH A COMMODORE 64 OR ATARI 2600.
NO, IF WE'RE GOING TO PROPERLY INVESTIGATE STEVE'S CONDITION I RECOMMEND WE MOVE HIM TO THE TOWER.
HE WANTS TO STAY HERE.

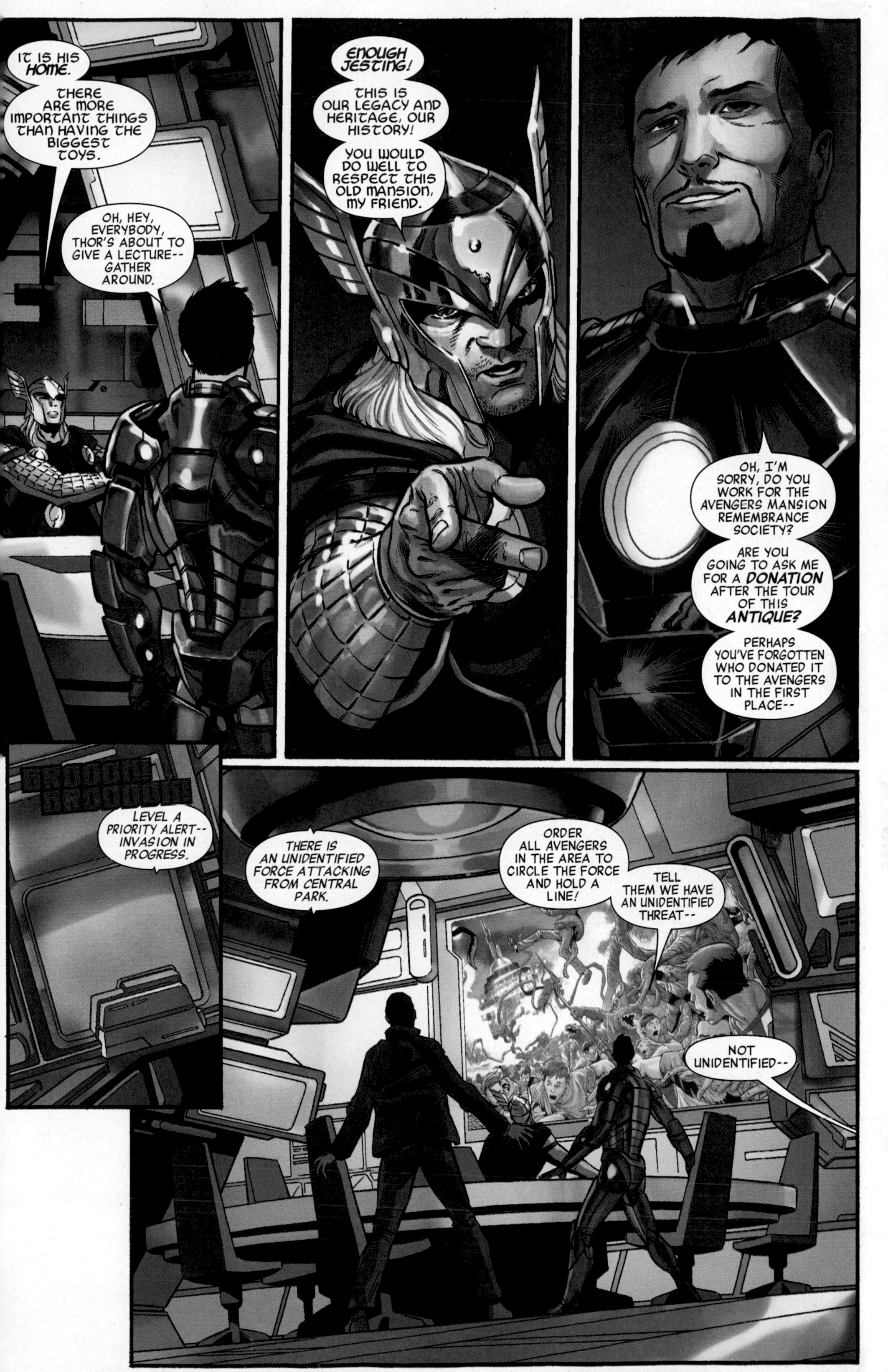
IT IS HIS HOME.
THERE ARE MORE IMPORTANT THINGS THAN HAVING THE BIGGEST TOYS.
OH, HEY, EVERYBODY, THOR'S ABOUT TO GIVE A LECTURE-- GATHER AROUND.
ENOUGH JESTING!
THIS IS OUR LEGACY AND HERITAGE, OUR HISTORY!
YOU WOULD DO WELL TO RESPECT THIS OLD MANSION, MY FRIEND.
OH, I'M SORRY, DO YOU WORK FOR THE AVENGERS MANSION REMEMBRANCE SOCIETY?
ARE YOU GOING TO ASK ME FOR A DONATION AFTER THE TOUR OF THIS ANTIQUE?
PERHAPS YOU'VE FORGOTTEN WHO DONATED IT TO THE AVENGERS IN THE FIRST PLACE--
LEVEL A PRIORITY ALERT-- INVASION IN PROGRESS.
THERE IS AN UNIDENTIFIED FORCE ATTACKING FROM CENTRAL PARK.
ORDER ALL AVENGERS IN THE AREA TO CIRCLE THE FORCE AND HOLD A LINE!
TELL THEM WE HAVE AN UNIDENTIFIED THREAT--
NOT UNIDENTIFIED--

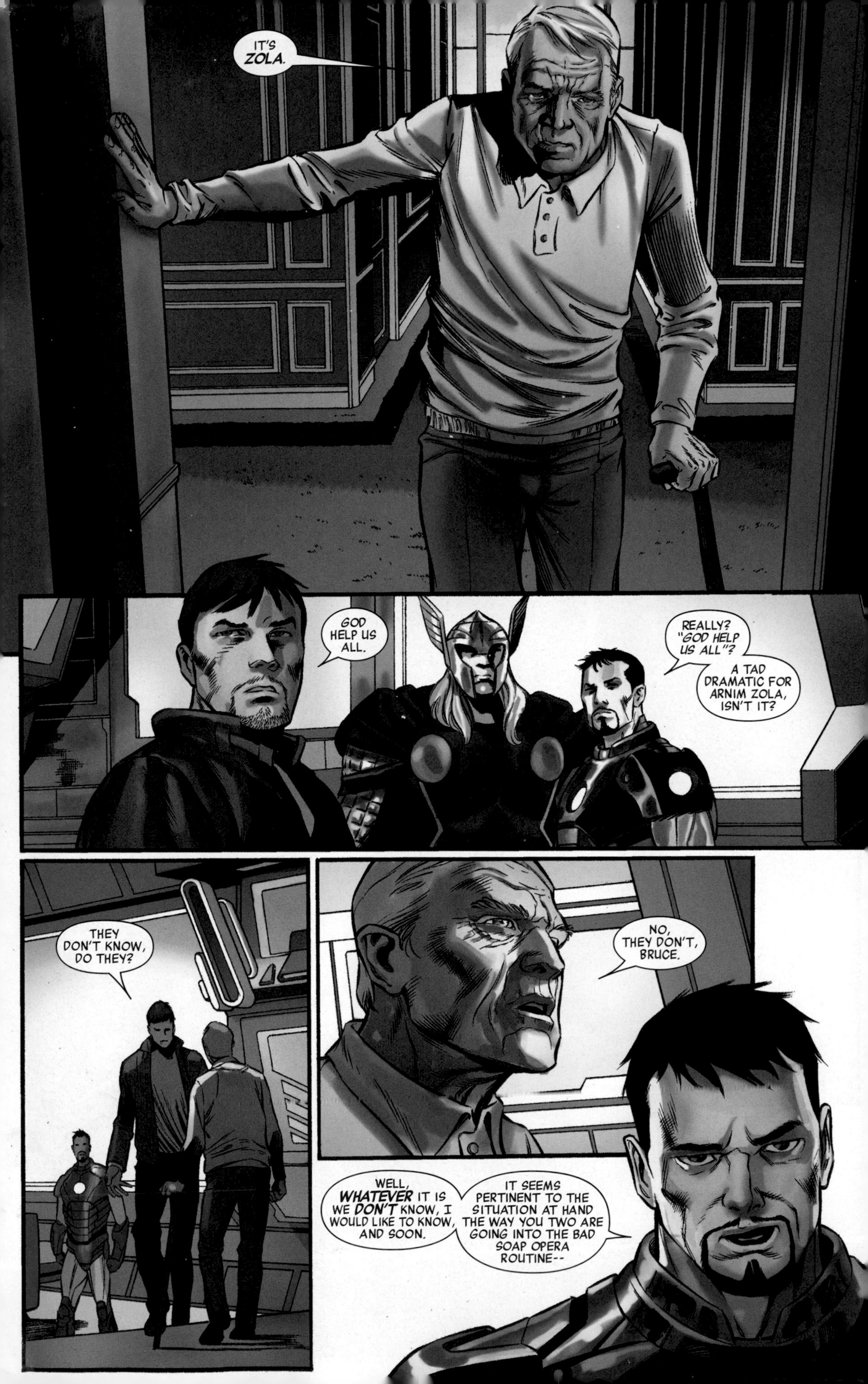
IT'S ZOLA.
GOD HELP US ALL.
REALLY? "GOD HELP US ALL"?
A TAD DRAMATIC FOR ARNIM ZOLA, ISN'T IT?
THEY DON'T KNOW, DO THEY?
NO, THEY DON'T, BRUCE.
WELL, WHATEVER IT IS WE DON'T KNOW, I WOULD LIKE TO KNOW, AND SOON.
IT SEEMS PERTINENT TO THE SITUATION AT HAND THE WAY YOU TWO ARE GOING INTO THE BAD SOAP OPERA ROUTINE--

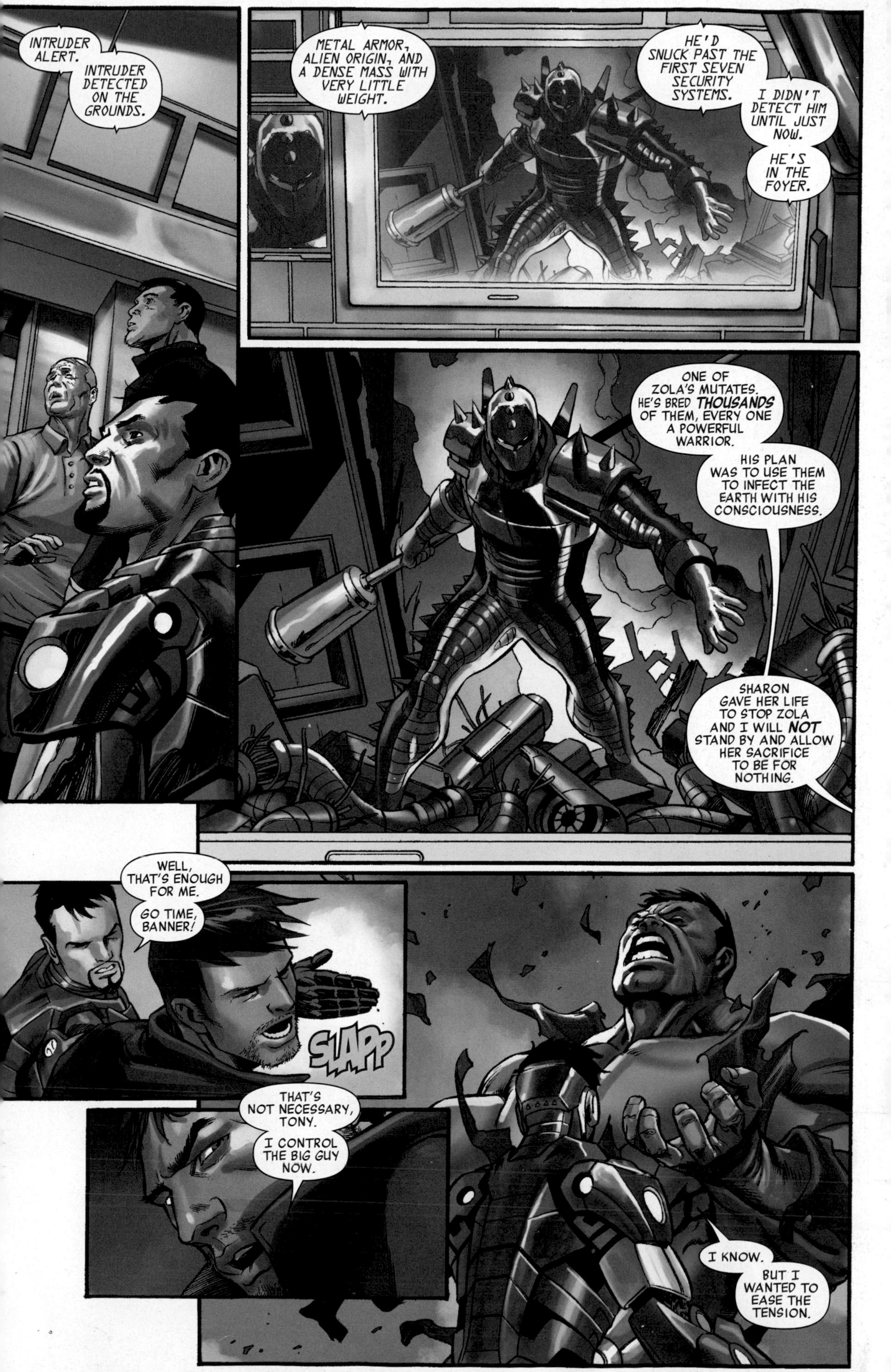
INTRUDER ALERT.
INTRUDER DETECTED ON THE GROUNDS.
METAL ARMOR, ALIEN ORIGIN, AND A DENSE MASS WITH VERY LITTLE WEIGHT.
HE'D SNUCK PAST THE FIRST SEVEN SECURITY SYSTEMS.
I DIDN'T DETECT HIM UNTIL JUST NOW.
HE'S IN THE FOYER.
ONE OF ZOLA'S MUTATES. HE'S BRED THOUSANDS OF THEM, EVERY ONE A POWERFUL WARRIOR.
HIS PLAN WAS TO USE THEM TO INFECT THE EARTH WITH HIS CONSCIOUSNESS.
SHARON GAVE HER LIFE TO STOP ZOLA AND I WILL NOT STAND BY AND ALLOW HER SACRIFICE TO BE FOR NOTHING.
WELL, THAT'S ENOUGH FOR ME.
GO TIME, BANNER!
SLAPP
THAT'S NOT NECESSARY, TONY.
I CONTROL THE BIG GUY NOW.
I KNOW.
BUT I WANTED TO EASE THE TENSION.

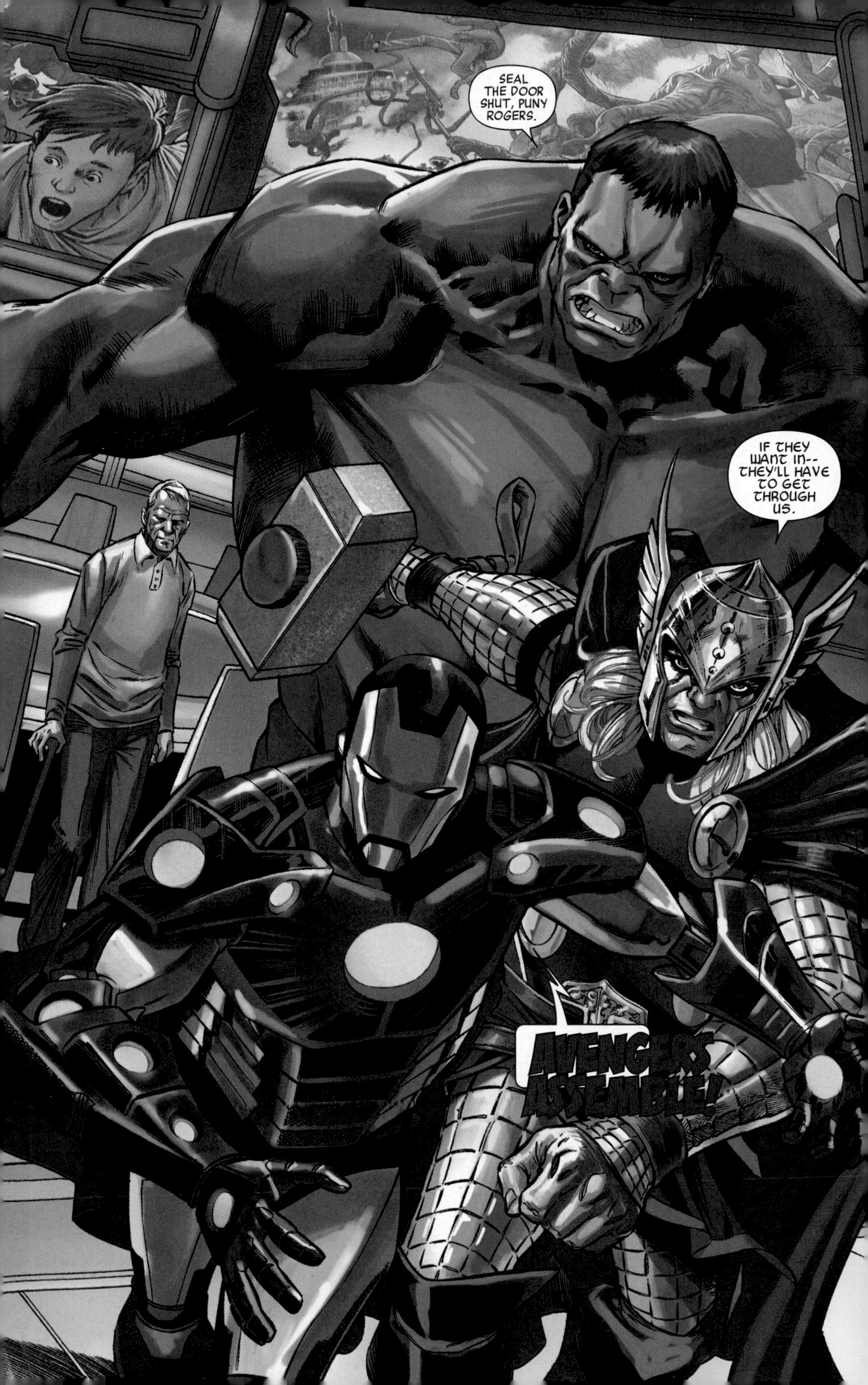
SEAL THE DOOR SHUT, PUNY ROGERS.
IF THEY WANT IN-- THEY'LL HAVE TO GET THROUGH US.
AVENGERS ASSEMBLE!

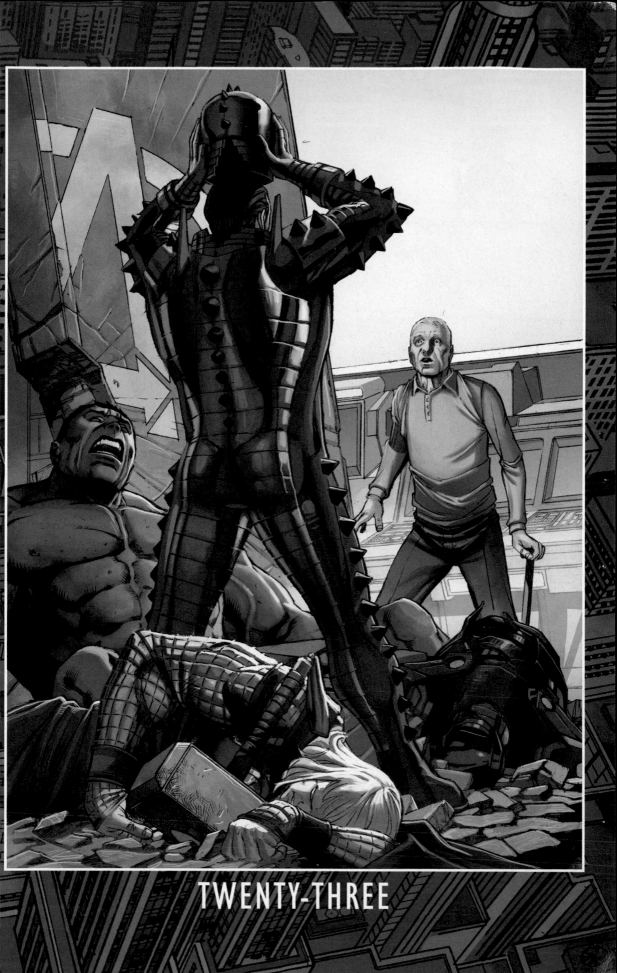

TWENTY-THREE

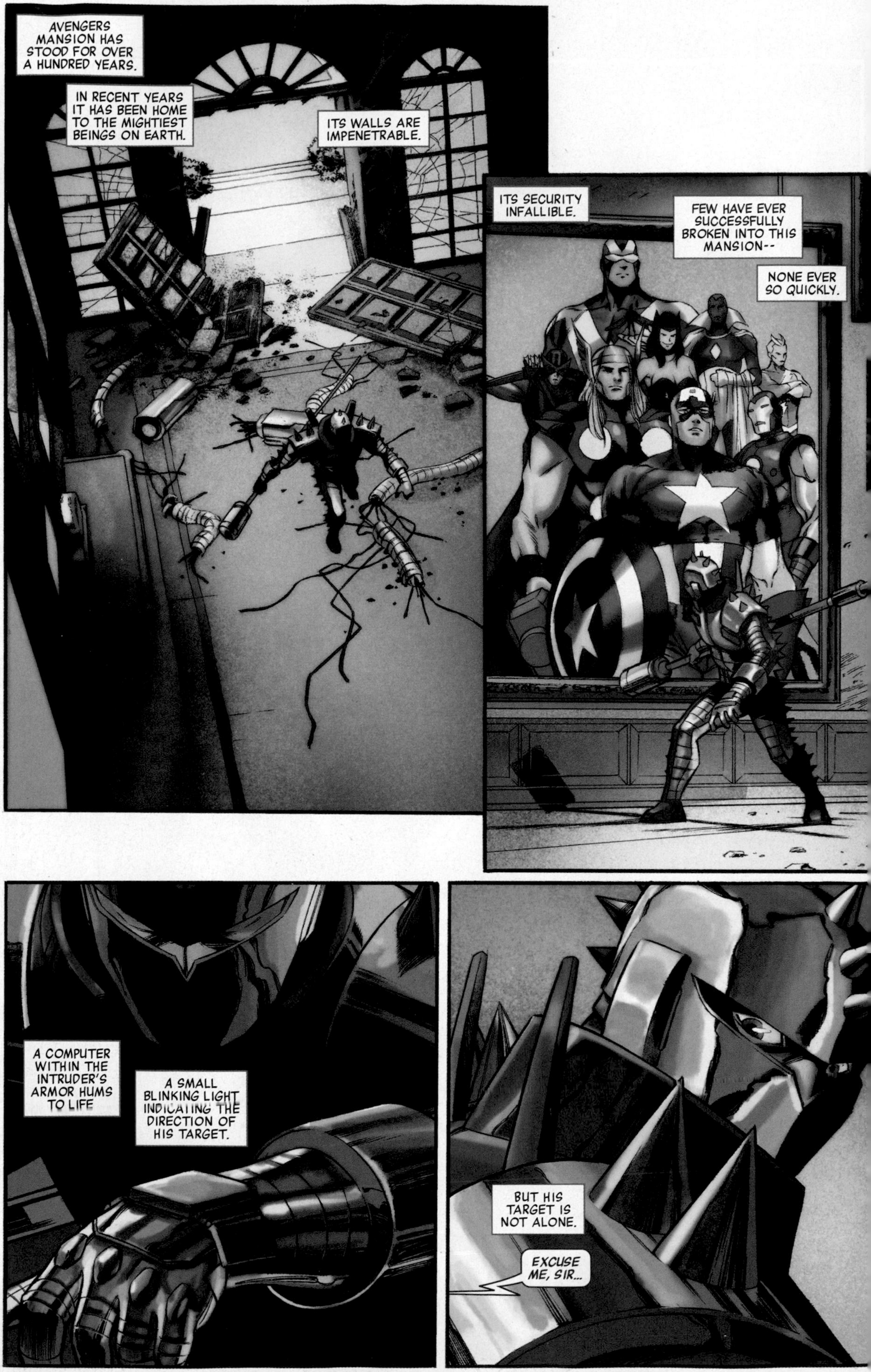
AVENGERS MANSION HAS STOOD FOR OVER A HUNDRED YEARS.
IN RECENT YEARS IT HAS BEEN HOME TO THE MIGHTIEST BEINGS ON EARTH.
ITS WALLS ARE IMPENETRABLE.
ITS SECURITY INFALLIBLE.
FEW HAVE EVER SUCCESSFULLY BROKEN INTO THIS MANSION--
NONE EVER SO QUICKLY.
A COMPUTER WITHIN THE INTRUDER'S ARMOR HUMS TO LIFE
A SMALL BLINKING LIGHT INDICATING THE DIRECTION OF HIS TARGET.
BUT HIS TARGET IS NOT ALONE.
EXCUSE ME, SIR...

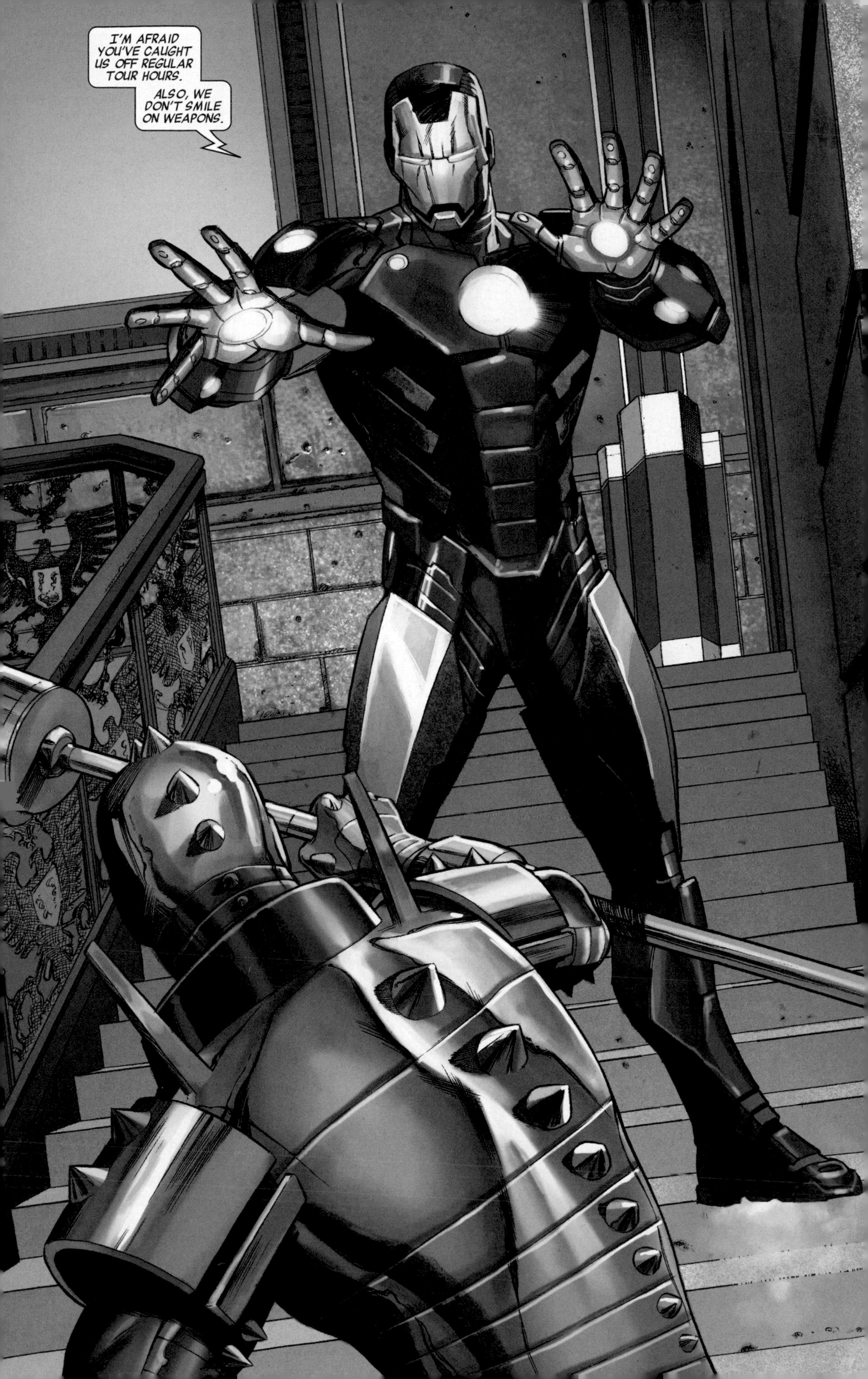
I'M AFRAID YOU'VE CAUGHT US OFF REGULAR TOUR HOURS.
ALSO, WE DON'T SMILE ON WEAPONS.

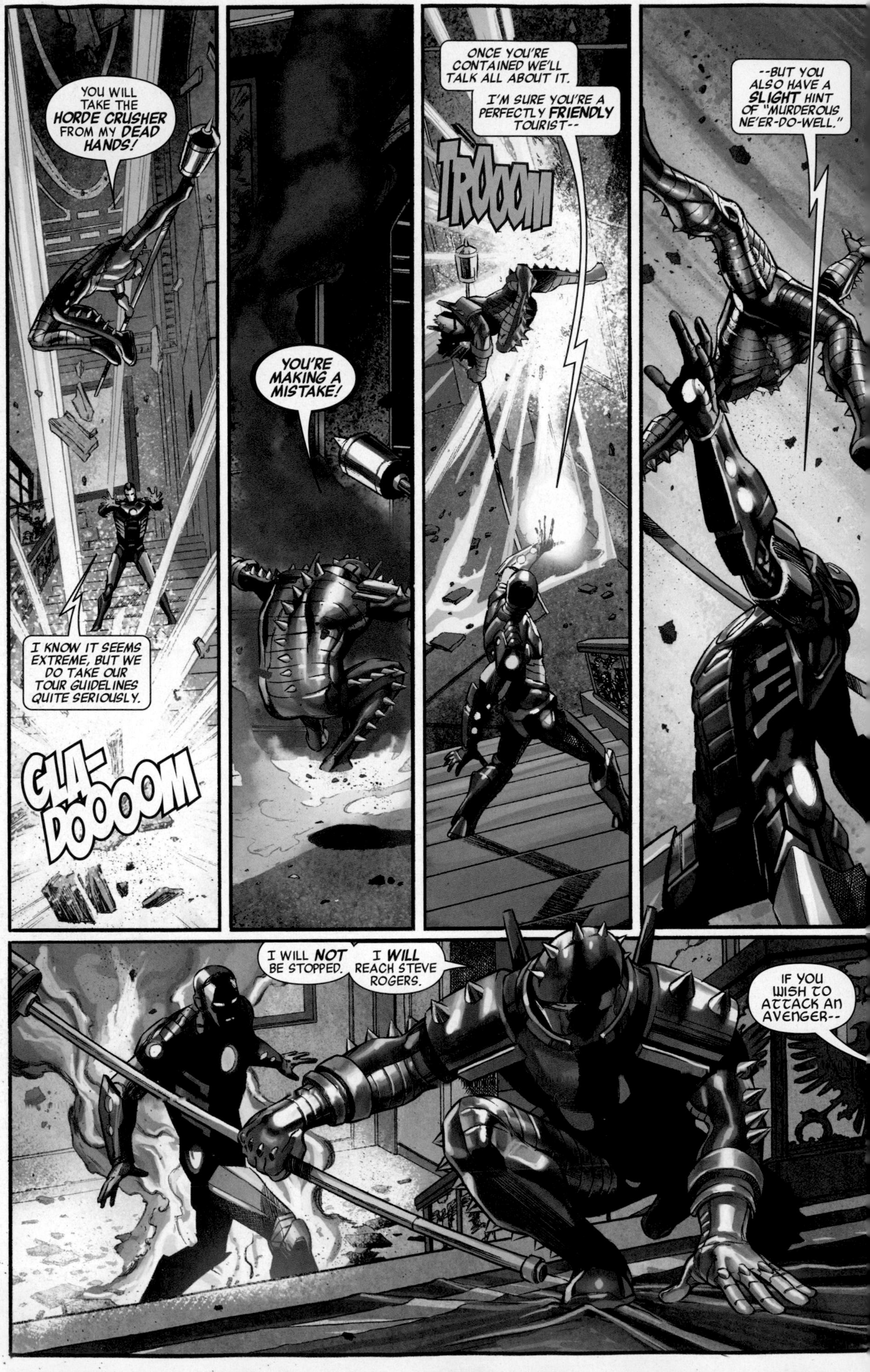
YOU WILL TAKE THE HORDE CRUSHER FROM MY DEAD HANDS!
I KNOW IT SEEMS EXTREME, BUT WE DO TAKE OUR TOUR GUIDELINES QUITE SERIOUSLY.
GLA-DOOOOM
YOU'RE MAKING A MISTAKE!
ONCE YOU'RE CONTAINED WE'LL TALK ALL ABOUT IT.
I'M SURE YOU'RE A PERFECTLY FRIENDLY TOURIST--
TROOOM
--BUT YOU ALSO HAVE A SLIGHT HINT OF "MURDEROUS NE'ER-DO-WELL."
I WILL NOT BE STOPPED.
I WILL REACH STEVE ROGERS.
IF YOU WISH TO ATTACK AN AVENGER--

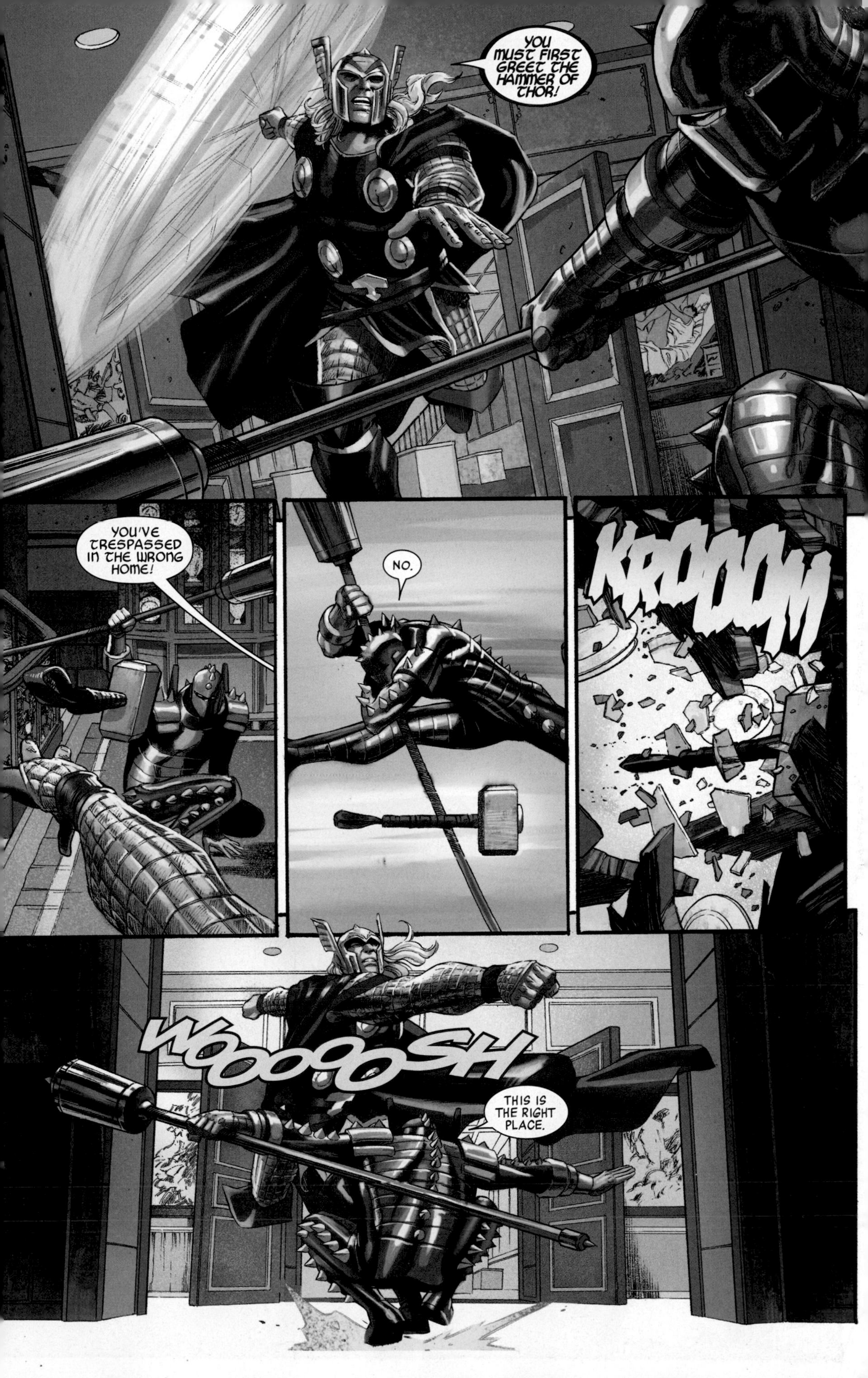
YOU MUST FIRST GREET THE HAMMER OF THOR!
YOU'VE TRESPASSED IN THE WRONG HOME!
NO.
KROOOM
WOOOOOSH
THIS IS THE RIGHT PLACE.

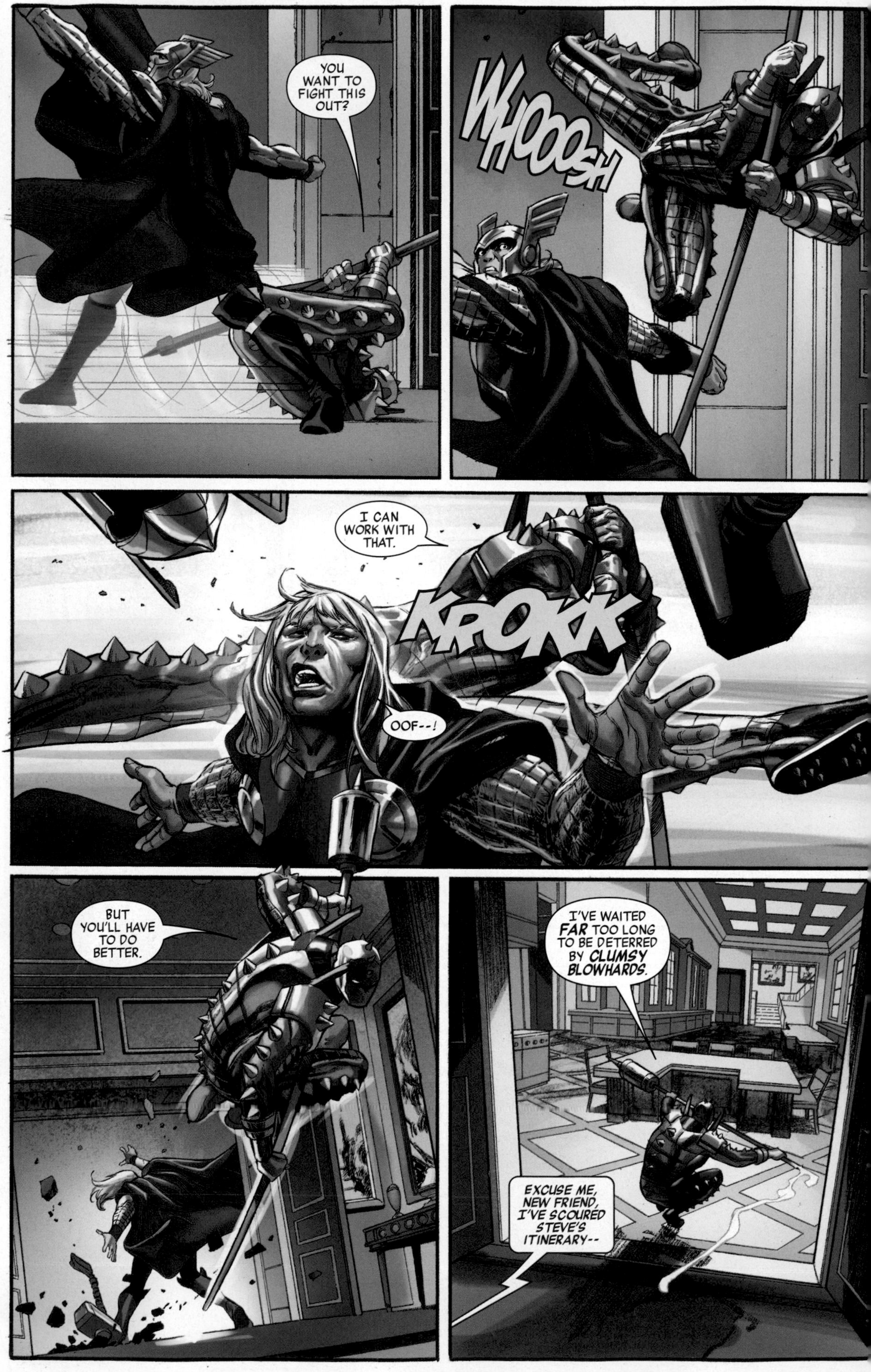
YOU WANT TO FIGHT THIS OUT?
WHOOOOSH
I CAN WORK WITH THAT.
KROKK
OOF--!
BUT YOU'LL HAVE TO DO BETTER.
I'VE WAITED FAR TOO LONG TO BE DETERRED BY CLUMSY BLOWHARDS.
EXCUSE ME, NEW FRIEND, I'VE SCOURED STEVE'S ITINERARY--

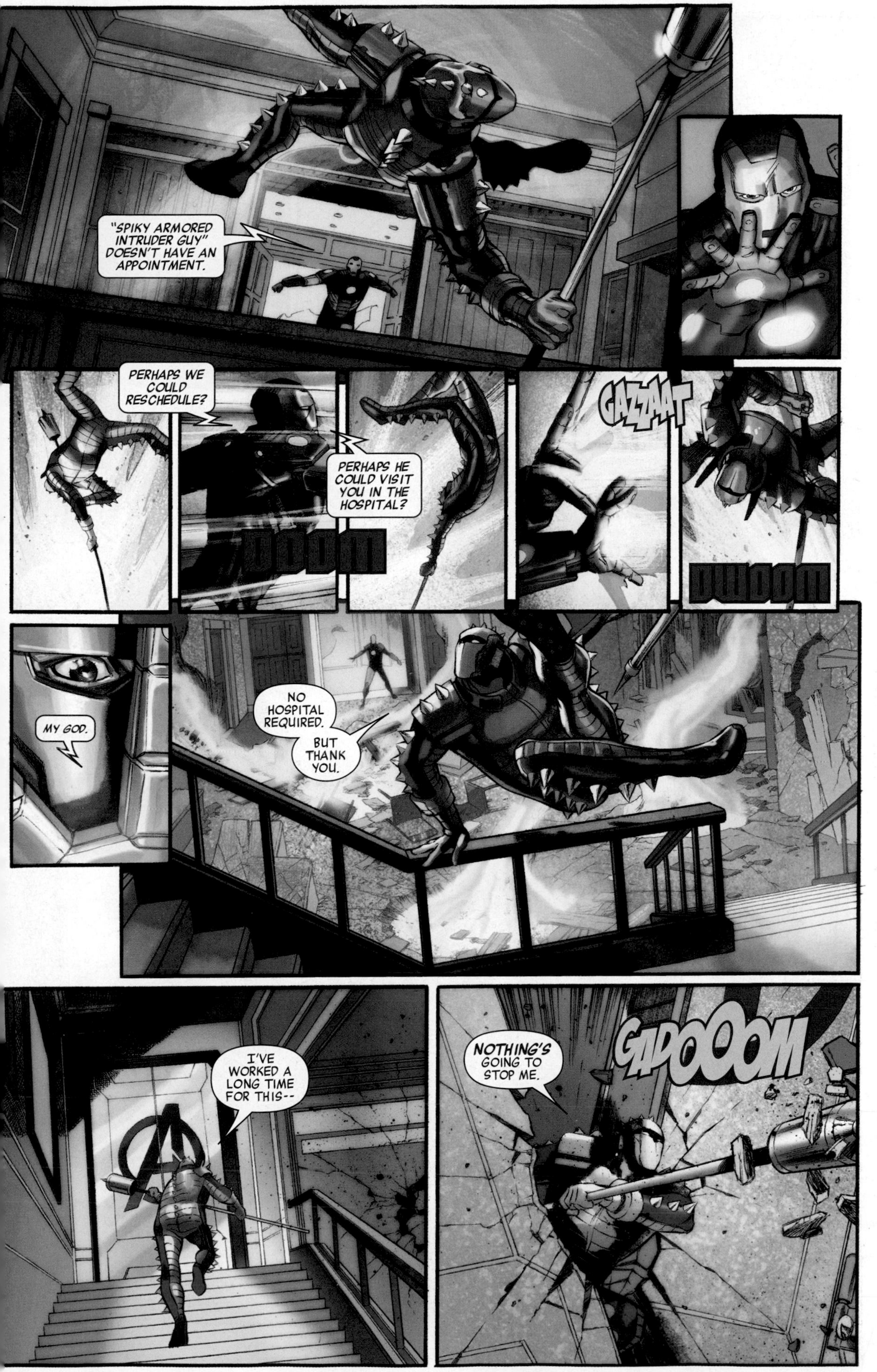
"SPIKY ARMORED INTRUDER GUY" DOESN'T HAVE AN APPOINTMENT.
PERHAPS WE COULD RESCHEDULE?
DOOM
PERHAPS HE COULD VISIT YOU IN THE HOSPITAL?
GAZZAAT
DWOOM
MY GOD.
NO HOSPITAL REQUIRED.
BUT THANK YOU.
I'VE WORKED A LONG TIME FOR THIS--
NOTHING'S GOING TO STOP ME.
GADOOOOM

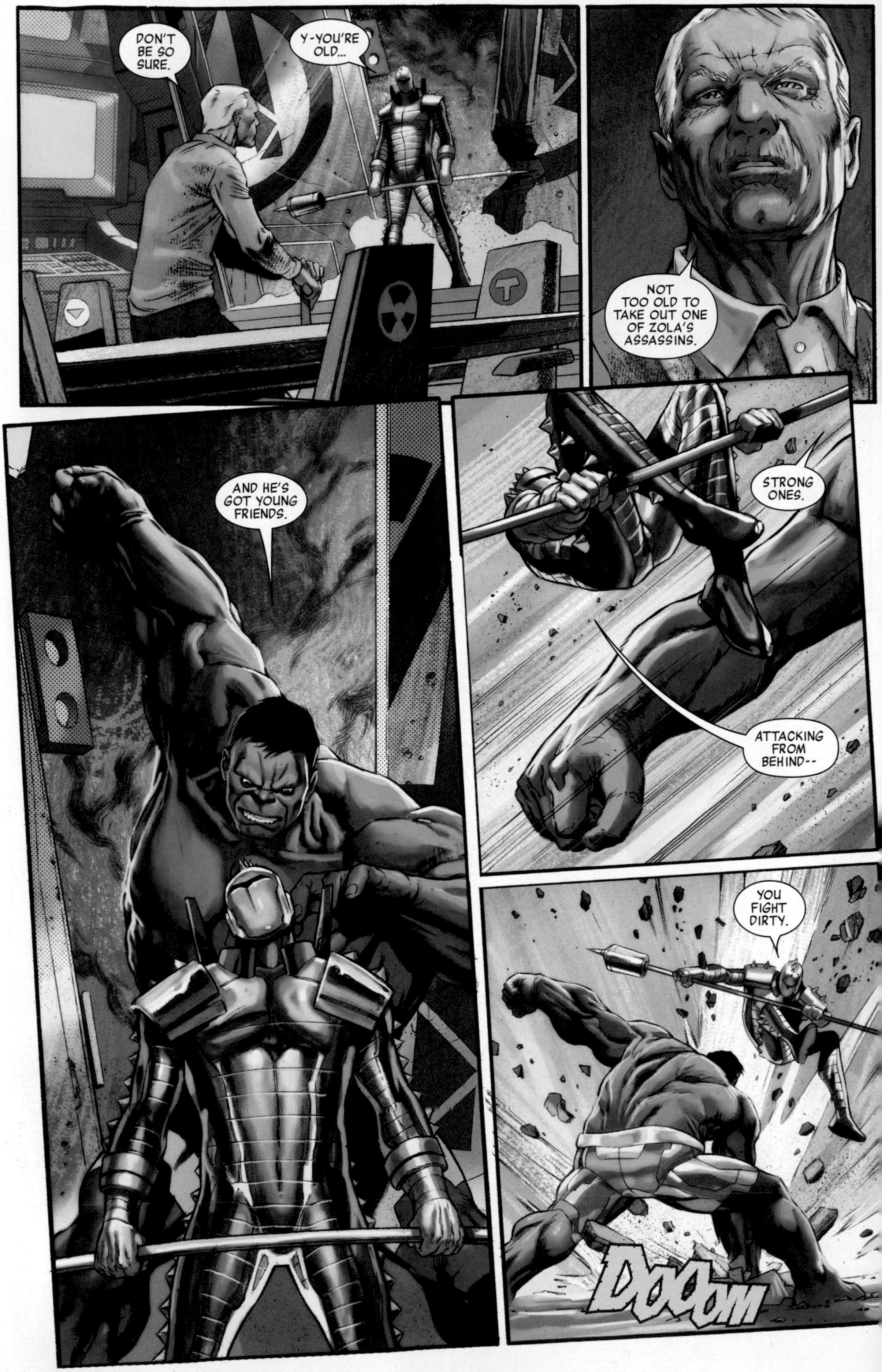
Y-YOU'RE OLD...
DON'T BE SO SURE.
NOT TOO OLD TO TAKE OUT ONE OF ZOLA'S ASSASSINS.
AND HE'S GOT YOUNG FRIENDS.
STRONG ONES.
ATTACKING FROM BEHIND--
YOU FIGHT DIRTY.
DOOOM

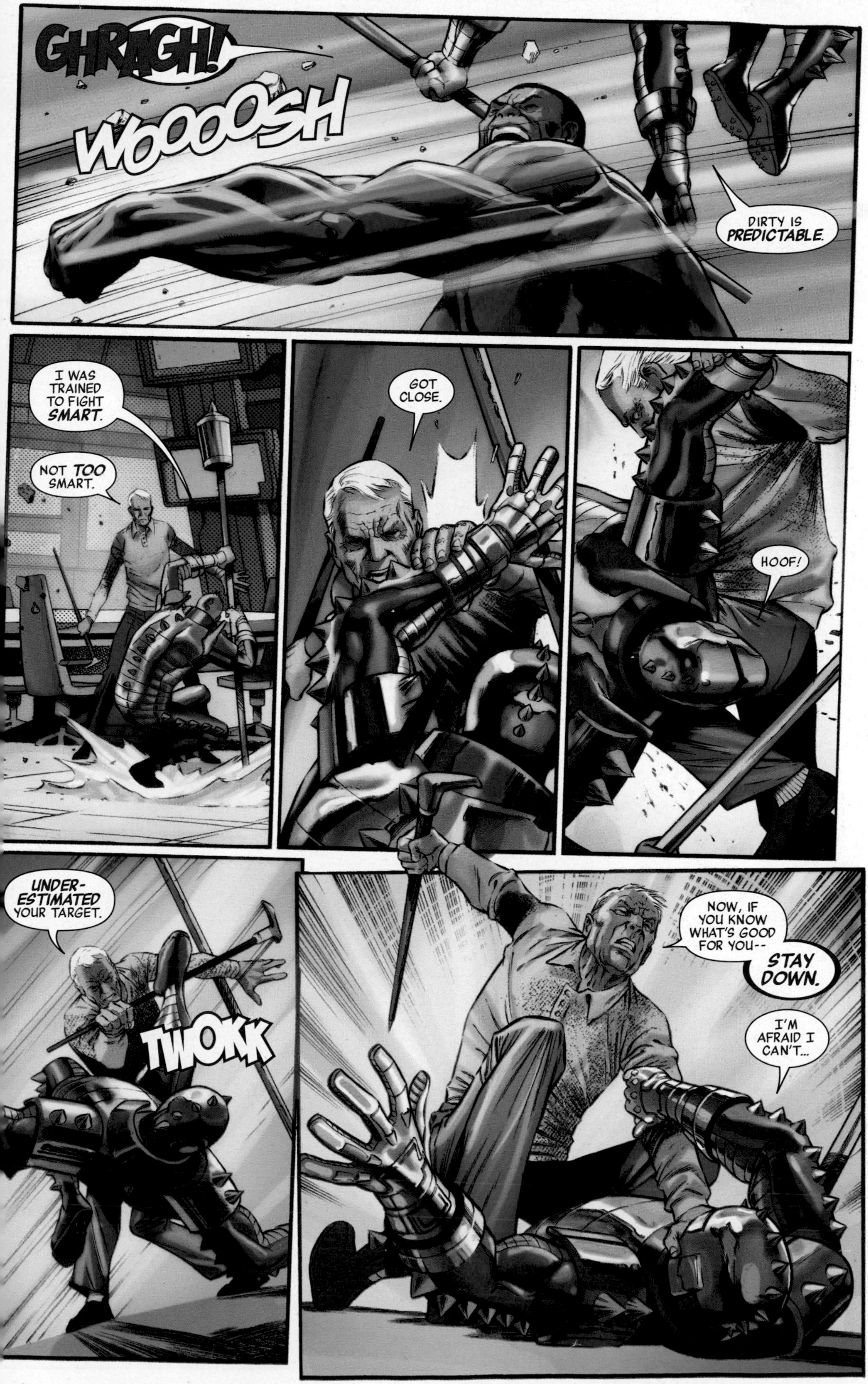
GHRAGH!
WOOOOOSH
DIRTY IS PREDICTABLE.
I WAS TRAINED TO FIGHT SMART.
NOT TOO SMART.
GOT CLOSE.
HOOF!
UNDER-ESTIMATED YOUR TARGET.
TWOKK
NOW, IF YOU KNOW WHAT'S GOOD FOR YOU--
STAY DOWN.
I'M AFRAID I CAN'T...

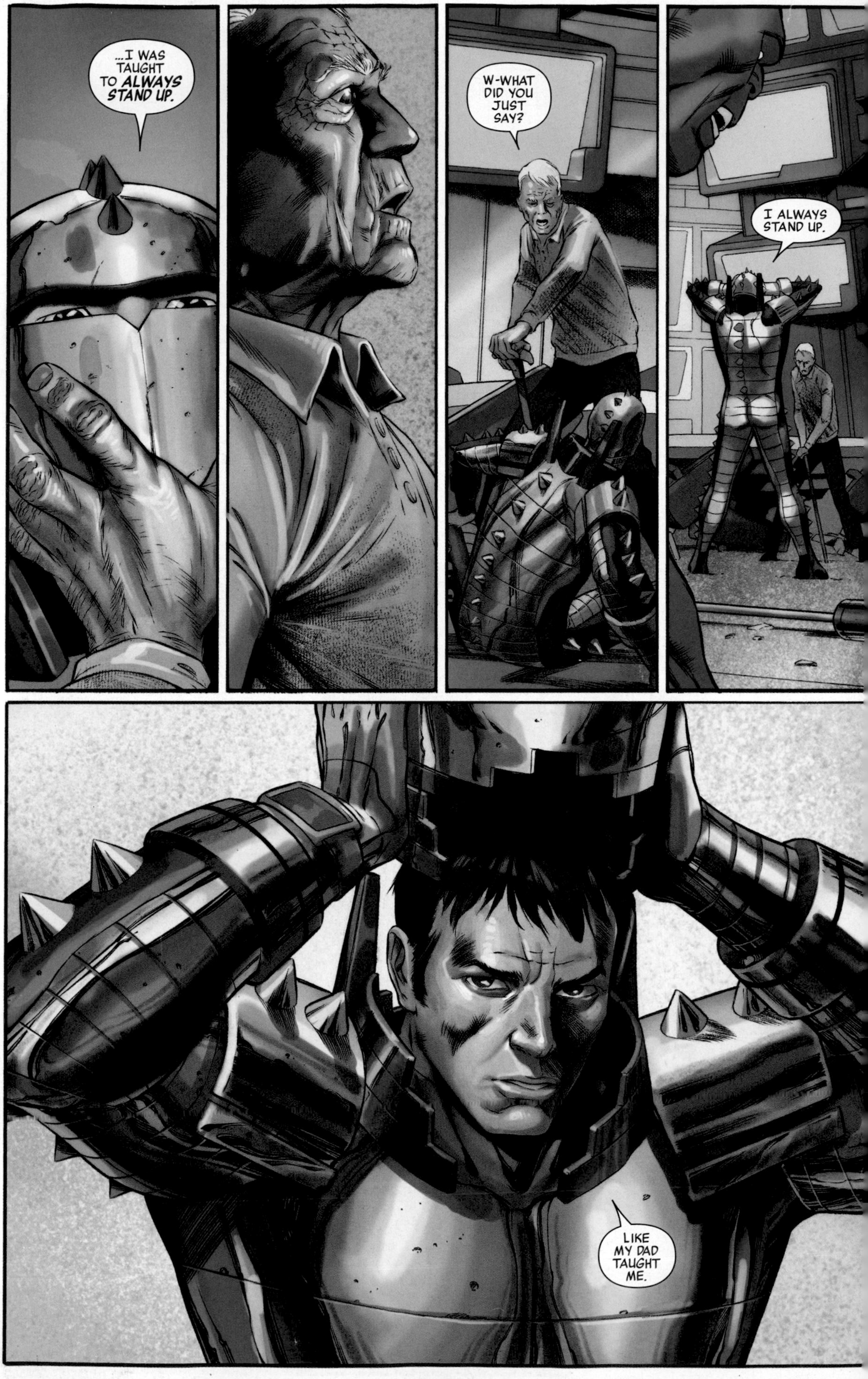
...I WAS TAUGHT TO ALWAYS STAND UP.
W-WHAT DID YOU JUST SAY?
I ALWAYS STAND UP.
LIKE MY DAD TAUGHT ME.

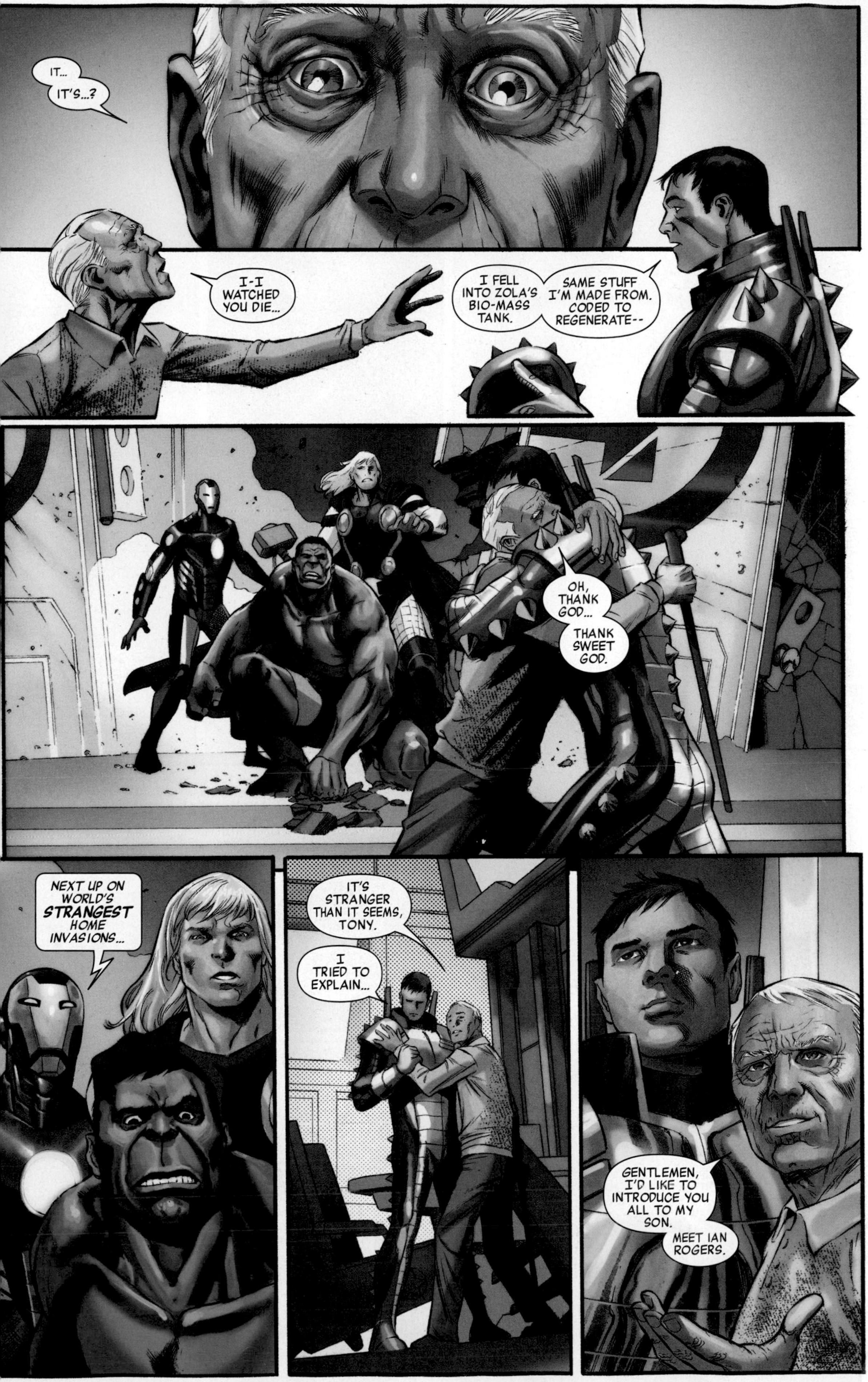
IT... IT'S...?
I-I WATCHED YOU DIE...
I FELL INTO ZOLA'S BIO-MASS TANK.
SAME STUFF I'M MADE FROM. CODED TO REGENERATE--
OH, THANK GOD...
THANK SWEET GOD.
NEXT UP ON WORLD'S STRANGEST HOME INVASIONS...
IT'S STRANGER THAN IT SEEMS, TONY.
I TRIED TO EXPLAIN...
GENTLEMEN, I'D LIKE TO INTRODUCE YOU ALL TO MY SON.
MEET IAN ROGERS.

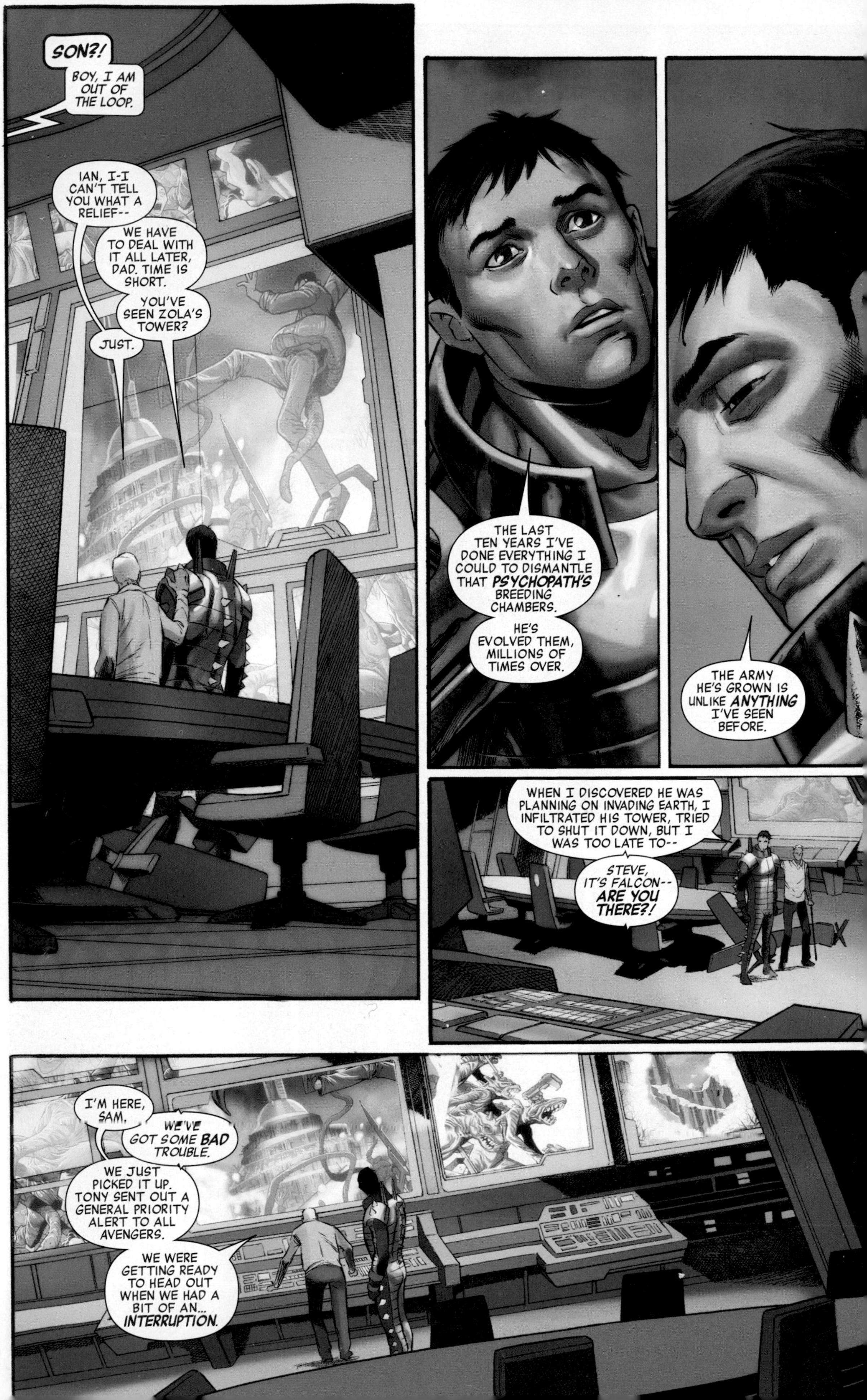
SON?!
BOY, I AM OUT OF THE LOOP.
IAN, I-I CAN'T TELL YOU WHAT A RELIEF--
WE HAVE TO DEAL WITH IT ALL LATER, DAD. TIME IS SHORT.
YOU'VE SEEN ZOLA'S TOWER?
JUST.
THE LAST TEN YEARS I'VE DONE EVERYTHING I COULD TO DISMANTLE THAT PSYCHOPATH'S BREEDING CHAMBERS.
HE'S EVOLVED THEM, MILLIONS OF TIMES OVER.
THE ARMY HE'S GROWN IS UNLIKE ANYTHING I'VE SEEN BEFORE.
WHEN I DISCOVERED HE WAS PLANNING ON INVADING EARTH, I INFILTRATED HIS TOWER, TRIED TO SHUT IT DOWN, BUT I WAS TOO LATE TO--
STEVE, IT'S FALCON-- ARE YOU THERE?!
I'M HERE, SAM.
WE'VE GOT SOME BAD TROUBLE.
WE JUST PICKED IT UP. TONY SENT OUT A GENERAL PRIORITY ALERT TO ALL AVENGERS.
WE WERE GETTING READY TO HEAD OUT WHEN WE HAD A BIT OF AN... INTERRUPTION.

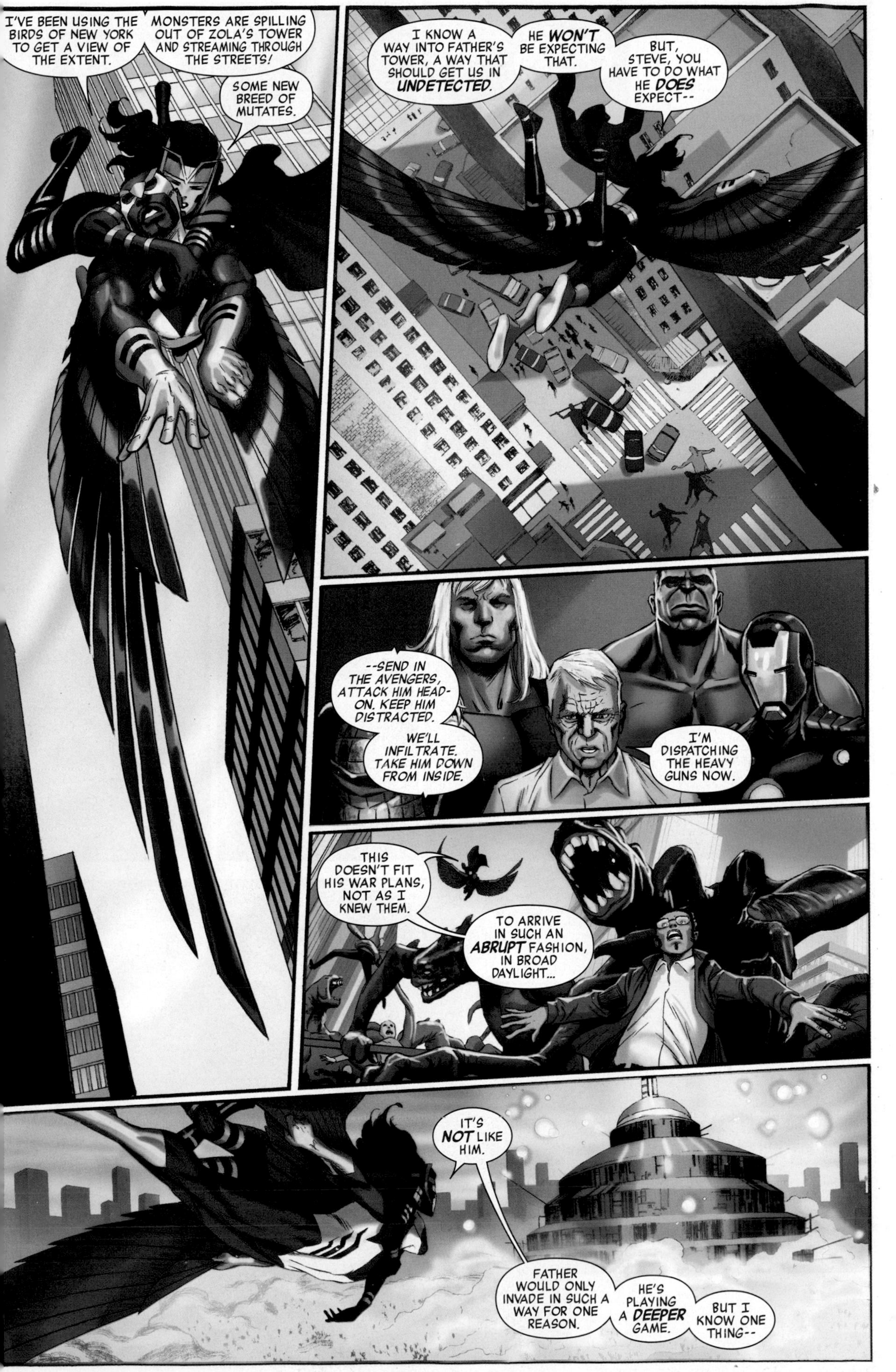
I'VE BEEN USING THE BIRDS OF NEW YORK TO GET A VIEW OF THE EXTENT.
MONSTERS ARE SPILLING OUT OF ZOLA'S TOWER AND STREAMING THROUGH THE STREETS!
SOME NEW BREED OF MUTATES.
I KNOW A WAY INTO FATHER'S TOWER, A WAY THAT SHOULD GET US IN UNDETECTED.
HE WON'T BE EXPECTING THAT.
BUT, STEVE, YOU HAVE TO DO WHAT HE DOES EXPECT--
--SEND IN THE AVENGERS, ATTACK HIM HEAD-ON. KEEP HIM DISTRACTED.
WE'LL INFILTRATE. TAKE HIM DOWN FROM INSIDE.
I'M DISPATCHING THE HEAVY GUNS NOW.
THIS DOESN'T FIT HIS WAR PLANS, NOT AS I KNEW THEM.
TO ARRIVE IN SUCH AN ABRUPT FASHION, IN BROAD DAYLIGHT...
IT'S NOT LIKE HIM.
FATHER WOULD ONLY INVADE IN SUCH A WAY FOR ONE REASON.
HE'S PLAYING A DEEPER GAME.
BUT I KNOW ONE THING--

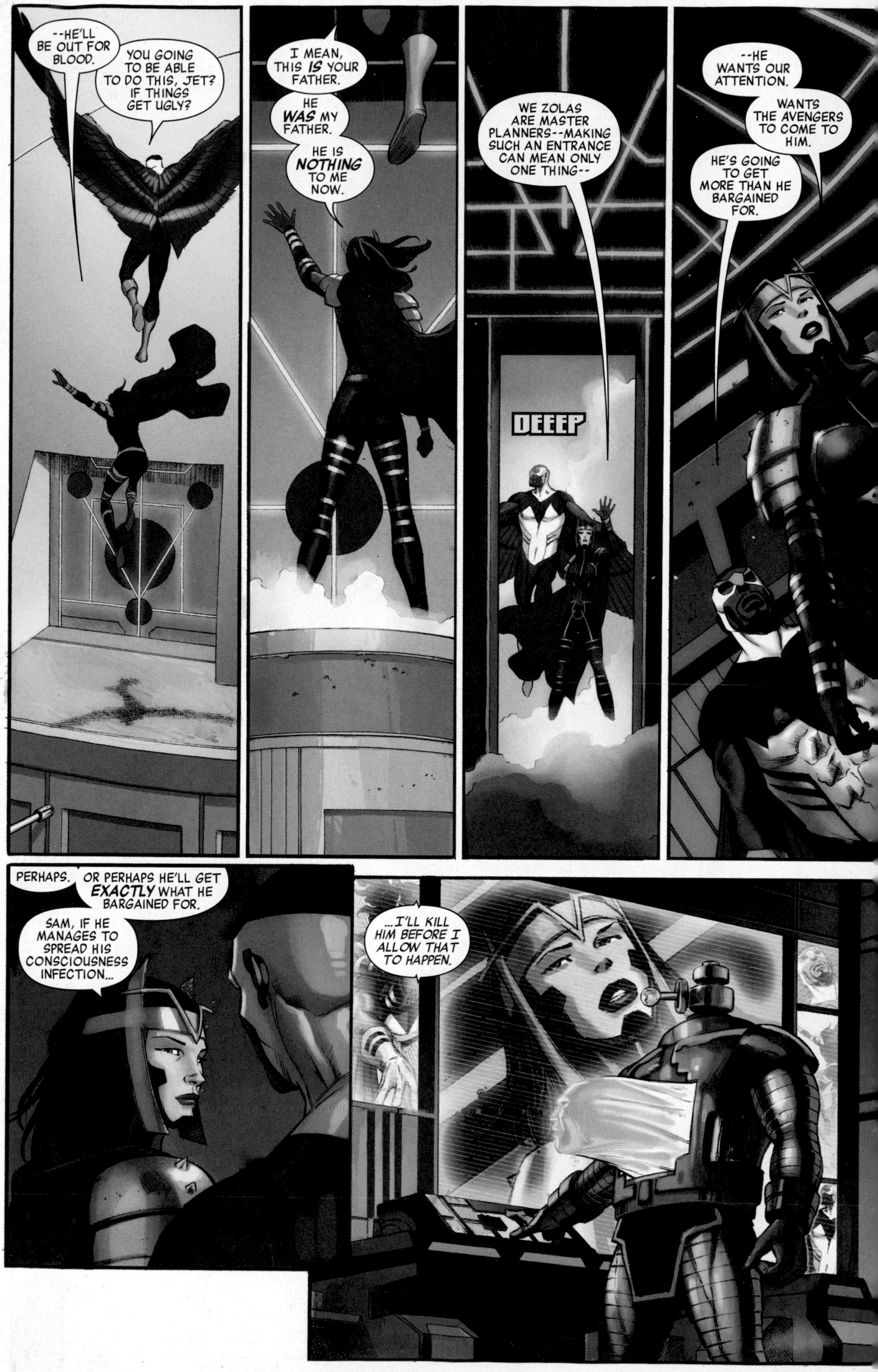
--HE'LL BE OUT FOR BLOOD.
YOU GOING TO BE ABLE TO DO THIS, JET? IF THINGS GET UGLY?
I MEAN, THIS IS YOUR FATHER.
HE WAS MY FATHER.
HE IS NOTHING TO ME NOW.
WE ZOLAS ARE MASTER PLANNERS--MAKING SUCH AN ENTRANCE CAN MEAN ONLY ONE THING--
DEEEP
--HE WANTS OUR ATTENTION.
WANTS THE AVENGERS TO COME TO HIM.
HE'S GOING TO GET MORE THAN HE BARGAINED FOR.
PERHAPS.
OR PERHAPS HE'LL GET EXACTLY WHAT HE BARGAINED FOR.
SAM, IF HE MANAGES TO SPREAD HIS CONSCIOUSNESS INFECTION...
...I'LL KILL HIM BEFORE I ALLOW THAT TO HAPPEN.

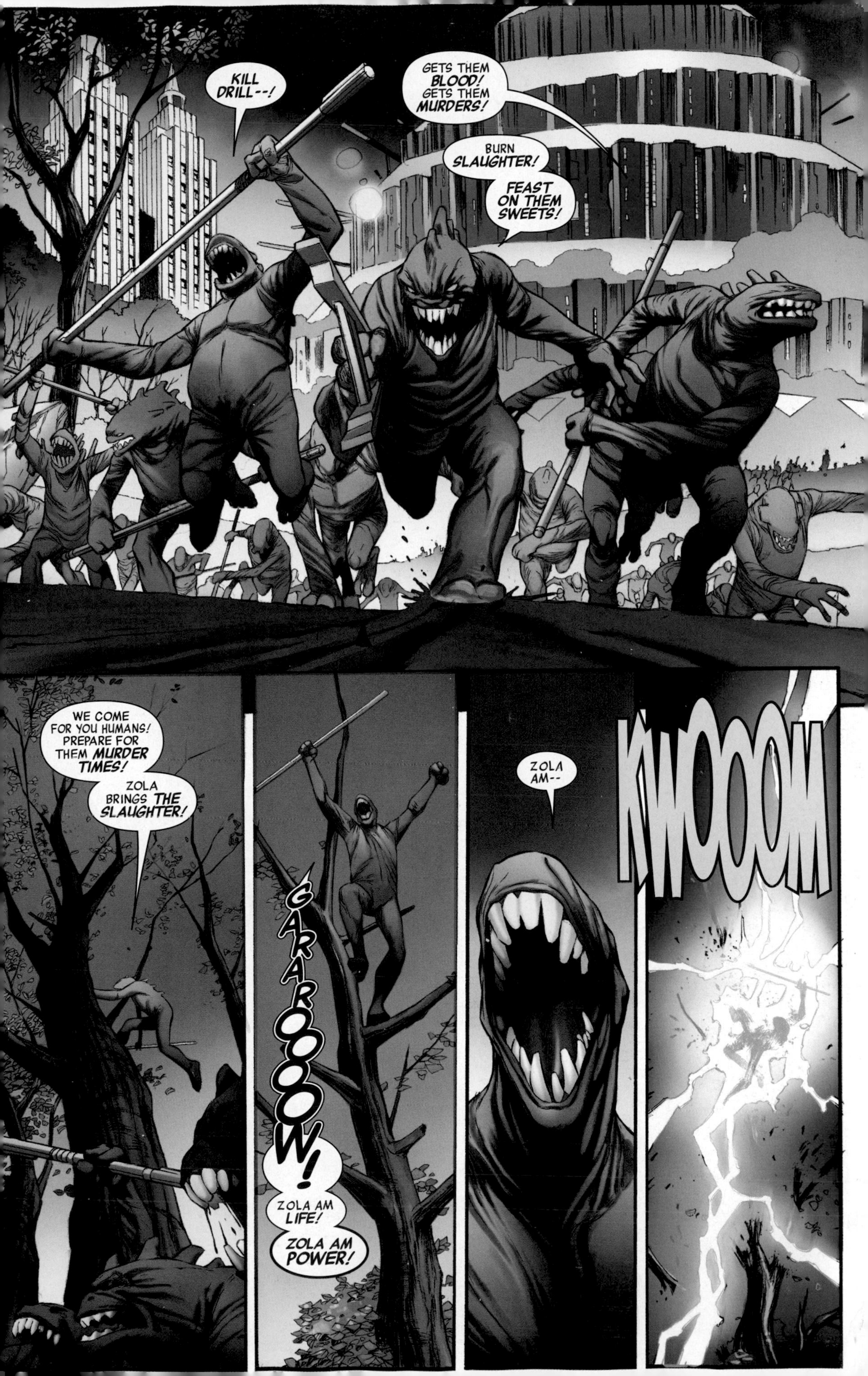
KILL DRILL--!
GETS THEM BLOOD! GETS THEM MURDERS!
BURN SLAUGHTER!
FEAST ON THEM SWEETS!
WE COME FOR YOU HUMANS! PREPARE FOR THEM MURDER TIMES!
ZOLA BRINGS THE SLAUGHTER!
GARAROOOOW!
ZOLA AM LIFE!
ZOLA AM POWER!
ZOLA AM--
KWOOOM

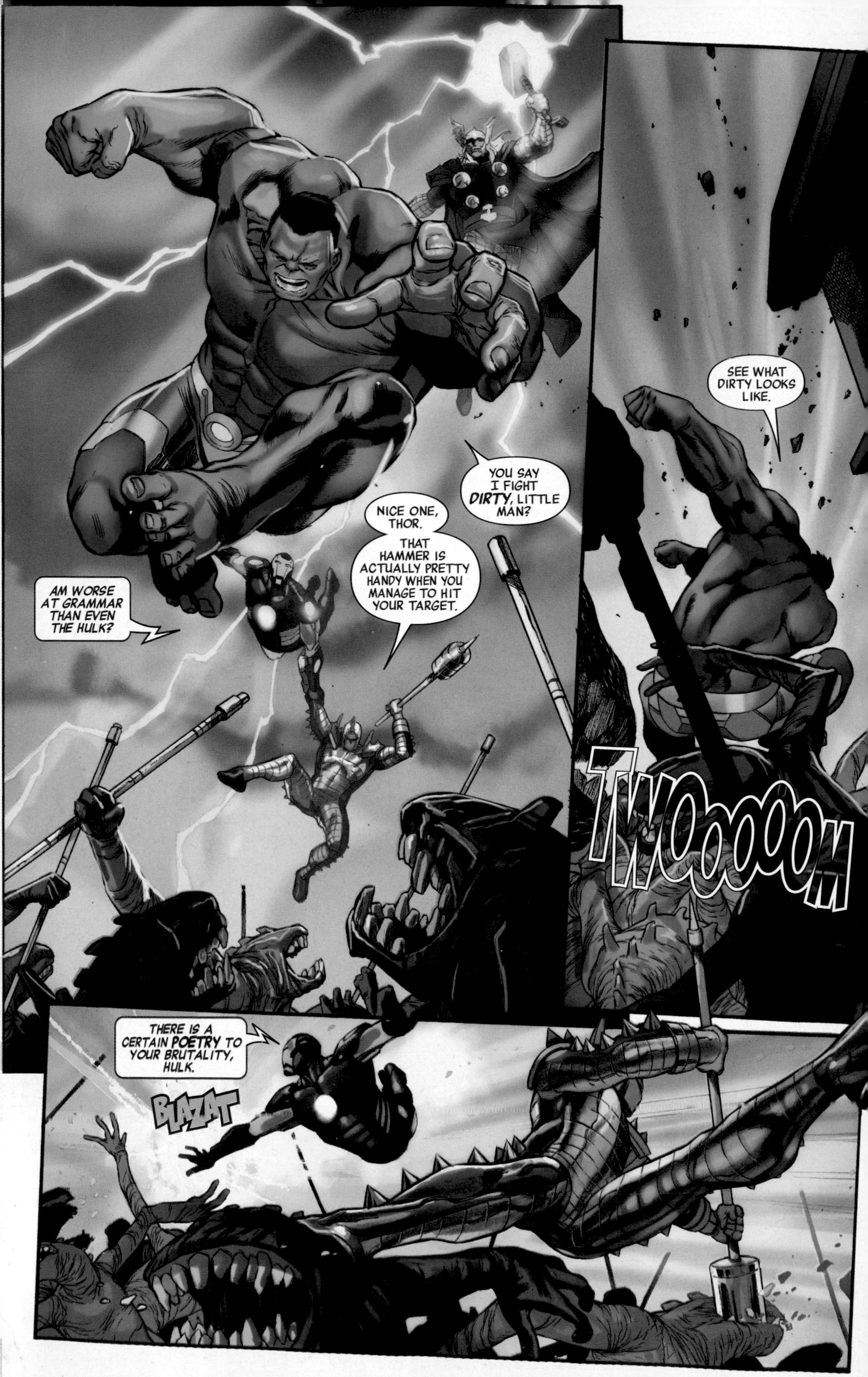
YOU SAY
I FIGHT
DIRTY, LITTLE
MAN?
AM WORSE
AT GRAMMAR
THAN EVEN
THE HULK?
NICE ONE,
THOR.
THAT
HAMMER IS
ACTUALLY PRETTY
HANDY WHEN YOU
MANAGE TO HIT
YOUR TARGET.
SEE WHAT
DIRTY LOOKS
LIKE.
TWOOOOOM
THERE IS A
CERTAIN POETRY TO
YOUR BRUTALITY,
HULK.
BLAZAT

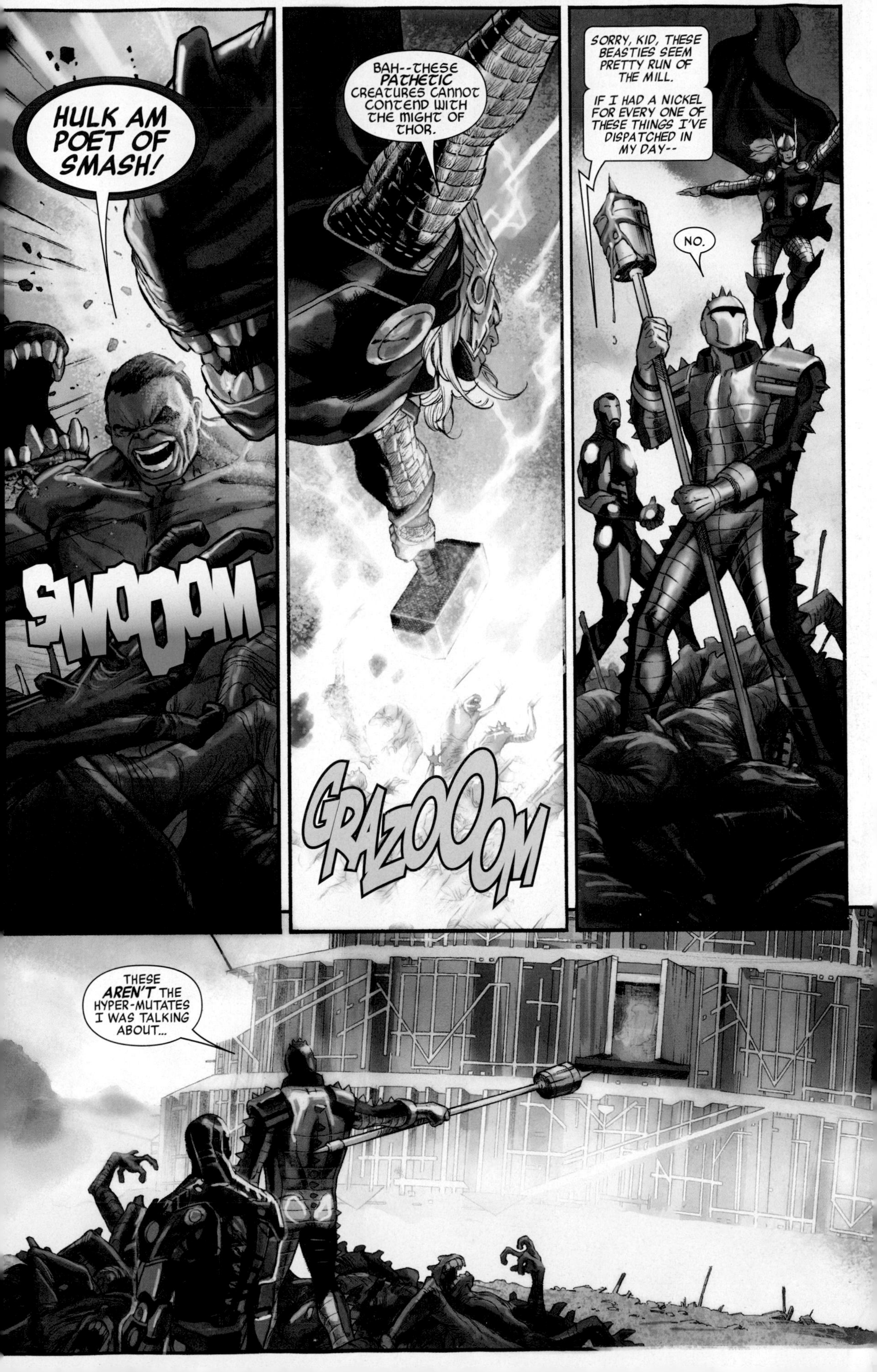

HULK AM POET OF SMASH!
SWOOOM
BAH--THESE *PATHETIC* CREATURES CANNOT CONTEND WITH THE MIGHT OF THOR.
GRAZOOOOM
SORRY, KID, THESE BEASTIES SEEM PRETTY RUN OF THE MILL.
IF I HAD A NICKEL FOR EVERY ONE OF THESE THINGS I'VE DISPATCHED IN MY DAY--
NO.
THESE *AREN'T* THE HYPER-MUTATES I WAS TALKING ABOUT...

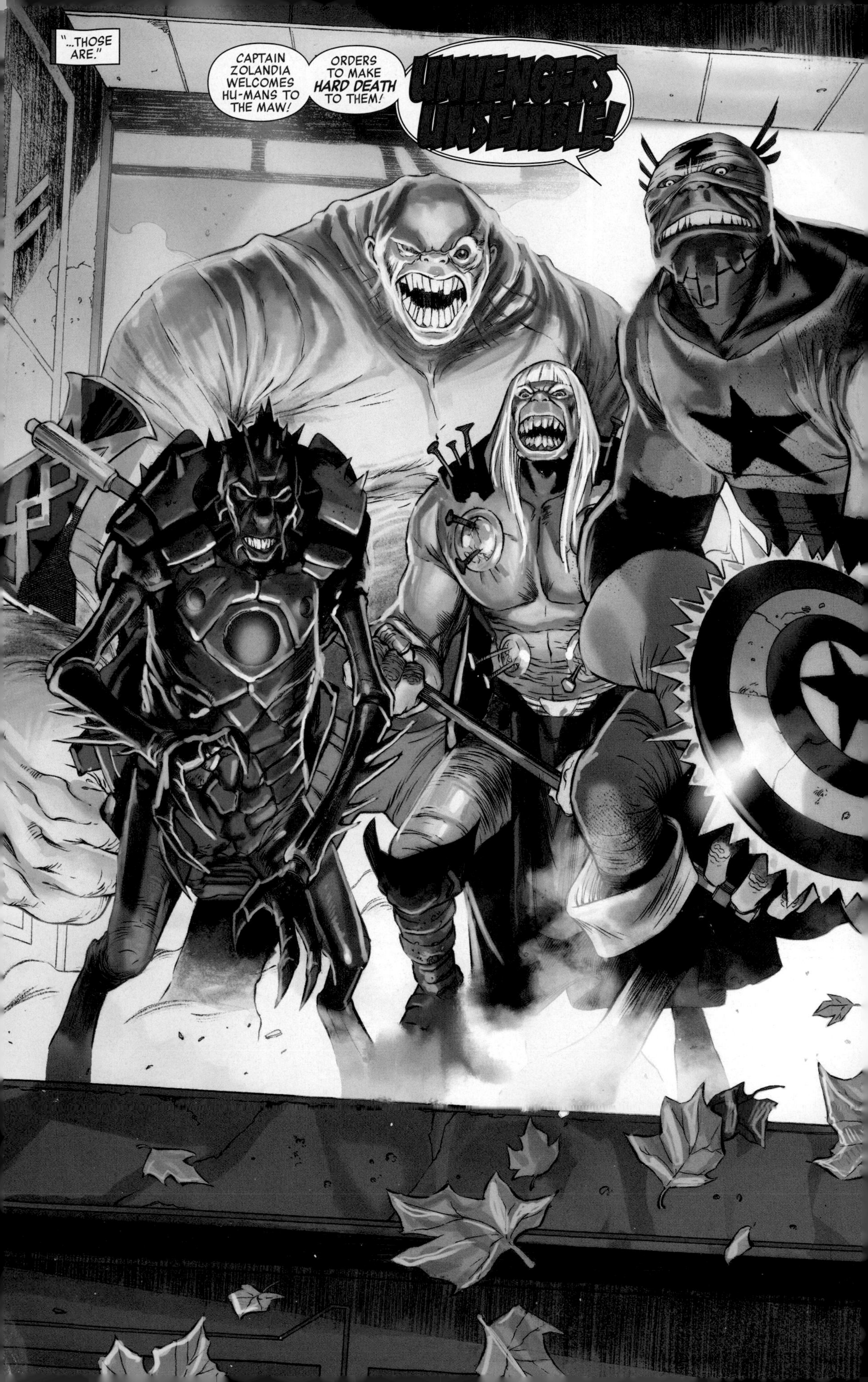
"...THOSE ARE."
CAPTAIN ZOLANDIA WELCOMES HU-MANS TO THE MAW!
ORDERS TO MAKE HARD DEATH TO THEM!
UNVENGERS UNSEMBLE!

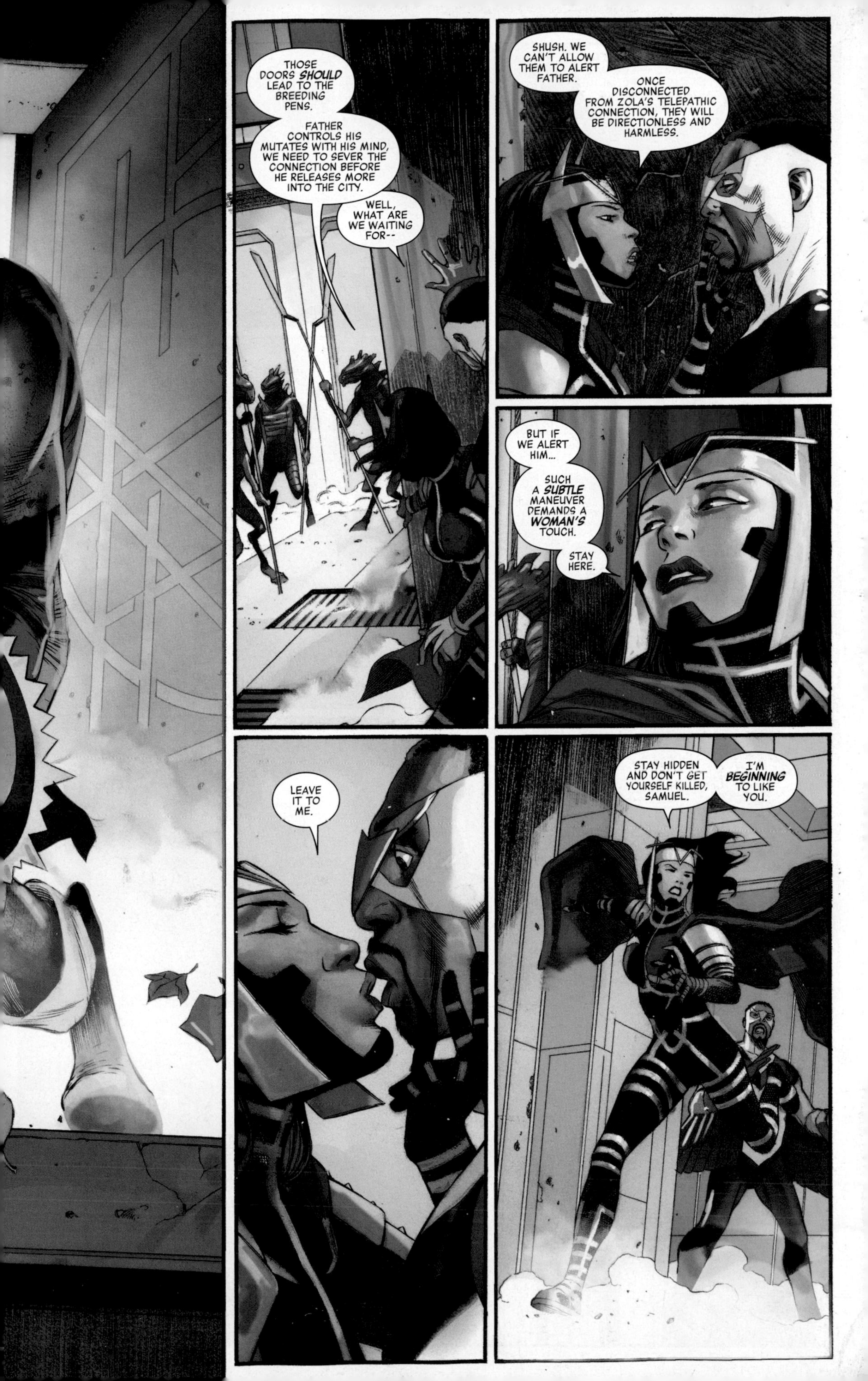
THOSE DOORS SHOULD LEAD TO THE BREEDING PENS.
FATHER CONTROLS HIS MUTATES WITH HIS MIND, WE NEED TO SEVER THE CONNECTION BEFORE HE RELEASES MORE INTO THE CITY.
WELL, WHAT ARE WE WAITING FOR--
SHUSH. WE CAN'T ALLOW THEM TO ALERT FATHER.
ONCE DISCONNECTED FROM ZOLA'S TELEPATHIC CONNECTION, THEY WILL BE DIRECTIONLESS AND HARMLESS.
BUT IF WE ALERT HIM...
SUCH A SUBTLE MANEUVER DEMANDS A WOMAN'S TOUCH.
STAY HERE.
LEAVE IT TO ME.
STAY HIDDEN AND DON'T GET YOURSELF KILLED, SAMUEL.
I'M BEGINNING TO LIKE YOU.

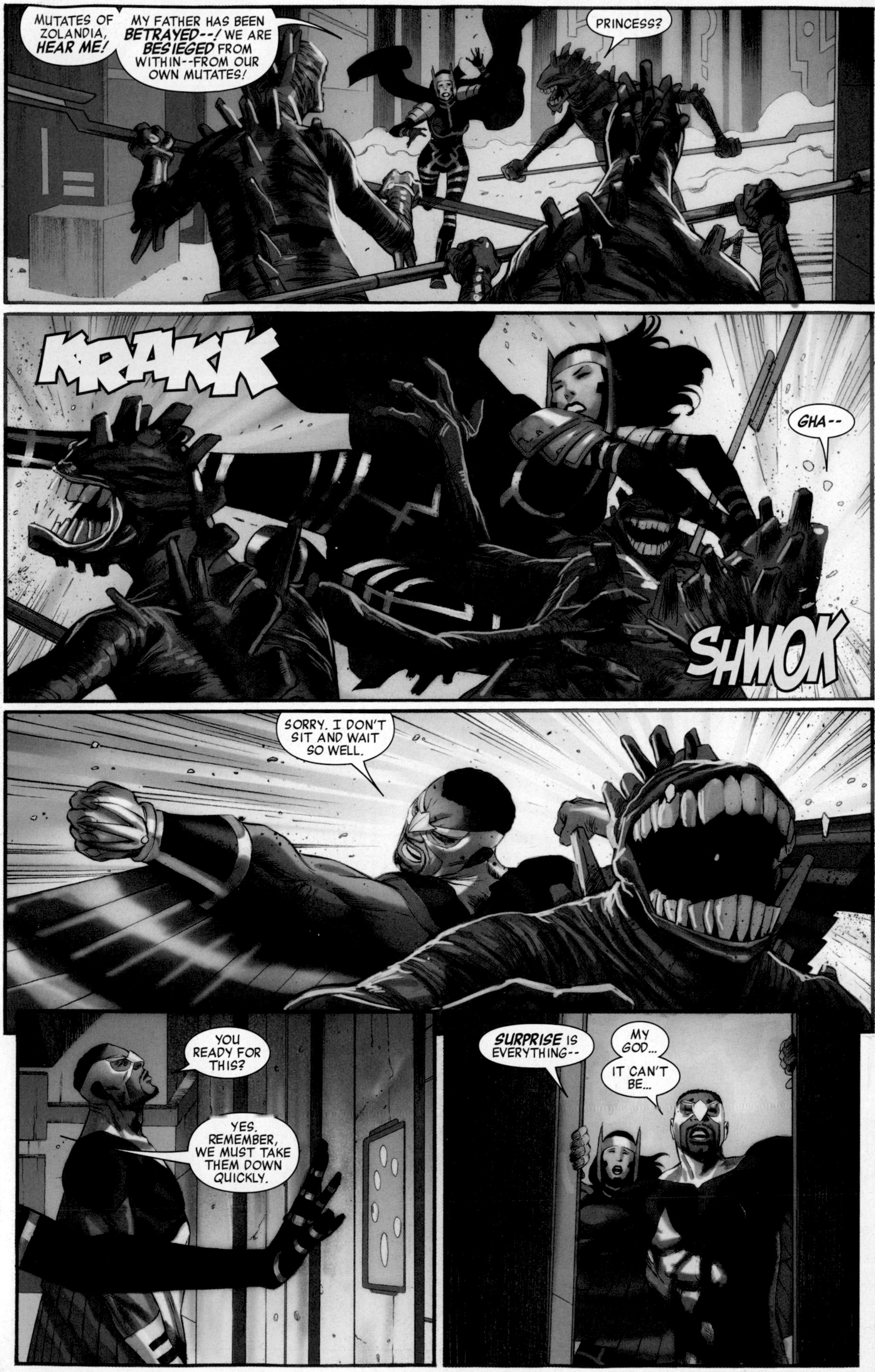
MUTATES OF ZOLANDIA, HEAR ME!
MY FATHER HAS BEEN BETRAYED--! WE ARE BESIEGED FROM WITHIN--FROM OUR OWN MUTATES!
PRINCESS?
KRAKK
GHA--
SHWOK
SORRY. I DON'T SIT AND WAIT SO WELL.
YOU READY FOR THIS?
YES. REMEMBER, WE MUST TAKE THEM DOWN QUICKLY.
SURPRISE IS EVERYTHING--
MY GOD... IT CAN'T BE...

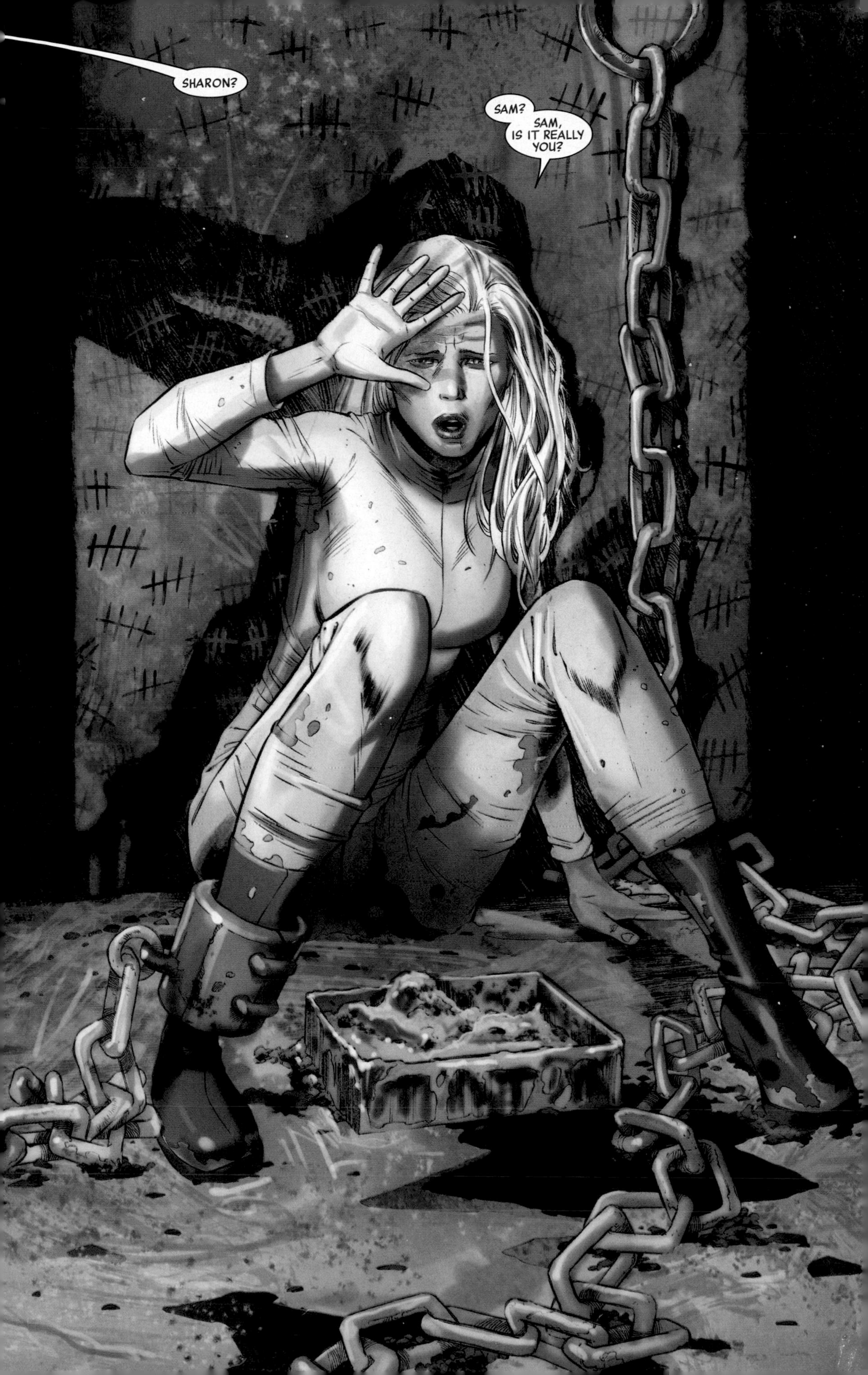
SHARON?
SAM?
SAM, IS IT REALLY YOU?

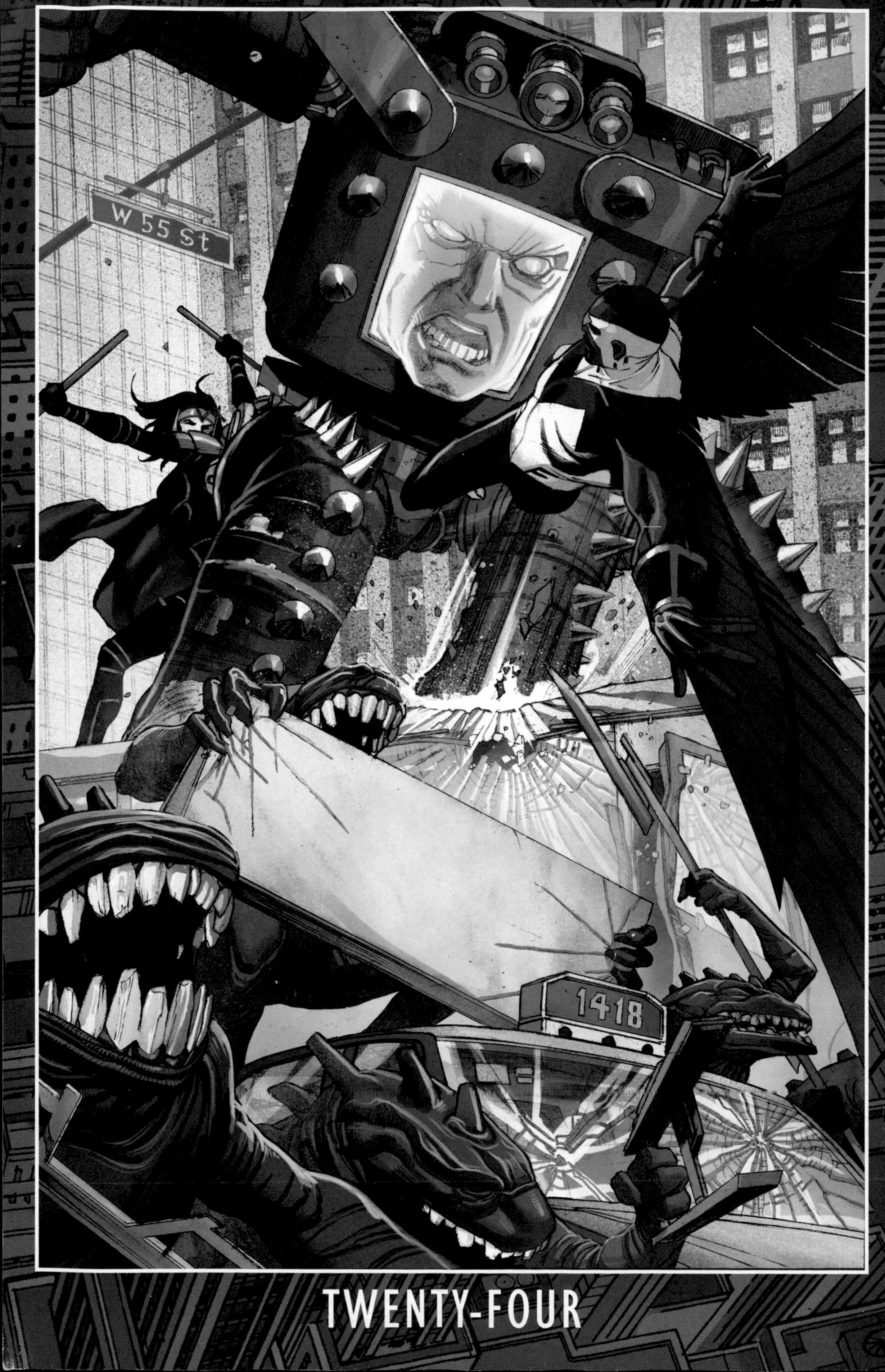
W 55 St
1418

# TWENTY-FOUR

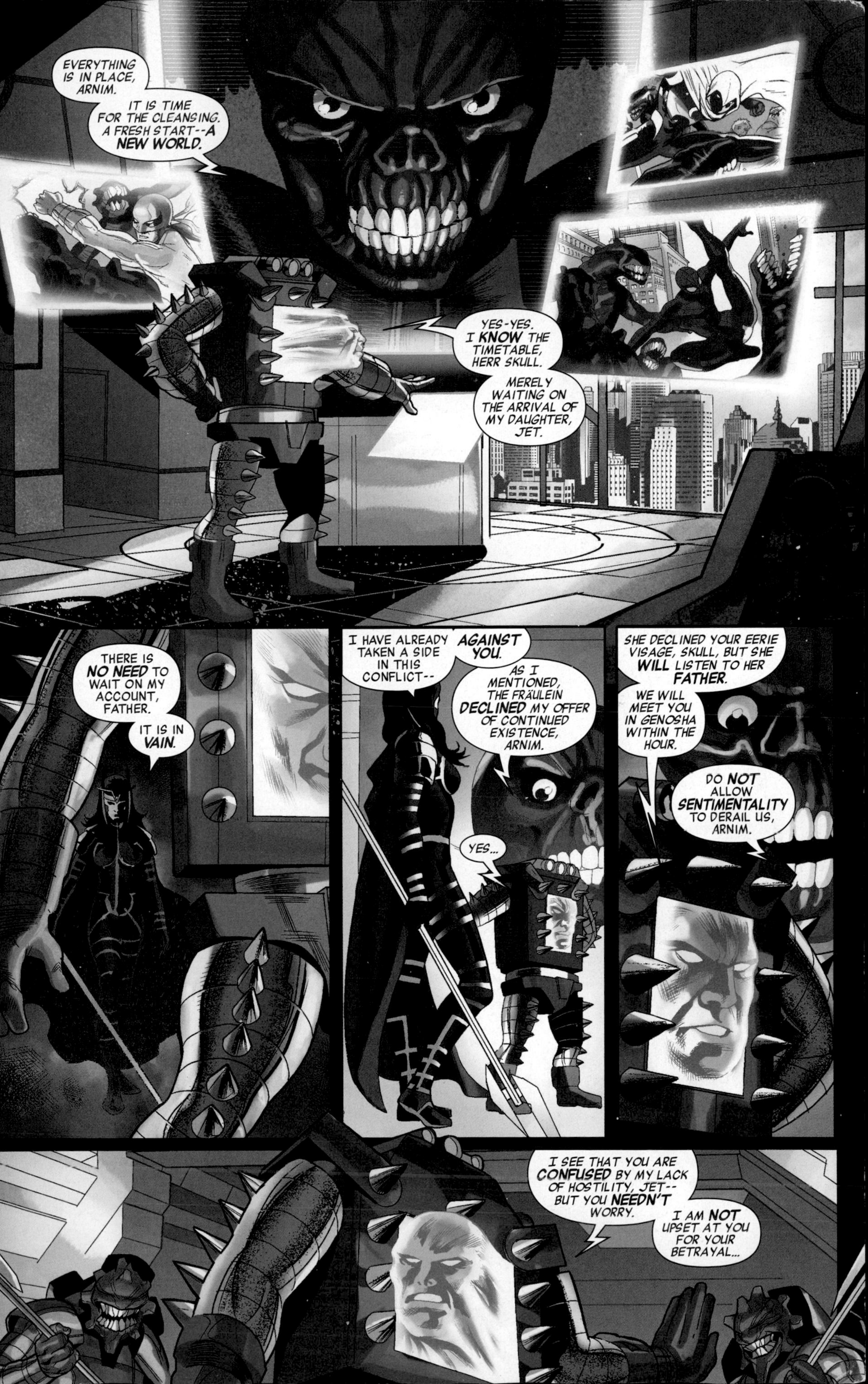
EVERYTHING IS IN PLACE, ARNIM.
IT IS TIME FOR THE CLEANSING. A FRESH START--A **NEW WORLD.**
YES-YES. I **KNOW** THE TIMETABLE, HERR SKULL.
MERELY WAITING ON THE ARRIVAL OF MY DAUGHTER, JET.
THERE IS **NO NEED** TO WAIT ON MY ACCOUNT, FATHER.
IT IS IN **VAIN**.
I HAVE ALREADY TAKEN A SIDE IN THIS CONFLICT--
**AGAINST YOU**.
AS I MENTIONED, THE FRÄULEIN **DECLINED** MY OFFER OF CONTINUED EXISTENCE, ARNIM.
YES...
SHE DECLINED YOUR EERIE VISAGE, SKULL, BUT SHE **WILL** LISTEN TO HER **FATHER**.
WE WILL MEET YOU IN GENOSHA WITHIN THE HOUR.
DO **NOT** ALLOW **SENTIMENTALITY** TO DERAIL US, ARNIM.
I SEE THAT YOU ARE **CONFUSED** BY MY LACK OF HOSTILITY, JET-- BUT YOU **NEEDN'T** WORRY.
I AM **NOT** UPSET AT YOU FOR YOUR BETRAYAL...

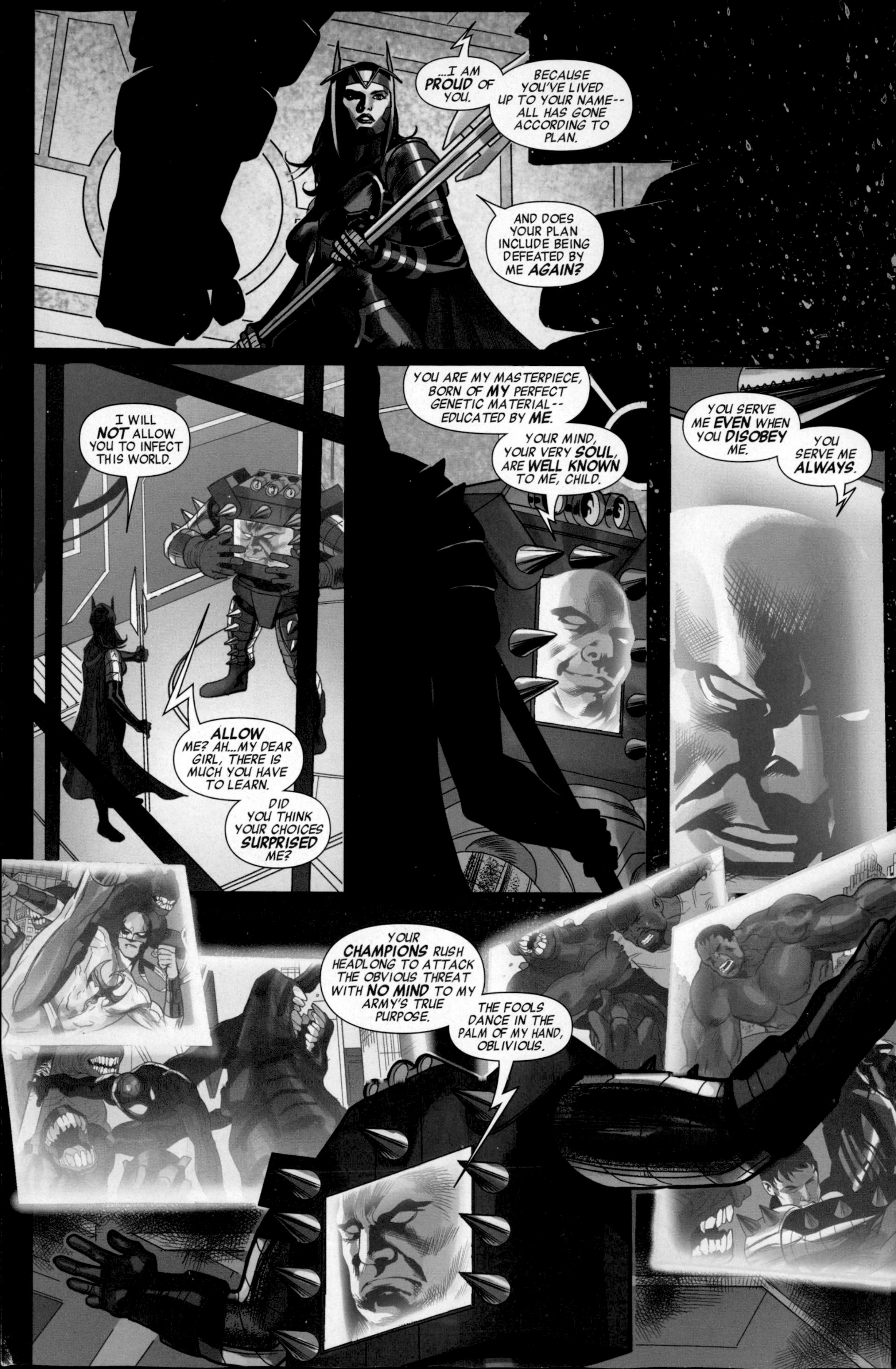
...I AM PROUD OF YOU.
BECAUSE YOU'VE LIVED UP TO YOUR NAME-- ALL HAS GONE ACCORDING TO PLAN.
AND DOES YOUR PLAN INCLUDE BEING DEFEATED BY ME AGAIN?
I WILL NOT ALLOW YOU TO INFECT THIS WORLD.
ALLOW ME? AH...MY DEAR GIRL, THERE IS MUCH YOU HAVE TO LEARN.
DID YOU THINK YOUR CHOICES SURPRISED ME?
YOU ARE MY MASTERPIECE, BORN OF MY PERFECT GENETIC MATERIAL-- EDUCATED BY ME.
YOUR MIND, YOUR VERY SOUL, ARE WELL KNOWN TO ME, CHILD.
YOU SERVE ME EVEN WHEN YOU DISOBEY ME.
YOU SERVE ME ALWAYS.
YOUR CHAMPIONS RUSH HEADLONG TO ATTACK THE OBVIOUS THREAT WITH NO MIND TO MY ARMY'S TRUE PURPOSE.
THE FOOLS DANCE IN THE PALM OF MY HAND, OBLIVIOUS.

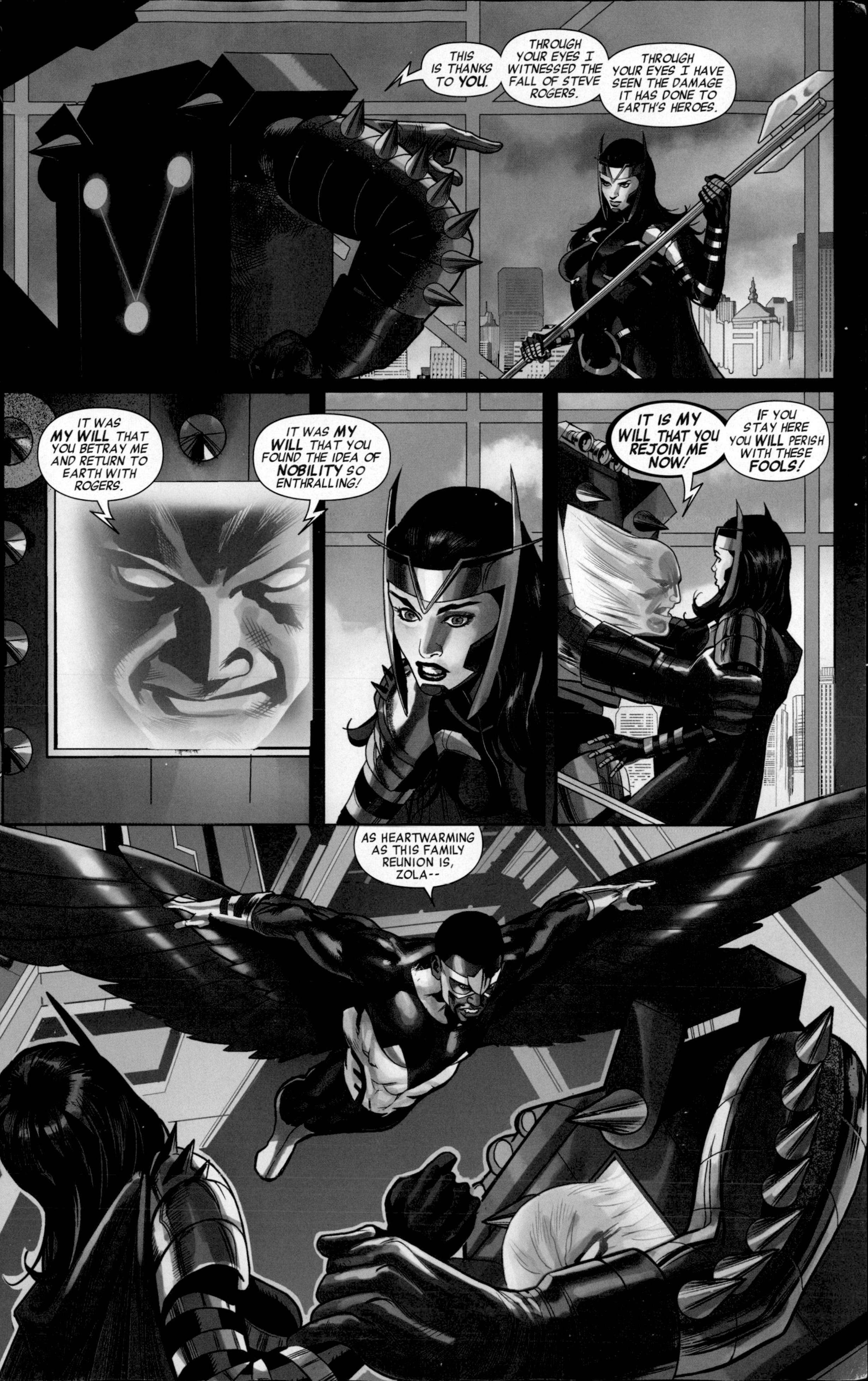
THIS IS THANKS TO YOU.
THROUGH YOUR EYES I WITNESSED THE FALL OF STEVE ROGERS.
THROUGH YOUR EYES I HAVE SEEN THE DAMAGE IT HAS DONE TO EARTH'S HEROES.
IT WAS MY WILL THAT YOU BETRAY ME AND RETURN TO EARTH WITH ROGERS.
IT WAS MY WILL THAT YOU FOUND THE IDEA OF NOBILITY SO ENTHRALLING!
IT IS MY WILL THAT YOU REJOIN ME NOW!
IF YOU STAY HERE YOU WILL PERISH WITH THESE FOOLS!
AS HEARTWARMING AS THIS FAMILY REUNION IS, ZOLA--

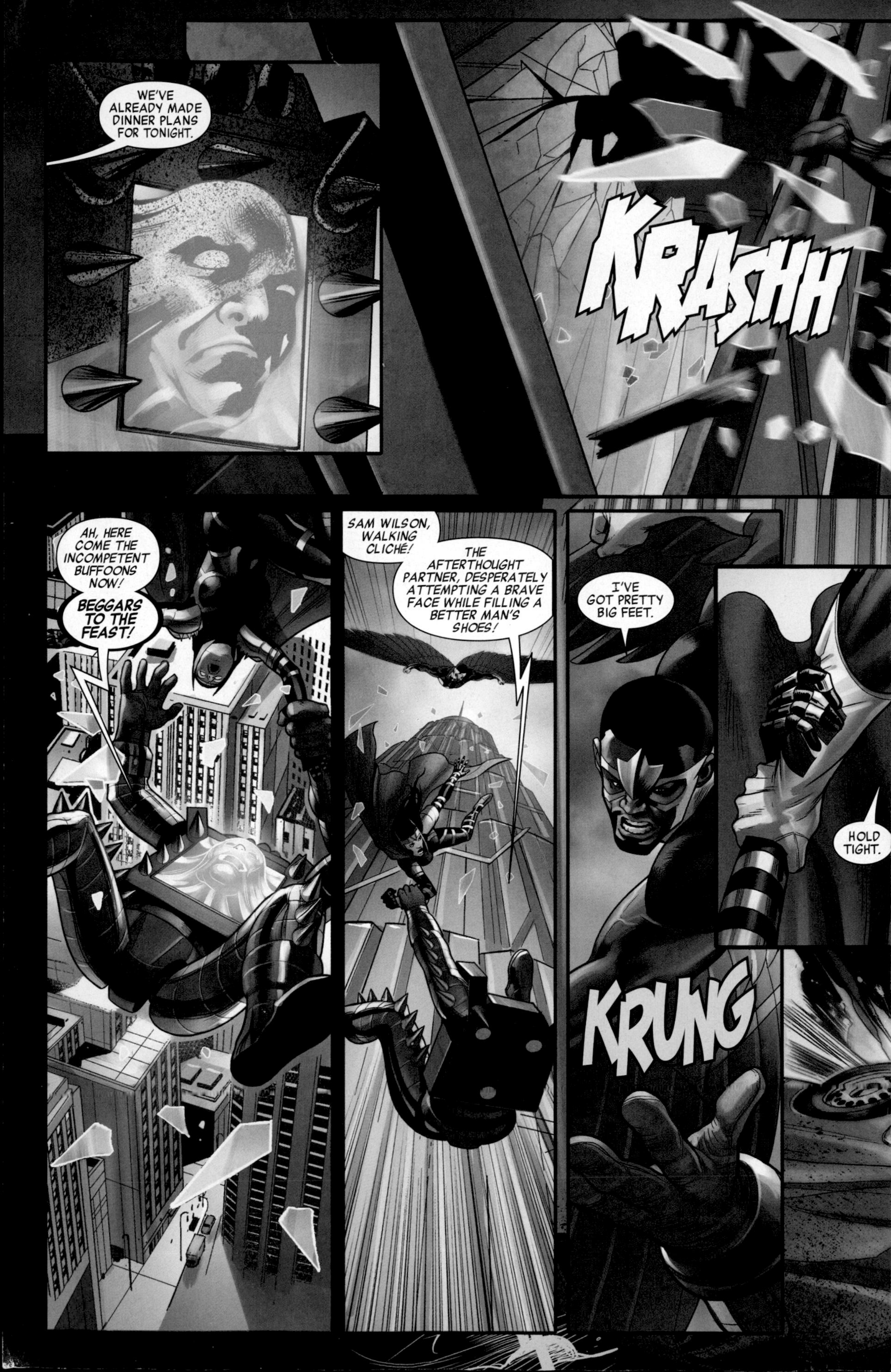
WE'VE ALREADY MADE DINNER PLANS FOR TONIGHT.
KRASHH
AH, HERE COME THE INCOMPETENT BUFFOONS NOW!
BEGGARS TO THE FEAST!
SAM WILSON, WALKING CLICHÉ!
THE AFTERTHOUGHT PARTNER, DESPERATELY ATTEMPTING A BRAVE FACE WHILE FILLING A BETTER MAN'S SHOES!
I'VE GOT PRETTY BIG FEET.
HOLD TIGHT.
KRUNG

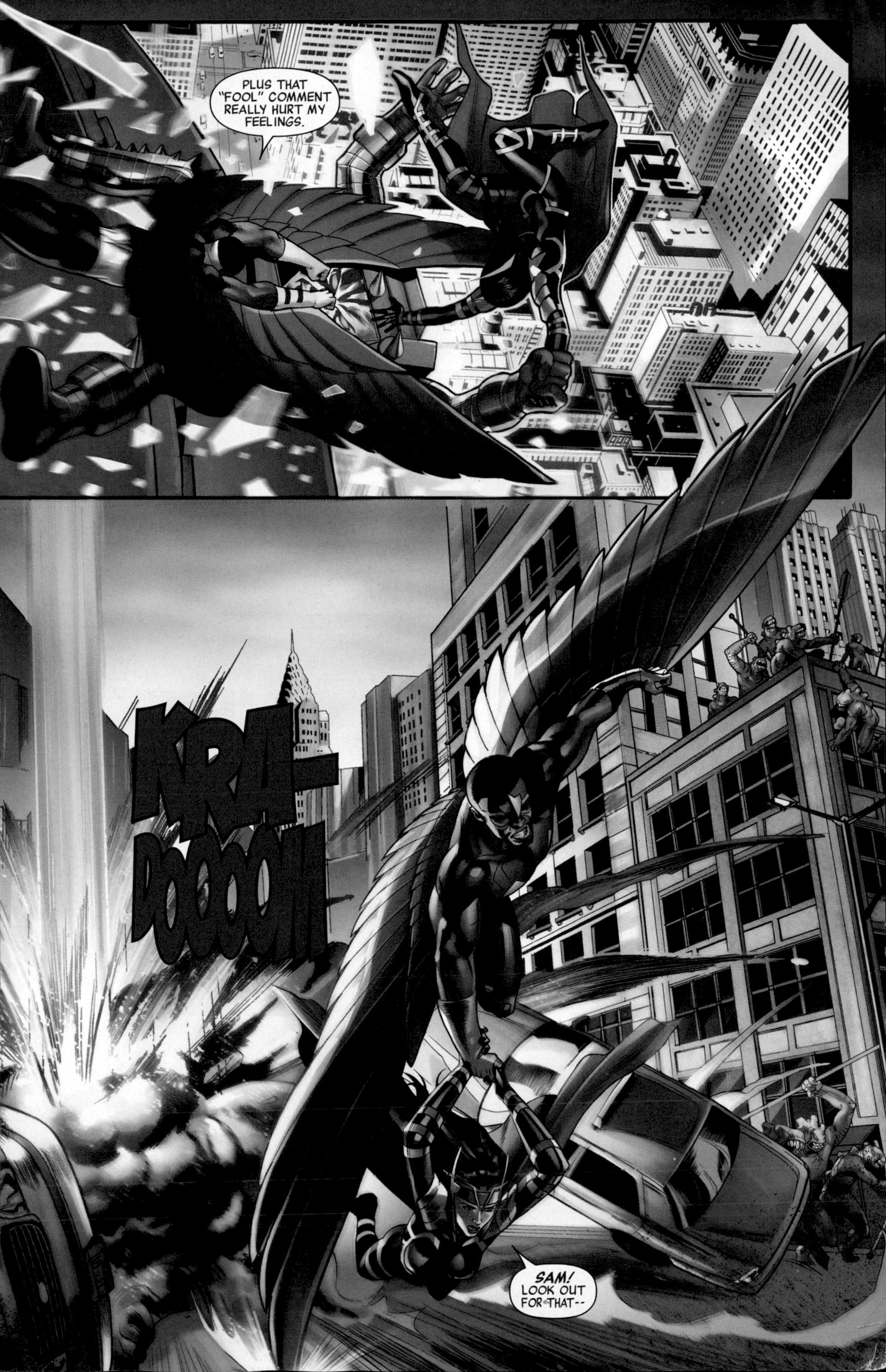
PLUS THAT "FOOL" COMMENT REALLY HURT MY FEELINGS.
KRA-DOOOOM
SAM! LOOK OUT FOR THAT--

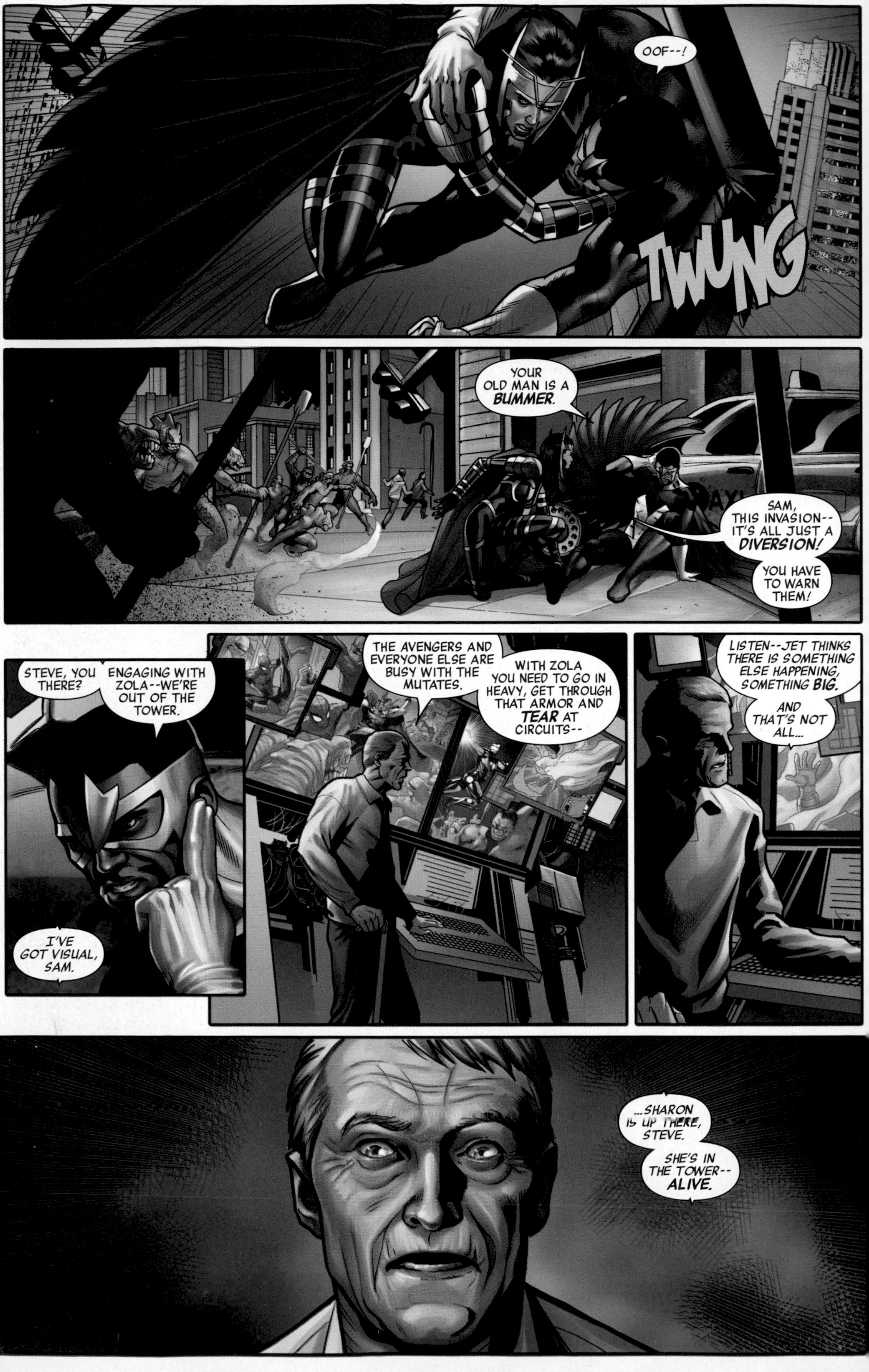
OOF--!
TWUNG
YOUR OLD MAN IS A BUMMER.
SAM, THIS INVASION--IT'S ALL JUST A DIVERSION!
YOU HAVE TO WARN THEM!
STEVE, YOU THERE?
ENGAGING WITH ZOLA--WE'RE OUT OF THE TOWER.
I'VE GOT VISUAL, SAM.
THE AVENGERS AND EVERYONE ELSE ARE BUSY WITH THE MUTATES.
WITH ZOLA YOU NEED TO GO IN HEAVY, GET THROUGH THAT ARMOR AND TEAR AT CIRCUITS--
LISTEN--JET THINKS THERE IS SOMETHING ELSE HAPPENING, SOMETHING BIG.
AND THAT'S NOT ALL...
...SHARON IS UP THERE, STEVE.
SHE'S IN THE TOWER--ALIVE.

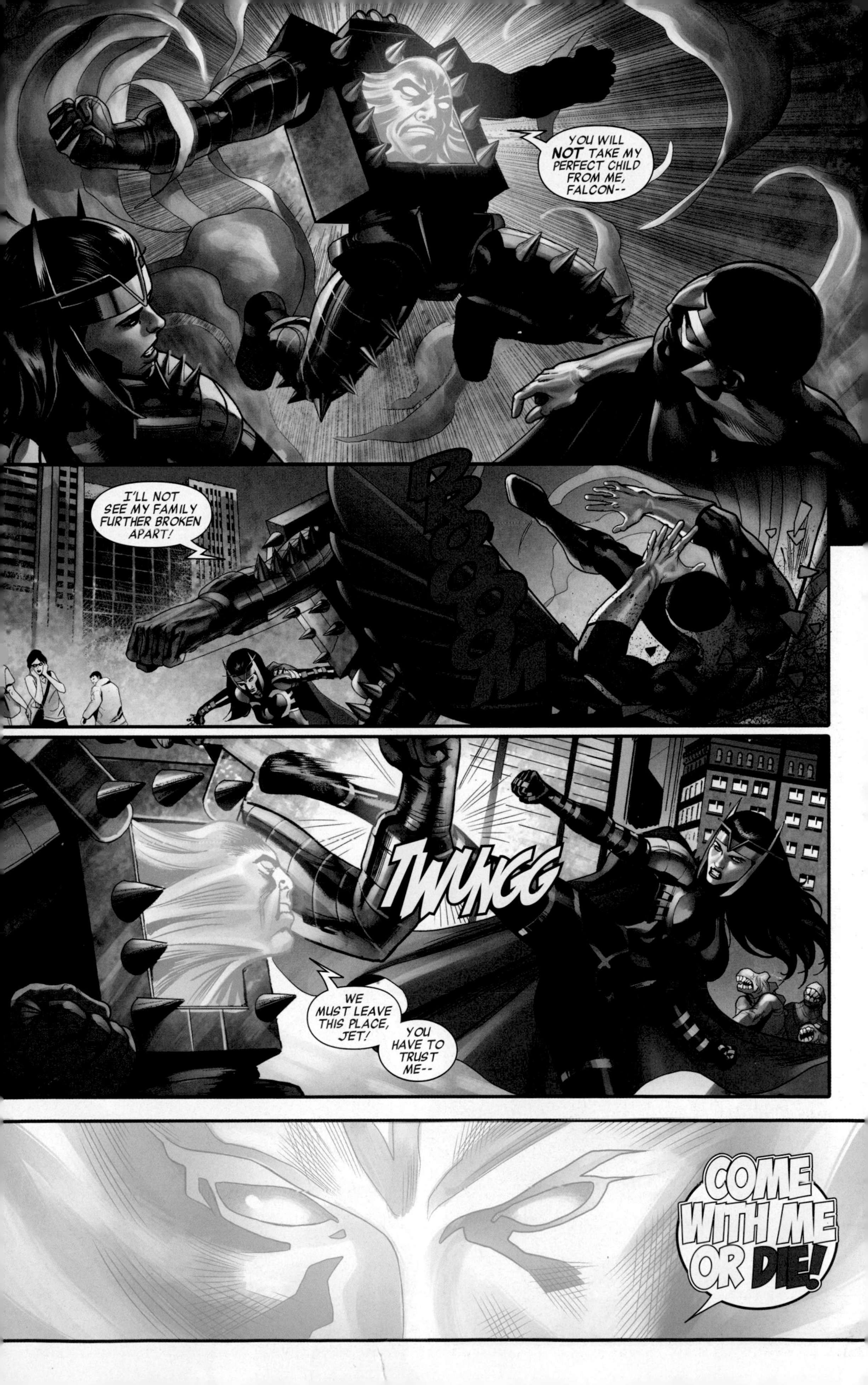
YOU WILL NOT TAKE MY PERFECT CHILD FROM ME, FALCON--
I'LL NOT SEE MY FAMILY FURTHER BROKEN APART!
BOOOOOM
TWUNGG
WE MUST LEAVE THIS PLACE, JET!
YOU HAVE TO TRUST ME--
COME WITH ME OR DIE!

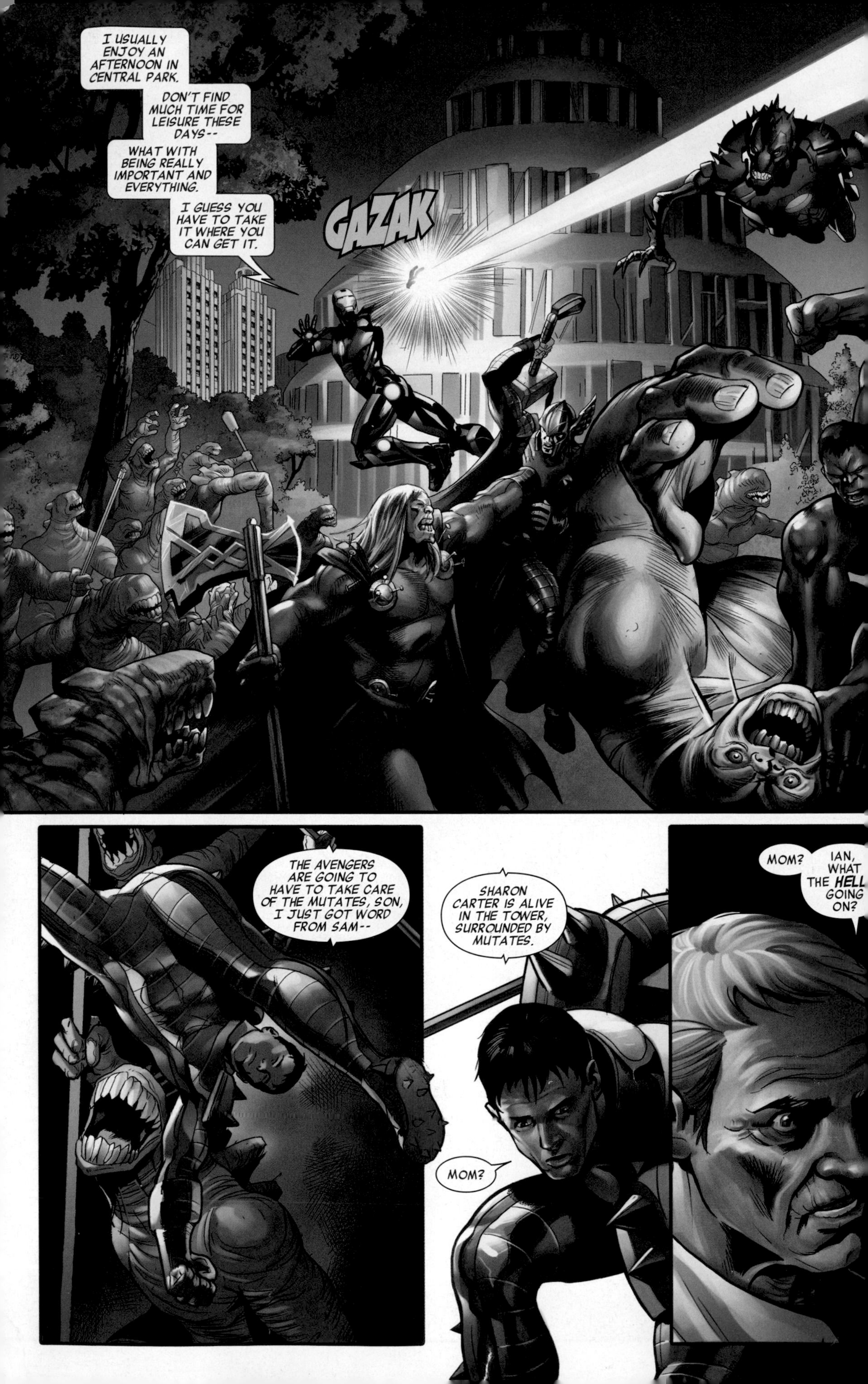

I USUALLY ENJOY AN AFTERNOON IN CENTRAL PARK.
DON'T FIND MUCH TIME FOR LEISURE THESE DAYS--
WHAT WITH BEING REALLY IMPORTANT AND EVERYTHING.
I GUESS YOU HAVE TO TAKE IT WHERE YOU CAN GET IT.
GAZAK
THE AVENGERS ARE GOING TO HAVE TO TAKE CARE OF THE MUTATES, SON, I JUST GOT WORD FROM SAM--
SHARON CARTER IS ALIVE IN THE TOWER, SURROUNDED BY MUTATES.
MOM?
MOM?
IAN, WHAT THE HELL GOING ON?

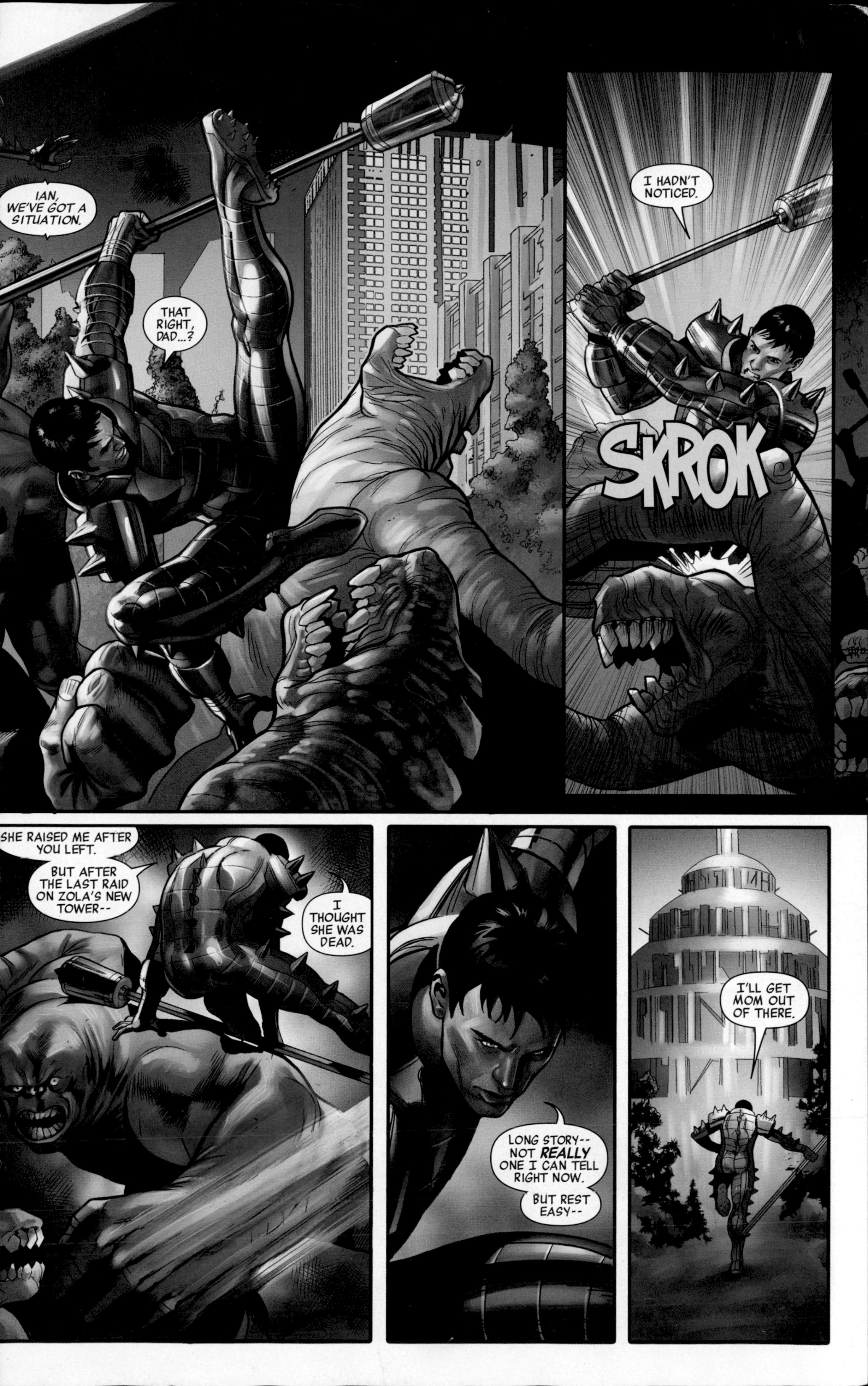
IAN, WE'VE GOT A SITUATION.
THAT RIGHT, DAD...?
I HADN'T NOTICED.
SKROK
SHE RAISED ME AFTER YOU LEFT.
BUT AFTER THE LAST RAID ON ZOLA'S NEW TOWER--
I THOUGHT SHE WAS DEAD.
LONG STORY-- NOT **REALLY** ONE I CAN TELL RIGHT NOW.
BUT REST EASY--
I'LL GET MOM OUT OF THERE.

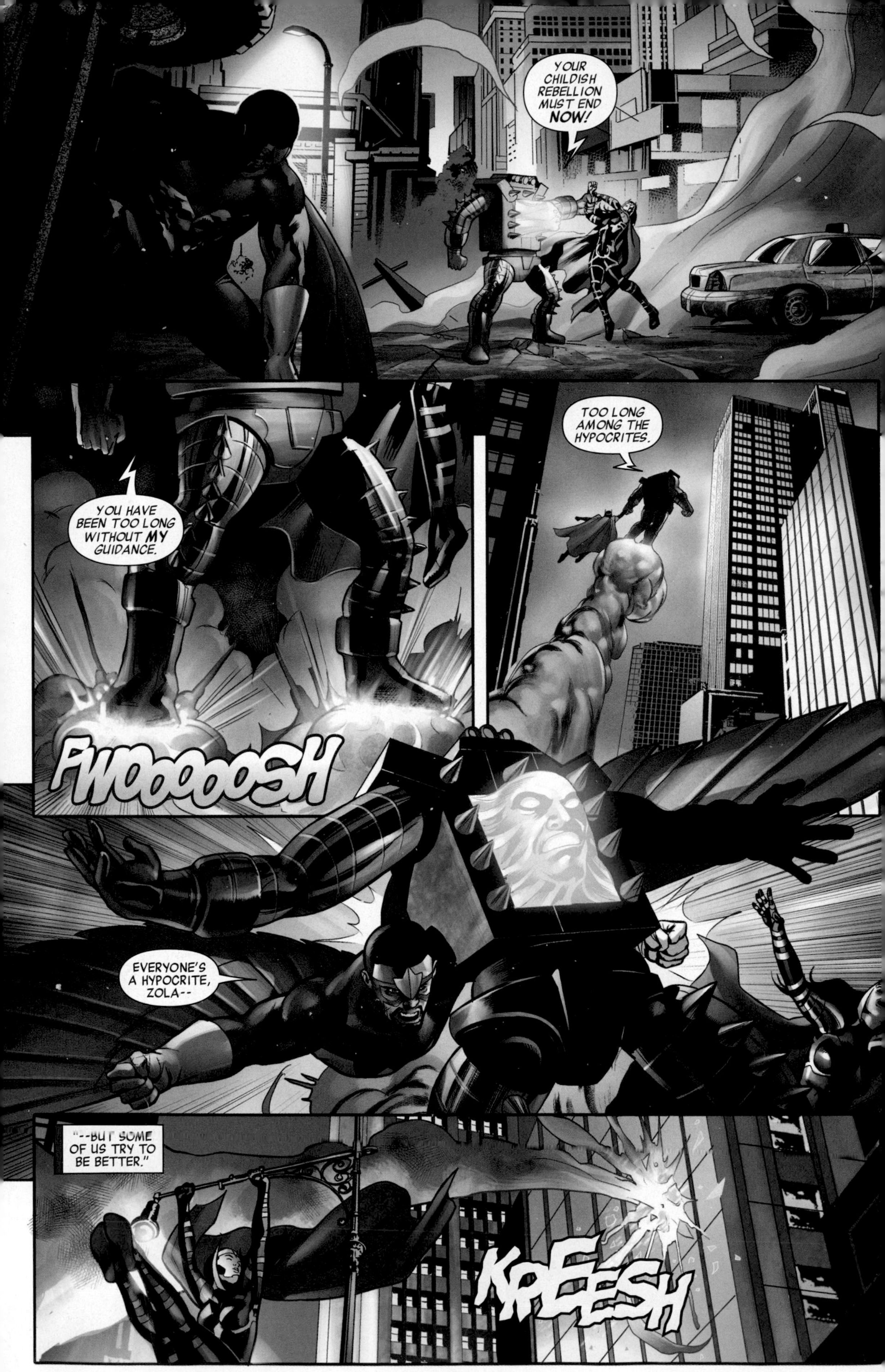
YOUR CHILDISH REBELLION MUST END NOW!
YOU HAVE BEEN TOO LONG WITHOUT MY GUIDANCE.
FWOOOOOSH
TOO LONG AMONG THE HYPOCRITES.
EVERYONE'S A HYPOCRITE, ZOLA--
"--BUT SOME OF US TRY TO BE BETTER."
KREEESH

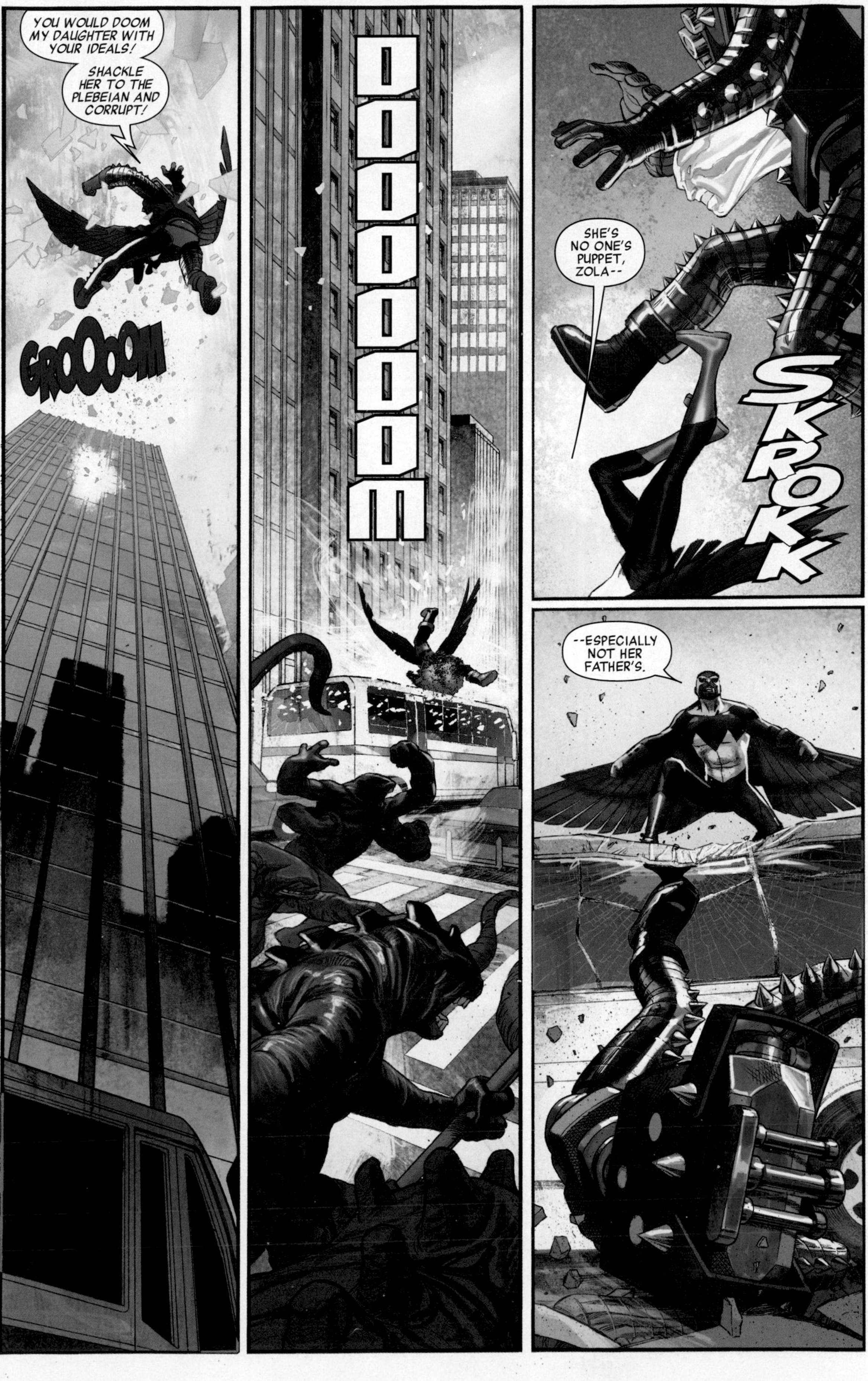
YOU WOULD DOOM MY DAUGHTER WITH YOUR IDEALS!
SHACKLE HER TO THE PLEBEIAN AND CORRUPT!
GROOOOM
DOOOOOOOM
SHE'S NO ONE'S PUPPET, ZOLA--
SKROKK
--ESPECIALLY NOT HER FATHER'S.

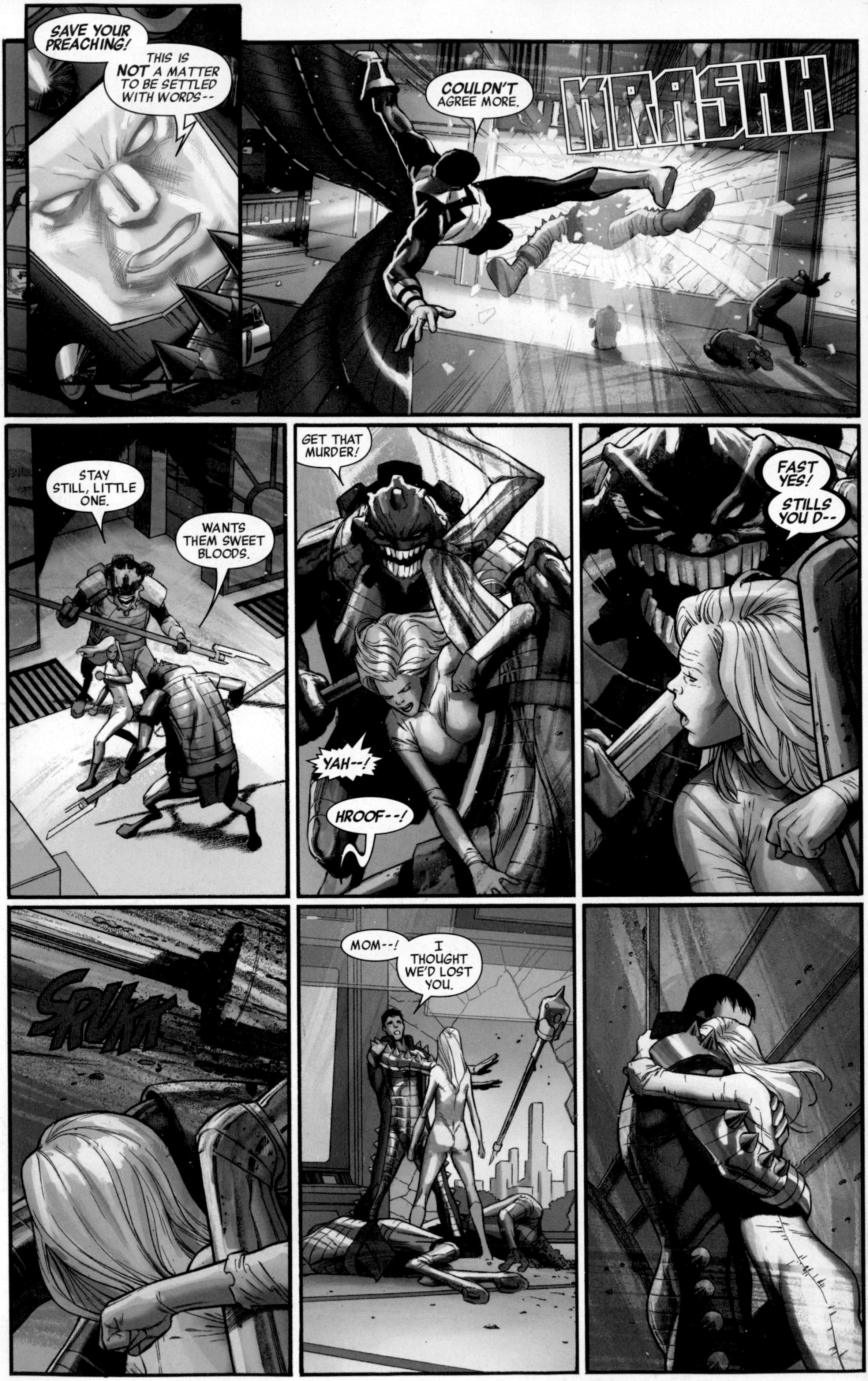
SAVE YOUR PREACHING!
THIS IS NOT A MATTER TO BE SETTLED WITH WORDS--
COULDN'T AGREE MORE.
KRASHH
STAY STILL, LITTLE ONE.
WANTS THEM SWEET BLOODS.
GET THAT MURDER!
YAH--!
HROOF--!
FAST YES!
STILLS YOU D--
SPLUNK
MOM--!
I THOUGHT WE'D LOST YOU.

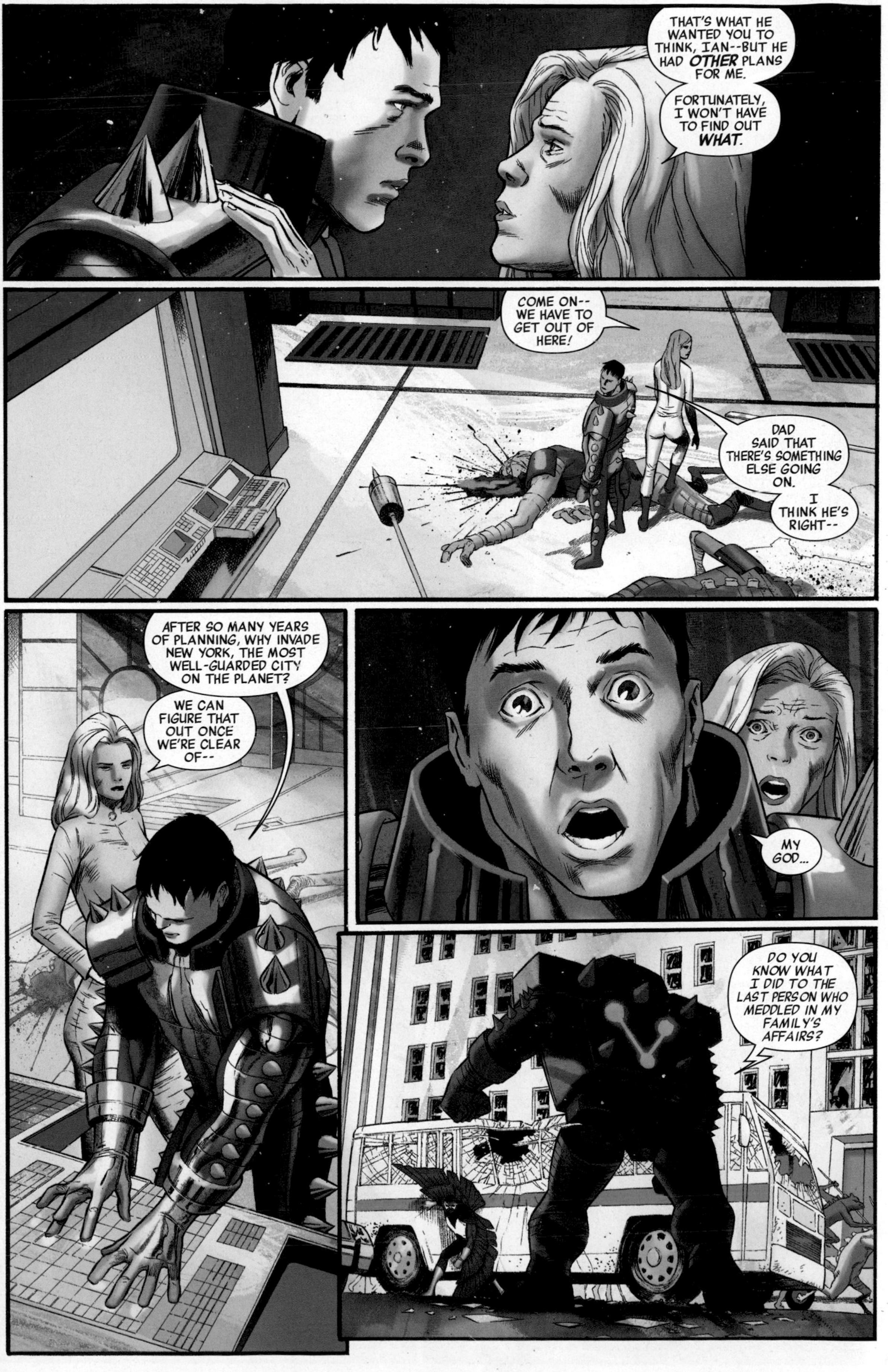
THAT'S WHAT HE WANTED YOU TO THINK, IAN--BUT HE HAD OTHER PLANS FOR ME.
FORTUNATELY, I WON'T HAVE TO FIND OUT WHAT.
COME ON-- WE HAVE TO GET OUT OF HERE!
DAD SAID THAT THERE'S SOMETHING ELSE GOING ON.
I THINK HE'S RIGHT--
AFTER SO MANY YEARS OF PLANNING, WHY INVADE NEW YORK, THE MOST WELL-GUARDED CITY ON THE PLANET?
WE CAN FIGURE THAT OUT ONCE WE'RE CLEAR OF--
MY GOD...
DO YOU KNOW WHAT I DID TO THE LAST PERSON WHO MEDDLED IN MY FAMILY'S AFFAIRS?

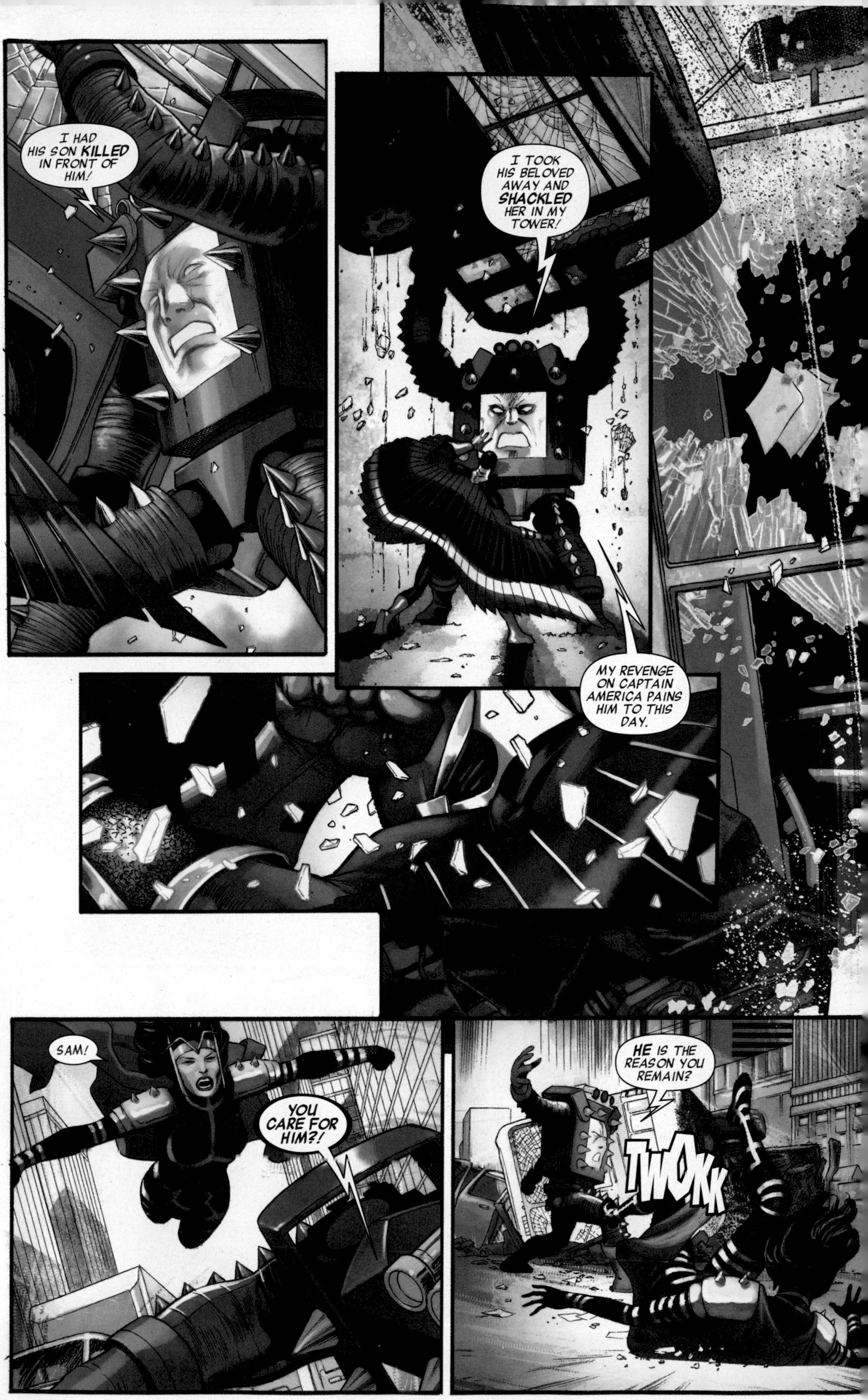

I HAD HIS SON KILLED IN FRONT OF HIM!
I TOOK HIS BELOVED AWAY AND SHACKLED HER IN MY TOWER!
MY REVENGE ON CAPTAIN AMERICA PAINS HIM TO THIS DAY.
SAM!
YOU CARE FOR HIM?!
HE IS THE REASON YOU REMAIN?
TWOKK

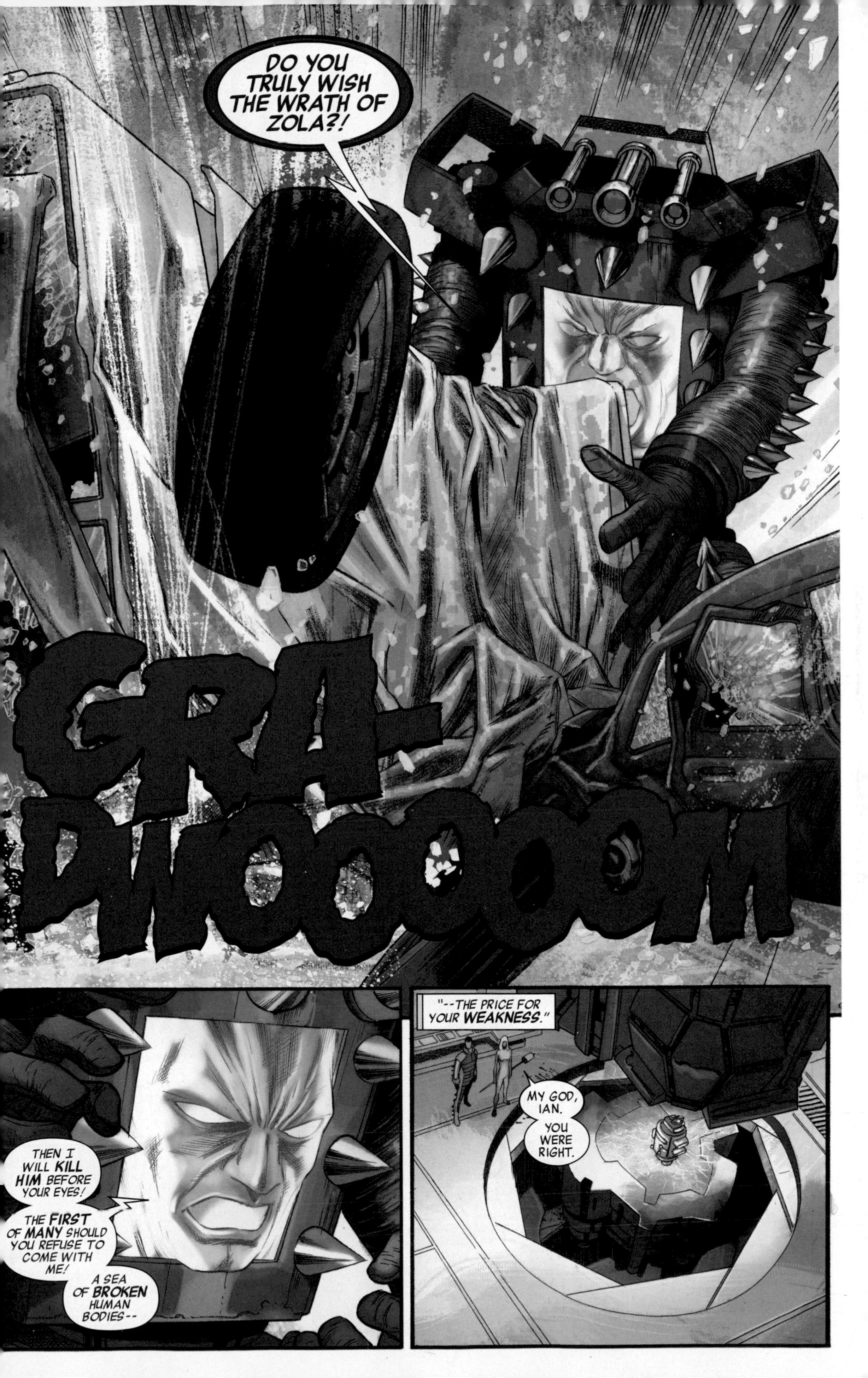
DO YOU TRULY WISH THE WRATH OF ZOLA?!
GRA-DWOOOOOM
THEN I WILL KILL HIM BEFORE YOUR EYES!
THE FIRST OF MANY SHOULD YOU REFUSE TO COME WITH ME!
A SEA OF BROKEN HUMAN BODIES--
"--THE PRICE FOR YOUR WEAKNESS."
MY GOD, IAN.
YOU WERE RIGHT.

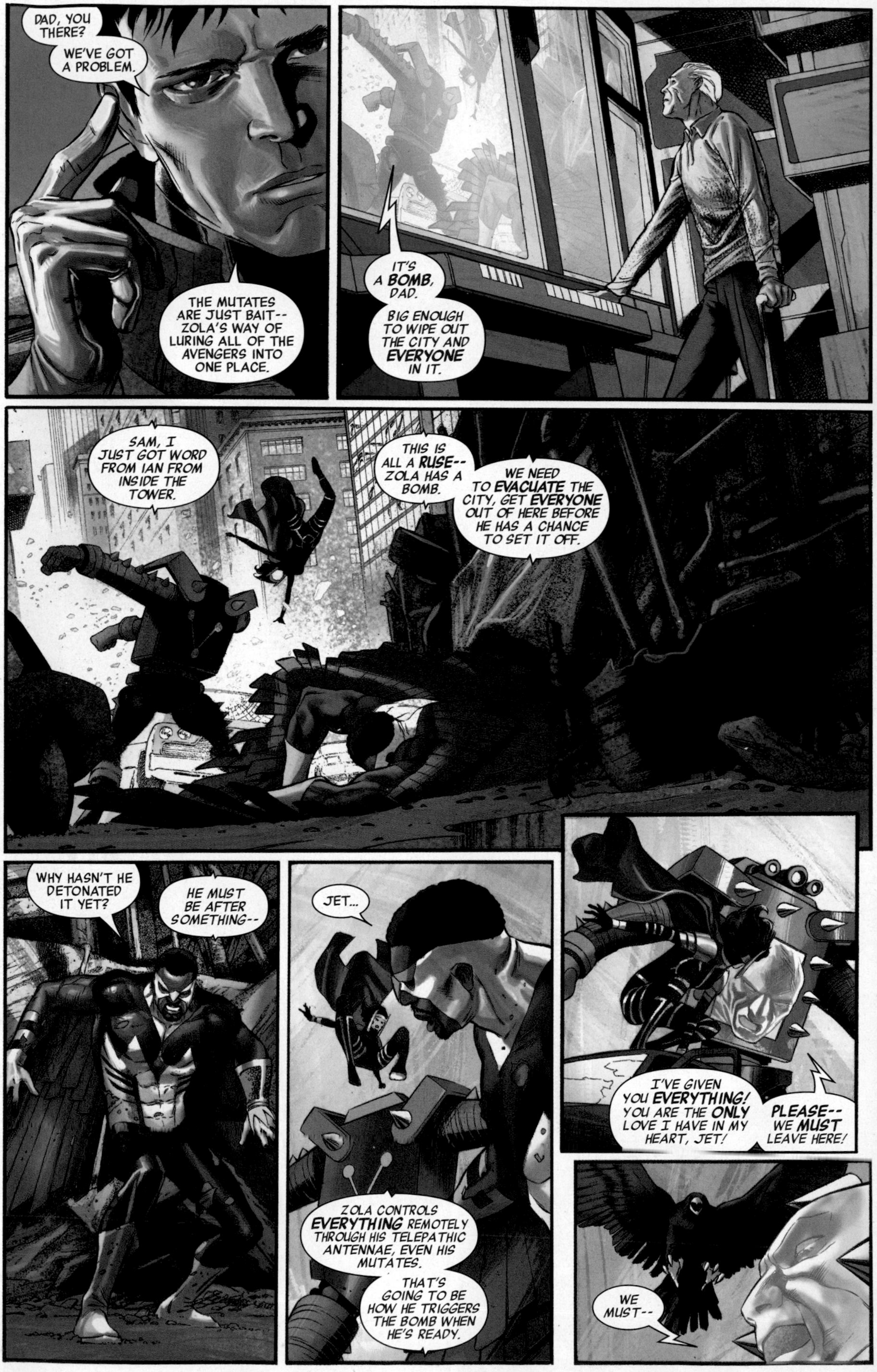
DAD, YOU THERE?
WE'VE GOT A PROBLEM.
THE MUTATES ARE JUST BAIT-- ZOLA'S WAY OF LURING ALL OF THE AVENGERS INTO ONE PLACE.
IT'S A **BOMB**, DAD.
BIG ENOUGH TO WIPE OUT THE CITY AND **EVERYONE** IN IT.
SAM, I JUST GOT WORD FROM IAN FROM INSIDE THE TOWER.
THIS IS ALL A **RUSE**-- ZOLA HAS A BOMB.
WE NEED TO **EVACUATE** THE CITY, GET **EVERYONE** OUT OF HERE BEFORE HE HAS A CHANCE TO SET IT OFF.
WHY HASN'T HE DETONATED IT YET?
HE MUST BE AFTER SOMETHING--
JET...
ZOLA CONTROLS **EVERYTHING** REMOTELY THROUGH HIS TELEPATHIC ANTENNAE, EVEN HIS MUTATES.
THAT'S GOING TO BE HOW HE TRIGGERS THE BOMB WHEN HE'S READY.
I'VE GIVEN YOU **EVERYTHING**! YOU ARE THE **ONLY** LOVE I HAVE IN MY HEART, JET!
**PLEASE**-- WE **MUST** LEAVE HERE!
WE MUST--

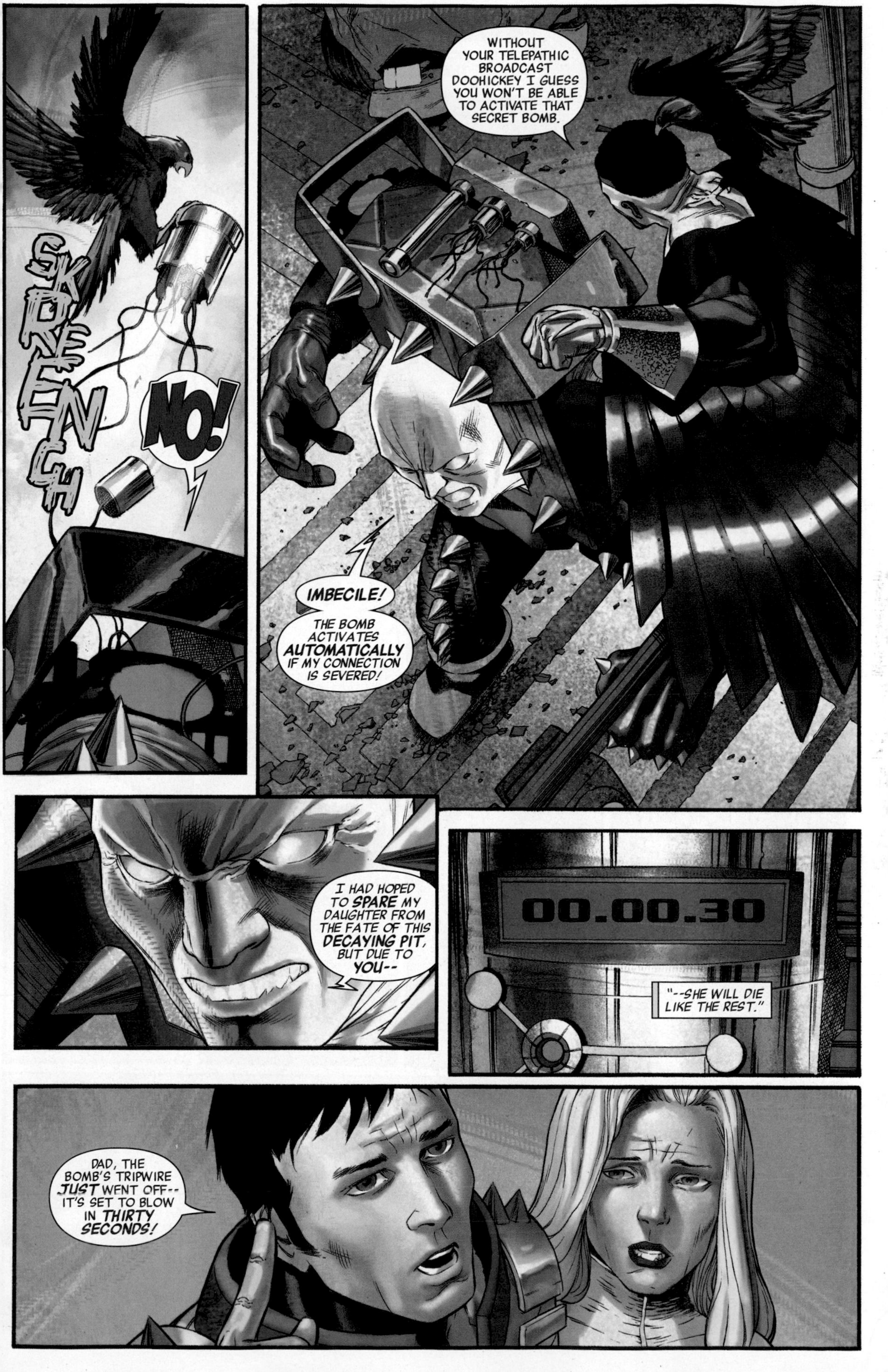

SKREENCH
NO!
WITHOUT YOUR TELEPATHIC BROADCAST DOOHICKEY I GUESS YOU WON'T BE ABLE TO ACTIVATE THAT SECRET BOMB.
IMBECILE!
THE BOMB ACTIVATES AUTOMATICALLY IF MY CONNECTION IS SEVERED!
I HAD HOPED TO SPARE MY DAUGHTER FROM THE FATE OF THIS DECAYING PIT, BUT DUE TO YOU--
00.00.30
"--SHE WILL DIE LIKE THE REST."
DAD, THE BOMB'S TRIPWIRE JUST WENT OFF--IT'S SET TO BLOW IN THIRTY SECONDS!

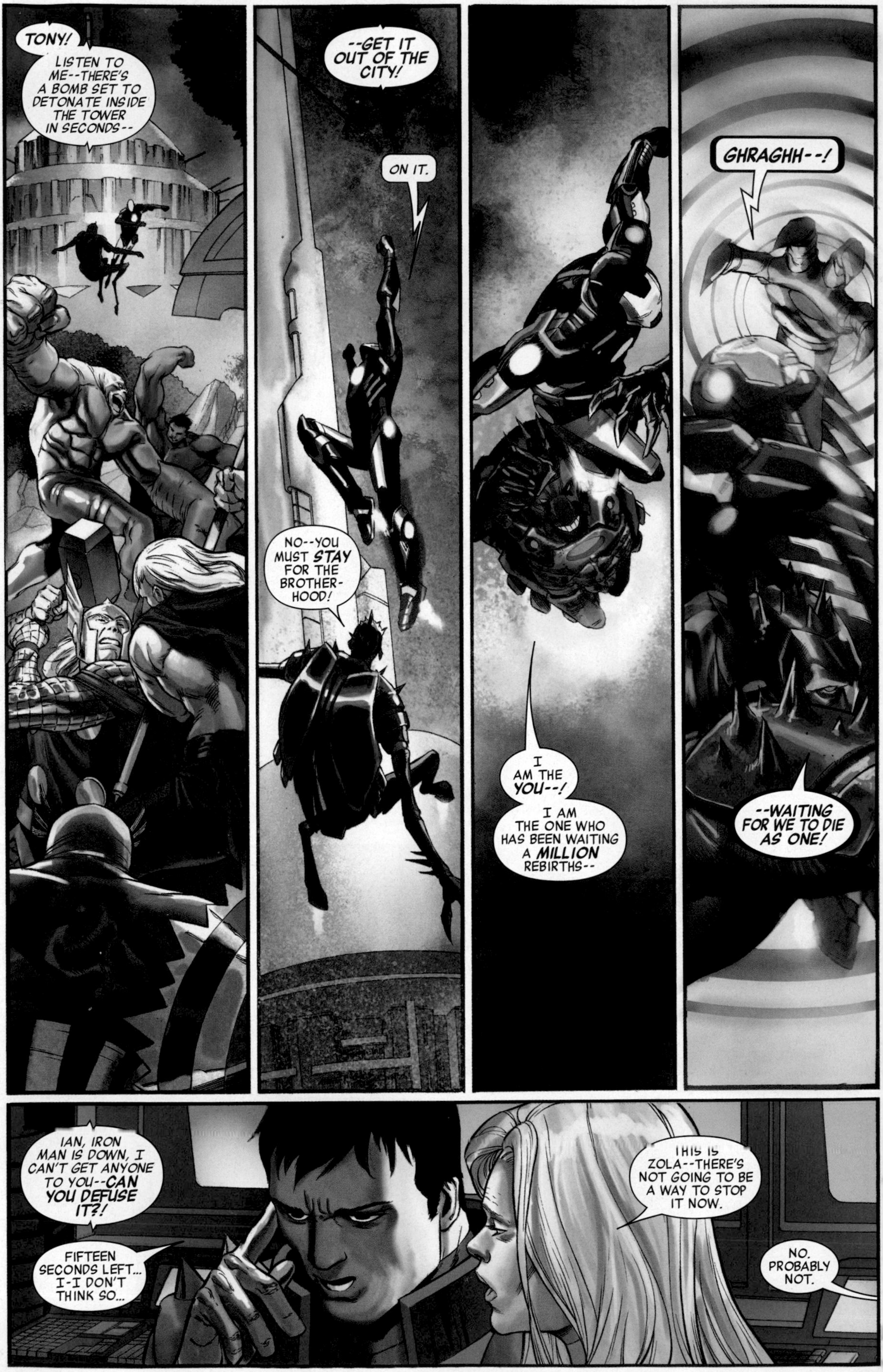
TONY!
LISTEN TO ME--THERE'S A BOMB SET TO DETONATE INSIDE THE TOWER IN SECONDS--
--GET IT OUT OF THE CITY!
ON IT.
NO--YOU MUST STAY FOR THE BROTHER-HOOD!
I AM THE YOU--!
I AM THE ONE WHO HAS BEEN WAITING A MILLION REBIRTHS--
GHRAGHH--!
--WAITING FOR WE TO DIE AS ONE!
IAN, IRON MAN IS DOWN, I CAN'T GET ANYONE TO YOU--CAN YOU DEFUSE IT?!
FIFTEEN SECONDS LEFT... I-I DON'T THINK SO...
THIS IS ZOLA--THERE'S NOT GOING TO BE A WAY TO STOP IT NOW.
NO. PROBABLY NOT.

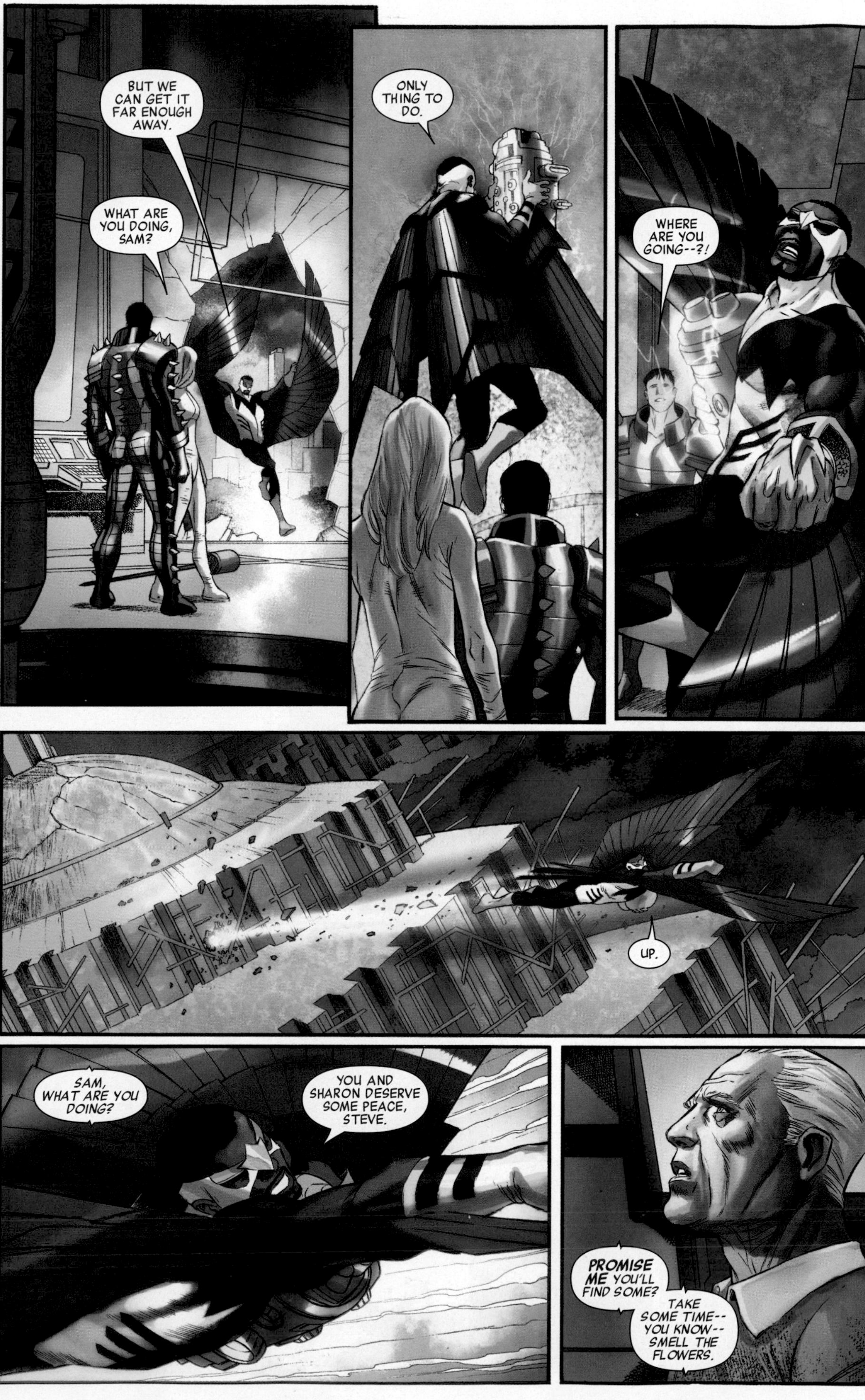

BUT WE CAN GET IT FAR ENOUGH AWAY.
WHAT ARE YOU DOING, SAM?
ONLY THING TO DO.
WHERE ARE YOU GOING--?!
UP.
SAM, WHAT ARE YOU DOING?
YOU AND SHARON DESERVE SOME PEACE, STEVE.
PROMISE ME YOU'LL FIND SOME?
TAKE SOME TIME-- YOU KNOW-- SMELL THE FLOWERS.

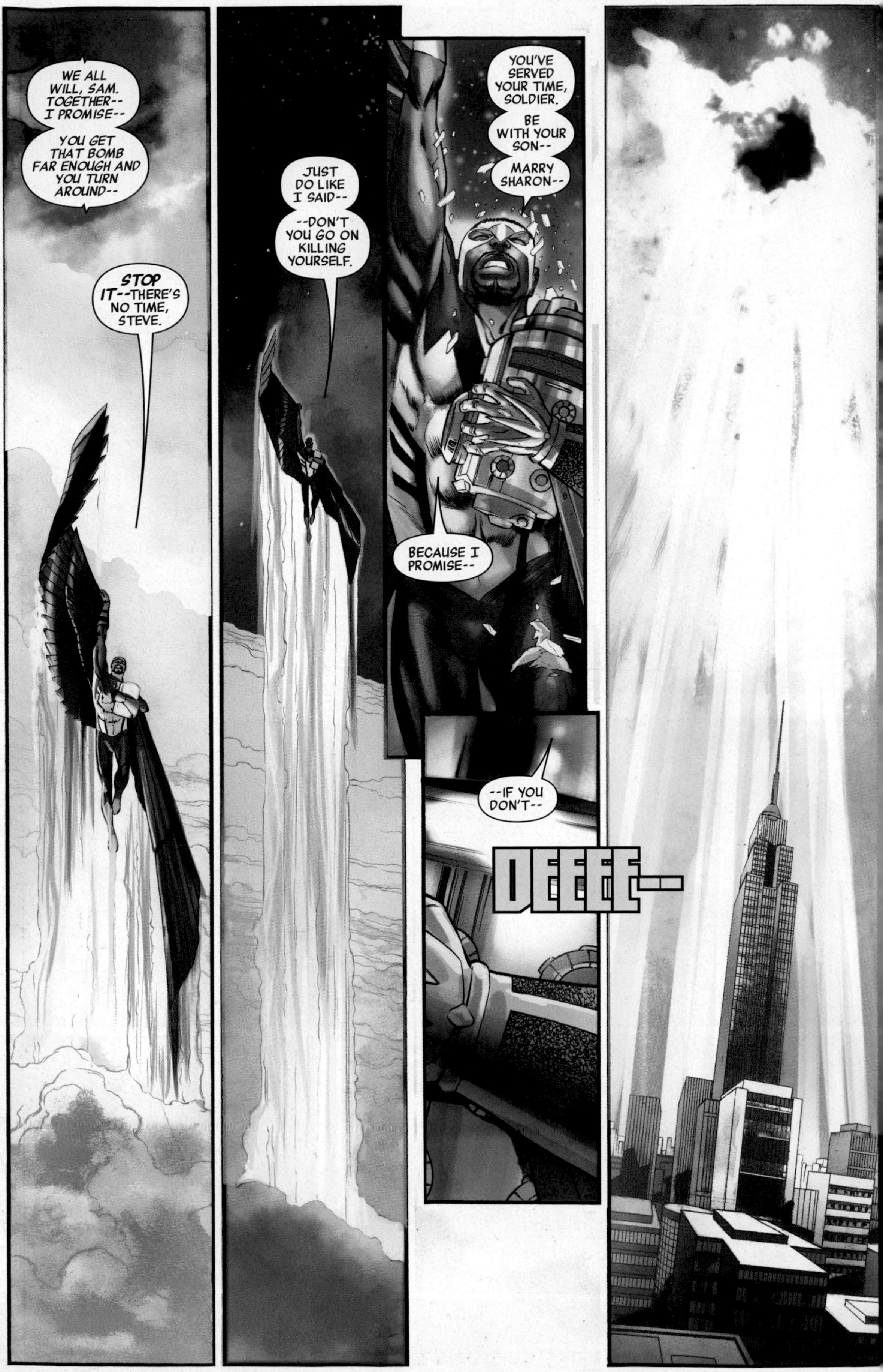
WE ALL WILL, SAM. TOGETHER-- I PROMISE--
YOU GET THAT BOMB FAR ENOUGH AND YOU TURN AROUND--
STOP IT--THERE'S NO TIME, STEVE.
JUST DO LIKE I SAID--
--DON'T YOU GO ON KILLING YOURSELF.
YOU'VE SERVED YOUR TIME, SOLDIER.
BE WITH YOUR SON--
MARRY SHARON--
BECAUSE I PROMISE--
--IF YOU DON'T--
DEEEE--

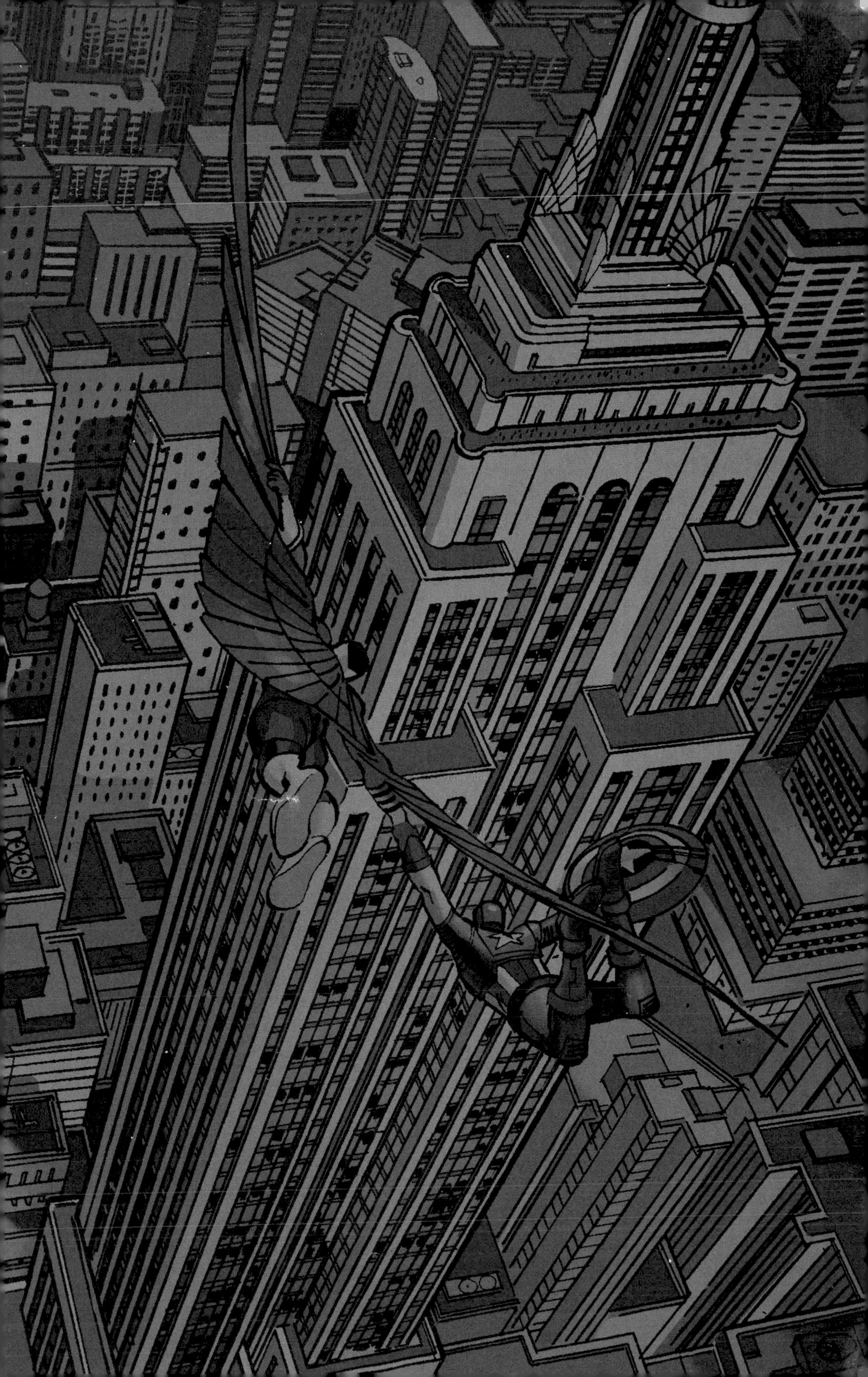

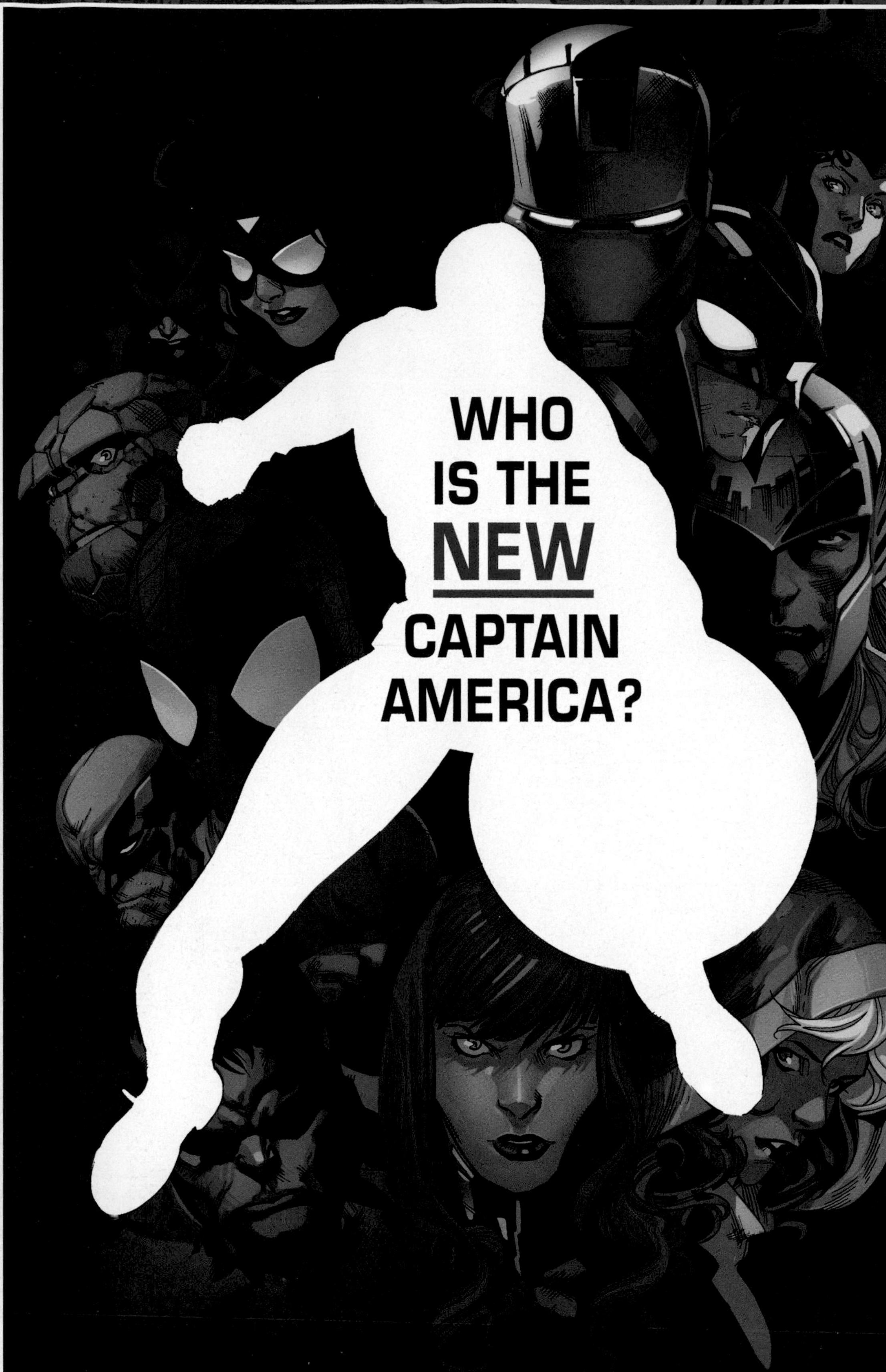
WHO
IS THE
NEW
CAPTAIN
AMERICA?

TWENTY-FIVE

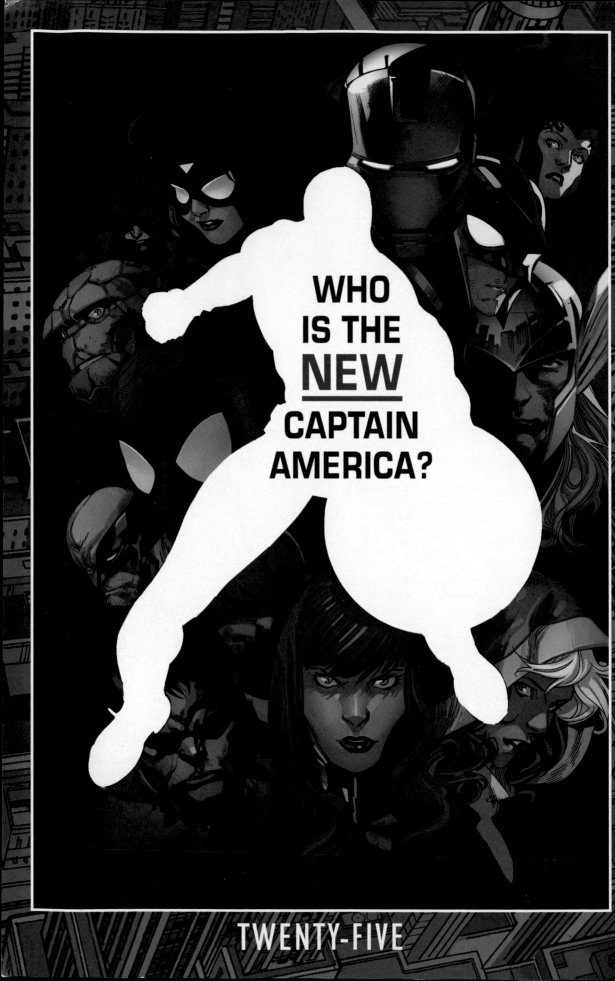

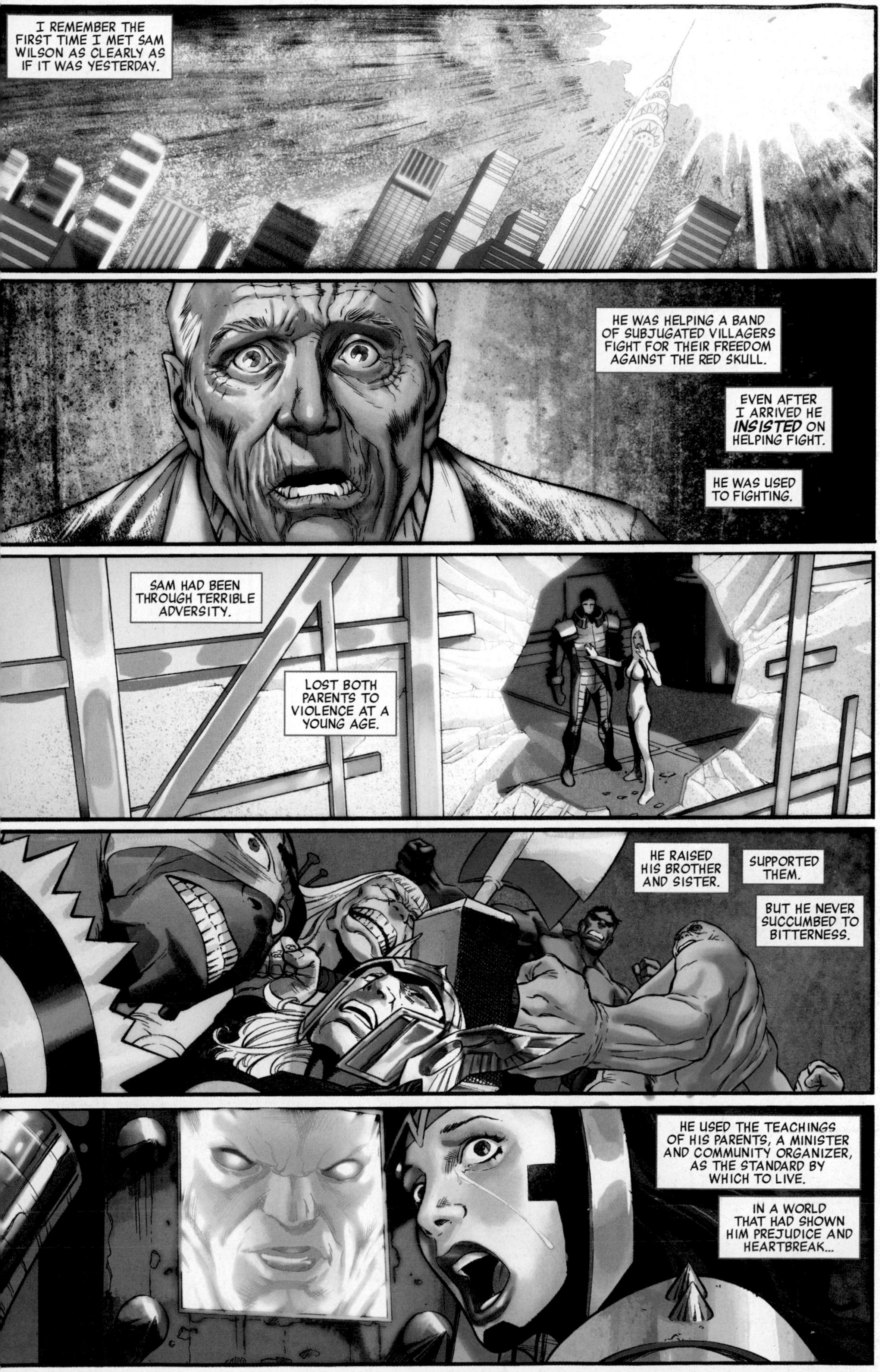
I REMEMBER THE FIRST TIME I MET SAM WILSON AS CLEARLY AS IF IT WAS YESTERDAY.
HE WAS HELPING A BAND OF SUBJUGATED VILLAGERS FIGHT FOR THEIR FREEDOM AGAINST THE RED SKULL.
EVEN AFTER I ARRIVED HE INSISTED ON HELPING FIGHT.
HE WAS USED TO FIGHTING.
SAM HAD BEEN THROUGH TERRIBLE ADVERSITY.
LOST BOTH PARENTS TO VIOLENCE AT A YOUNG AGE.
HE RAISED HIS BROTHER AND SISTER.
SUPPORTED THEM.
BUT HE NEVER SUCCUMBED TO BITTERNESS.
HE USED THE TEACHINGS OF HIS PARENTS, A MINISTER AND COMMUNITY ORGANIZER, AS THE STANDARD BY WHICH TO LIVE.
IN A WORLD THAT HAD SHOWN HIM PREJUDICE AND HEARTBREAK...

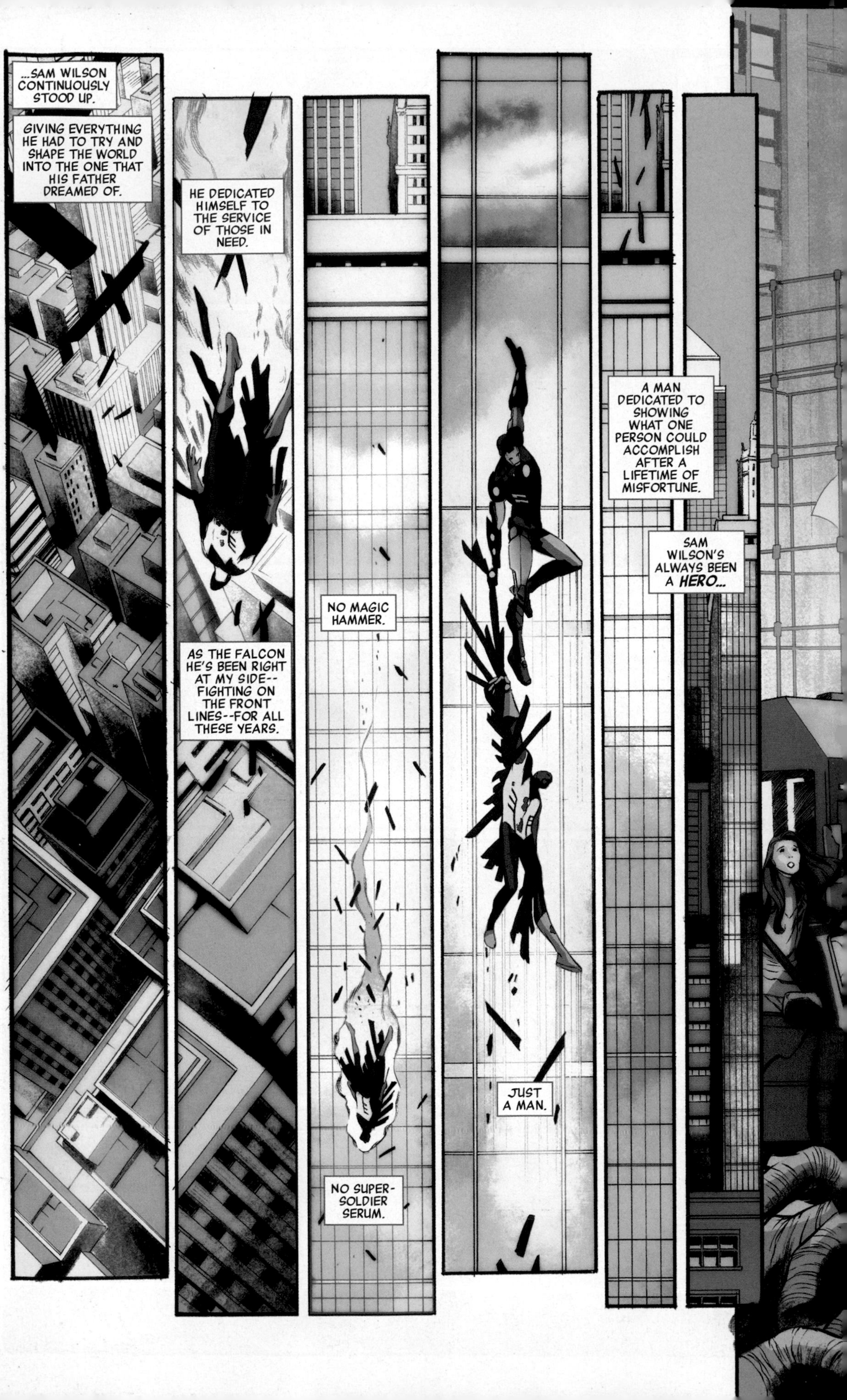
...SAM WILSON CONTINUOUSLY STOOD UP.
GIVING EVERYTHING HE HAD TO TRY AND SHAPE THE WORLD INTO THE ONE THAT HIS FATHER DREAMED OF.
HE DEDICATED HIMSELF TO THE SERVICE OF THOSE IN NEED.
AS THE FALCON HE'S BEEN RIGHT AT MY SIDE--FIGHTING ON THE FRONT LINES--FOR ALL THESE YEARS.
NO MAGIC HAMMER.
NO SUPER-SOLDIER SERUM.
JUST A MAN.
A MAN DEDICATED TO SHOWING WHAT ONE PERSON COULD ACCOMPLISH AFTER A LIFETIME OF MISFORTUNE.
SAM WILSON'S ALWAYS BEEN A HERO...

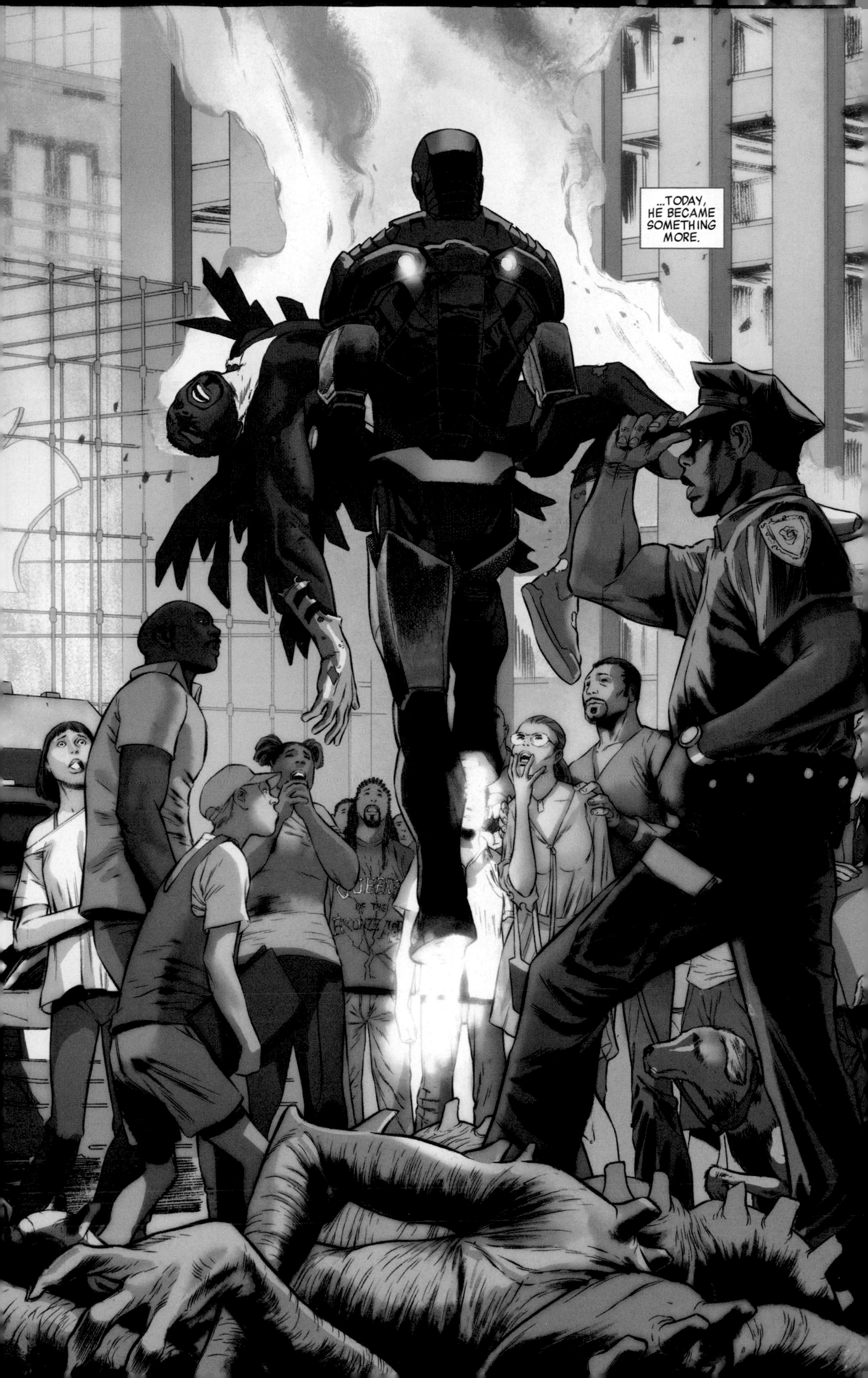
...TODAY, HE BECAME SOMETHING MORE.
QUEENS OF THE BRONZE AGE

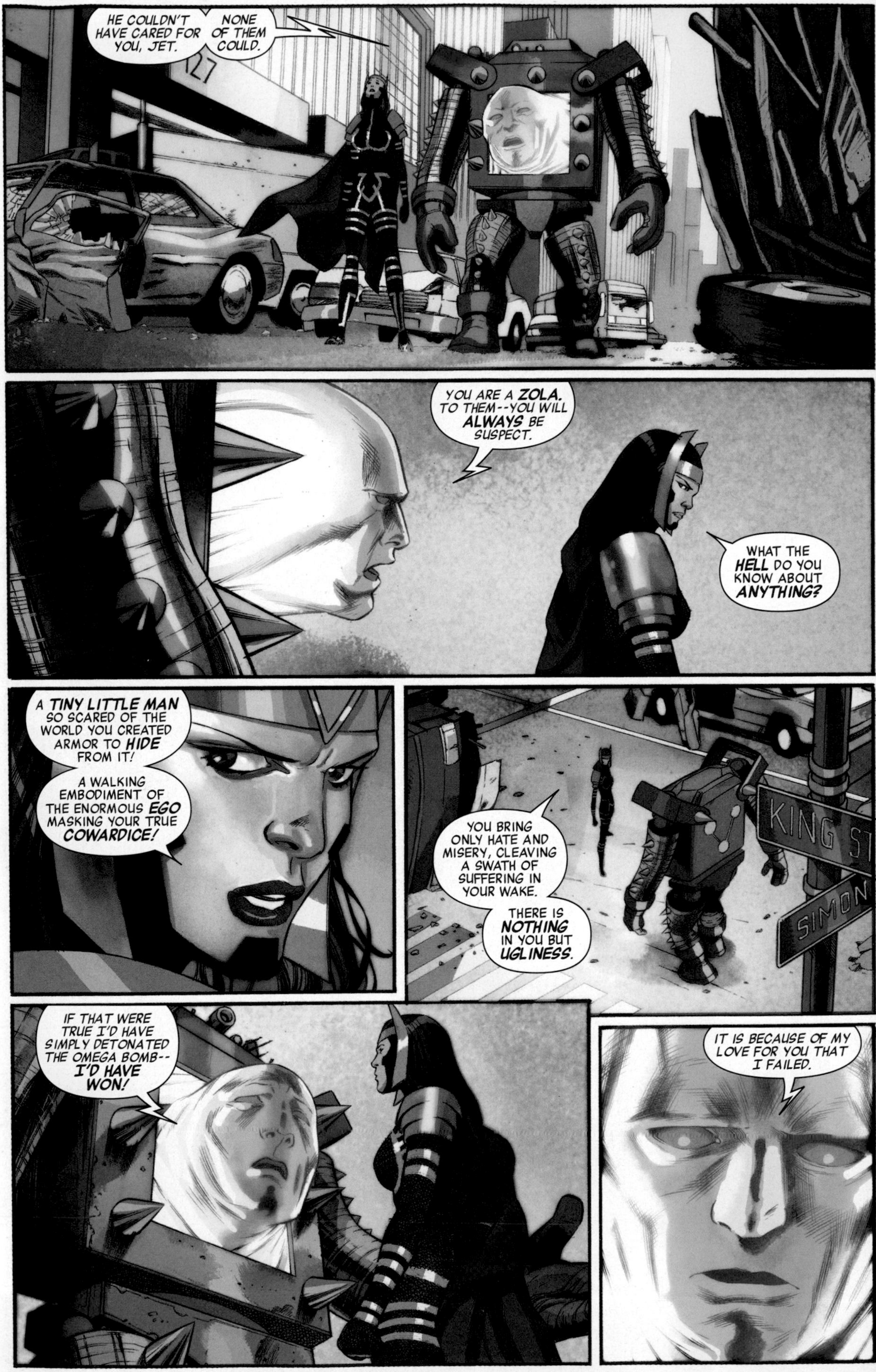
HE COULDN'T HAVE CARED FOR YOU, JET.
NONE OF THEM COULD.
YOU ARE A ZOLA. TO THEM--YOU WILL ALWAYS BE SUSPECT.
WHAT THE HELL DO YOU KNOW ABOUT ANYTHING?
A TINY LITTLE MAN SO SCARED OF THE WORLD YOU CREATED ARMOR TO HIDE FROM IT!
A WALKING EMBODIMENT OF THE ENORMOUS EGO MASKING YOUR TRUE COWARDICE!
YOU BRING ONLY HATE AND MISERY, CLEAVING A SWATH OF SUFFERING IN YOUR WAKE.
THERE IS NOTHING IN YOU BUT UGLINESS.
KING ST
SIMON
IF THAT WERE TRUE I'D HAVE SIMPLY DETONATED THE OMEGA BOMB-- I'D HAVE WON!
IT IS BECAUSE OF MY LOVE FOR YOU THAT I FAILED.

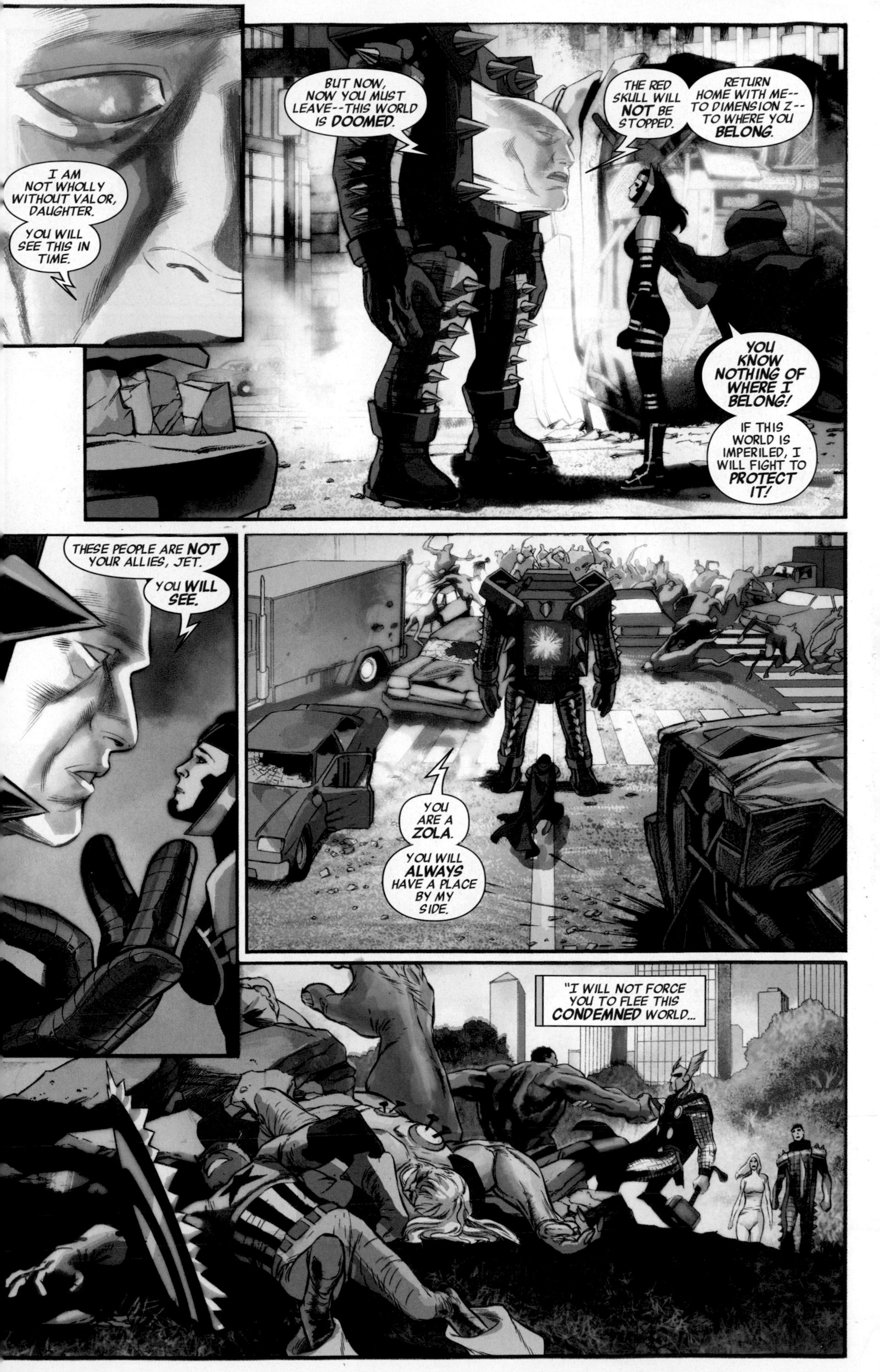
I AM NOT WHOLLY WITHOUT VALOR, DAUGHTER.
YOU WILL SEE THIS IN TIME.
BUT NOW, NOW YOU MUST LEAVE--THIS WORLD IS DOOMED.
THE RED SKULL WILL NOT BE STOPPED.
RETURN HOME WITH ME--TO DIMENSION Z--TO WHERE YOU BELONG.
YOU KNOW NOTHING OF WHERE I BELONG!
IF THIS WORLD IS IMPERILED, I WILL FIGHT TO PROTECT IT!
THESE PEOPLE ARE NOT YOUR ALLIES, JET.
YOU WILL SEE.
YOU ARE A ZOLA.
YOU WILL ALWAYS HAVE A PLACE BY MY SIDE.
"I WILL NOT FORCE YOU TO FLEE THIS CONDEMNED WORLD...

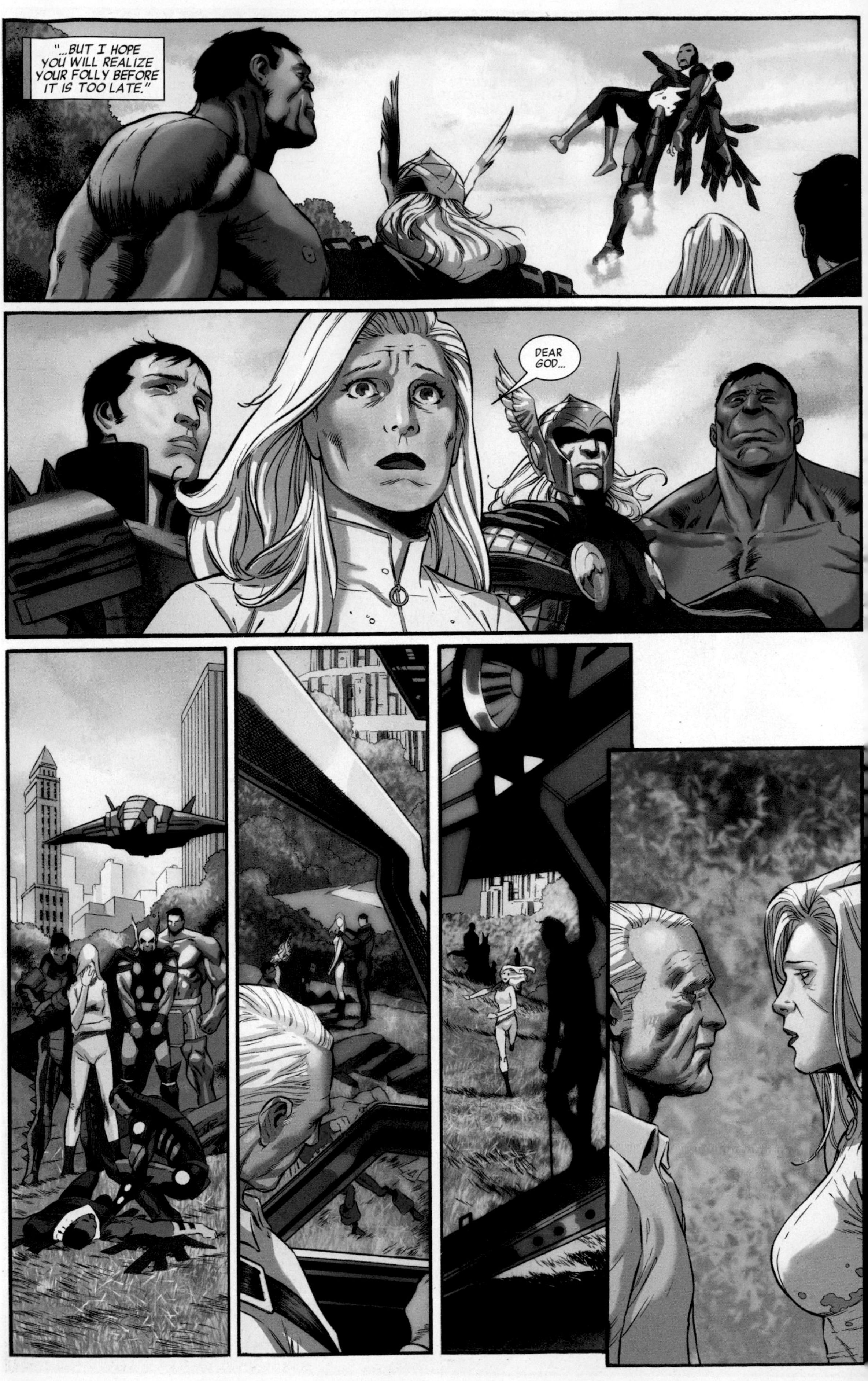
"...BUT I HOPE YOU WILL REALIZE YOUR FOLLY BEFORE IT IS TOO LATE."
DEAR GOD...

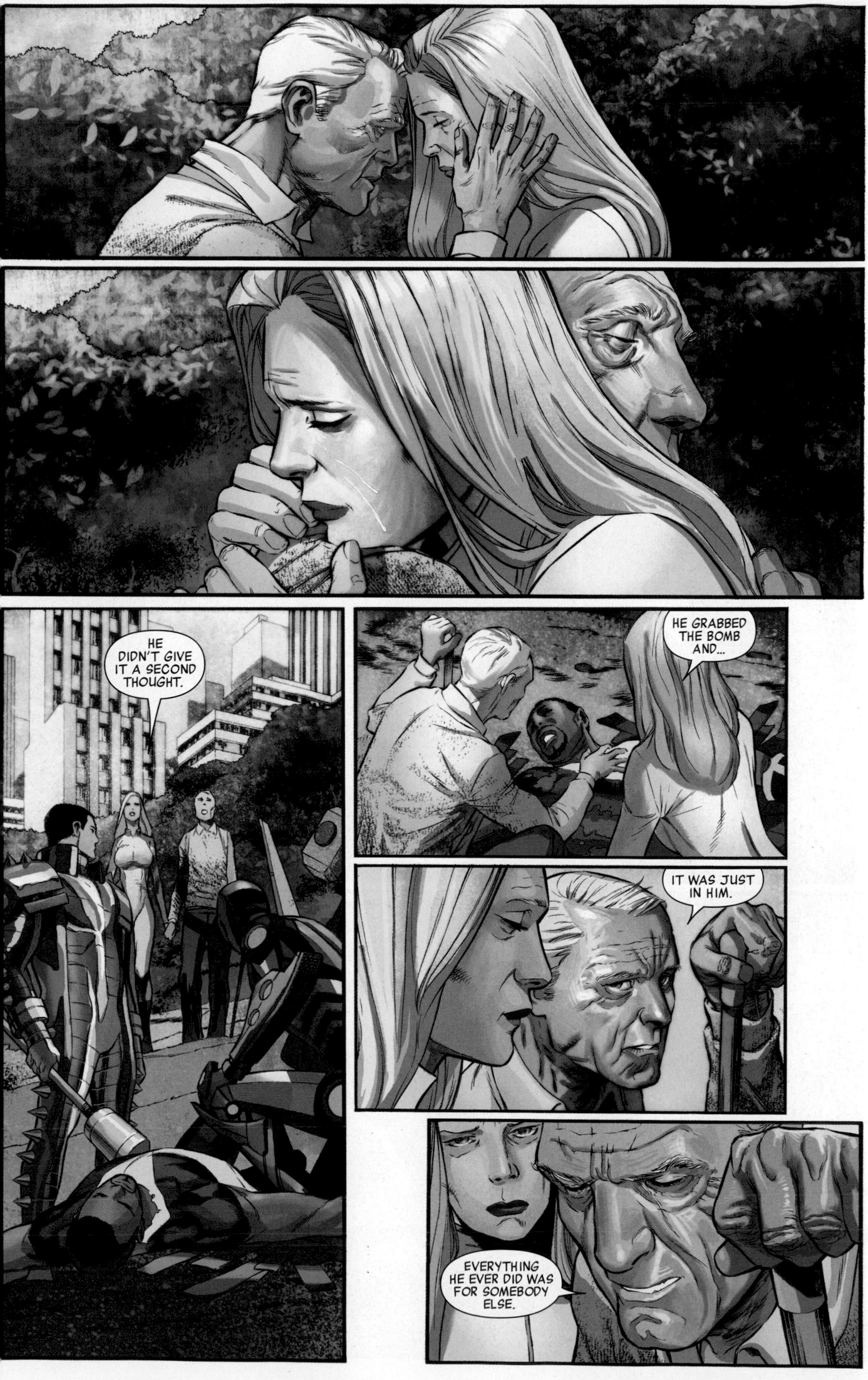
HE DIDN'T GIVE IT A SECOND THOUGHT.
HE GRABBED THE BOMB AND...
IT WAS JUST IN HIM.
EVERYTHING HE EVER DID WAS FOR SOMEBODY ELSE.

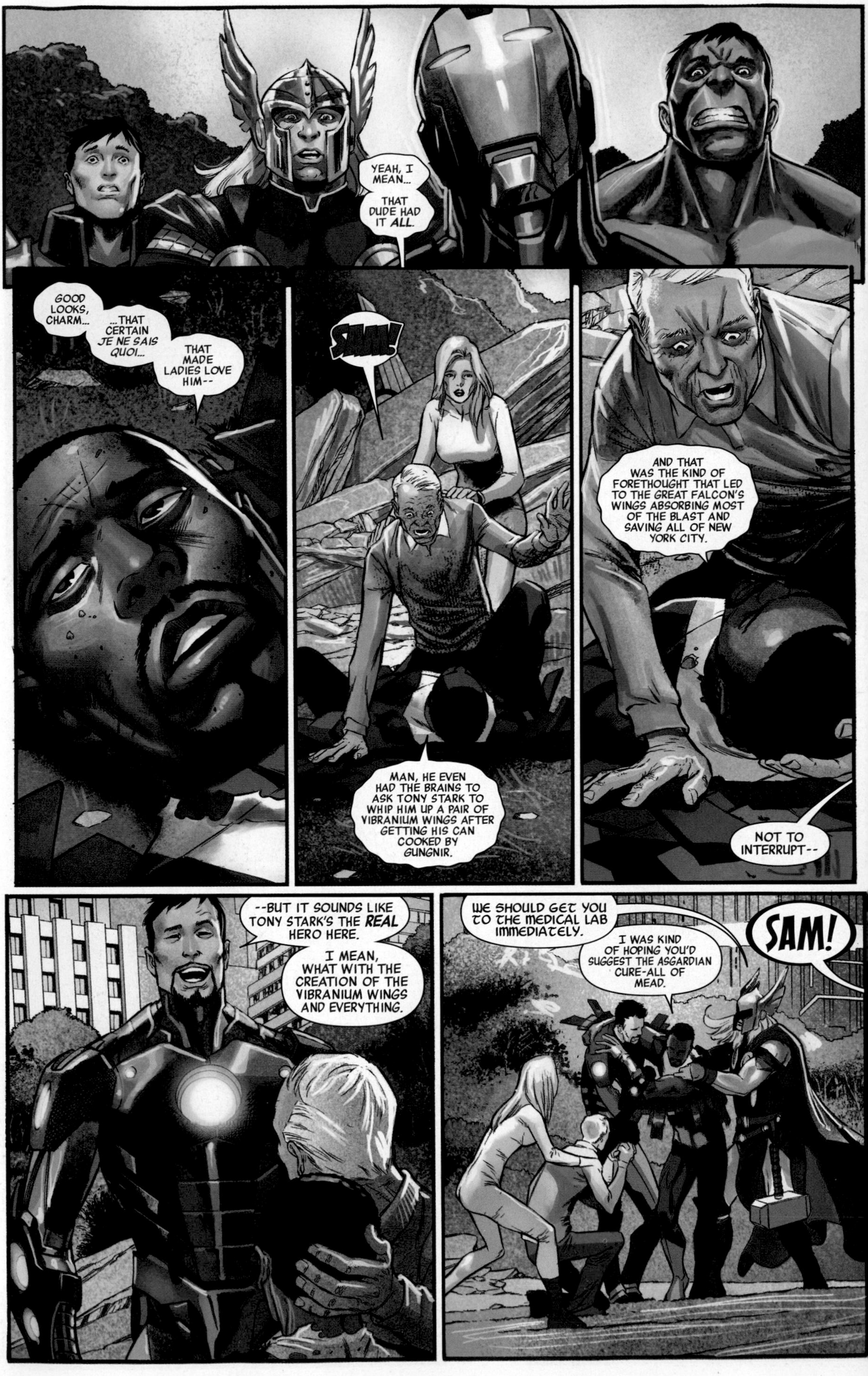
YEAH, I MEAN...
THAT DUDE HAD IT ALL.
GOOD LOOKS, CHARM...
...THAT CERTAIN JE NE SAIS QUOI...
THAT MADE LADIES LOVE HIM--
SAM!
MAN, HE EVEN HAD THE BRAINS TO ASK TONY STARK TO WHIP HIM UP A PAIR OF VIBRANIUM WINGS AFTER GETTING HIS CAN COOKED BY GUNGNIR.
AND THAT WAS THE KIND OF FORETHOUGHT THAT LED TO THE GREAT FALCON'S WINGS ABSORBING MOST OF THE BLAST AND SAVING ALL OF NEW YORK CITY.
NOT TO INTERRUPT--
--BUT IT SOUNDS LIKE TONY STARK'S THE REAL HERO HERE.
I MEAN, WHAT WITH THE CREATION OF THE VIBRANIUM WINGS AND EVERYTHING.
WE SHOULD GET YOU TO THE MEDICAL LAB IMMEDIATELY.
I WAS KIND OF HOPING YOU'D SUGGEST THE ASGARDIAN CURE-ALL OF MEAD.
SAM!

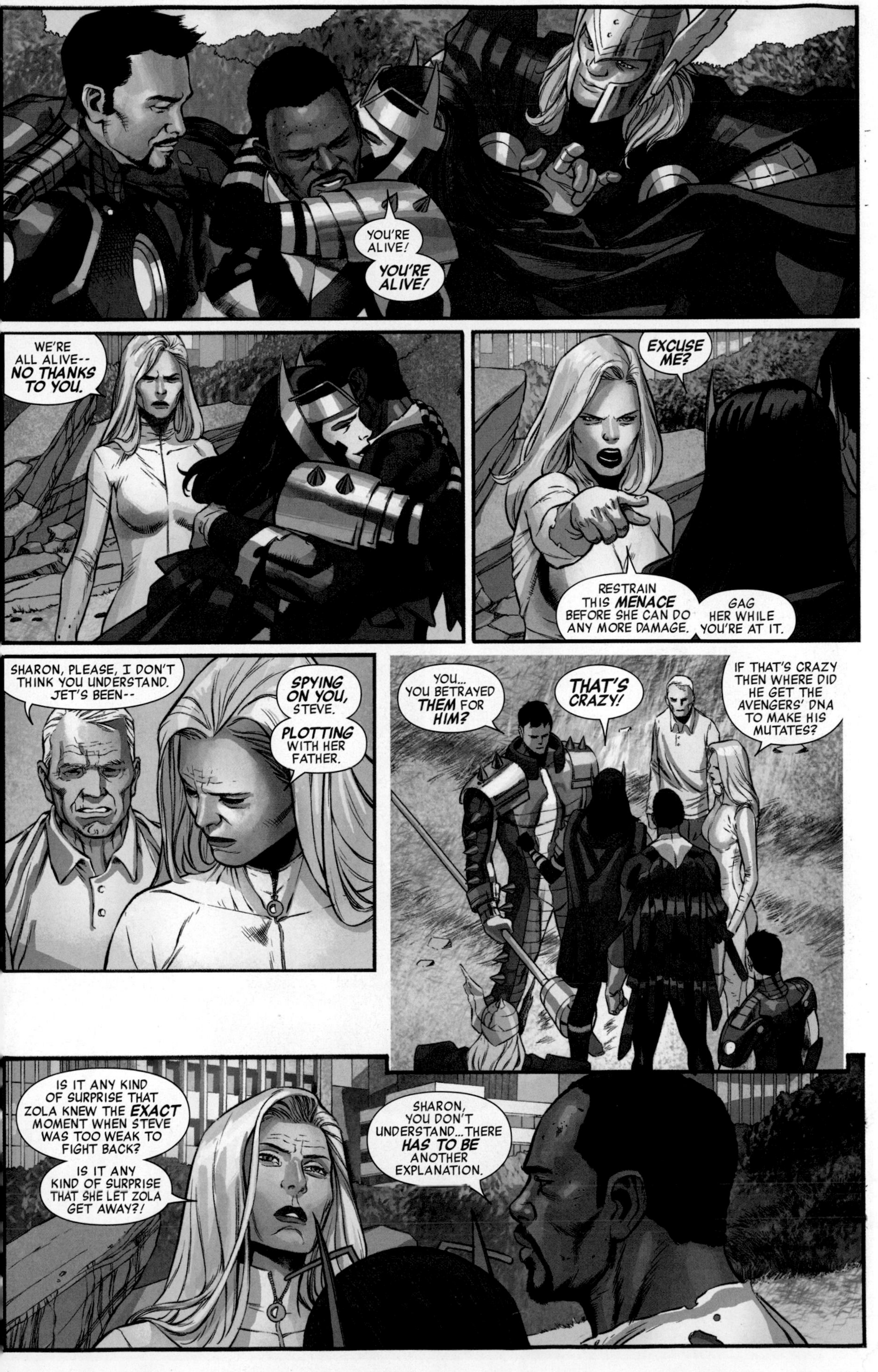
YOU'RE ALIVE!
YOU'RE ALIVE!
WE'RE ALL ALIVE-- NO THANKS TO YOU.
EXCUSE ME?
RESTRAIN THIS MENACE BEFORE SHE CAN DO ANY MORE DAMAGE.
GAG HER WHILE YOU'RE AT IT.
SHARON, PLEASE, I DON'T THINK YOU UNDERSTAND. JET'S BEEN--
SPYING ON YOU, STEVE.
PLOTTING WITH HER FATHER.
YOU... YOU BETRAYED THEM FOR HIM?
THAT'S CRAZY!
IF THAT'S CRAZY THEN WHERE DID HE GET THE AVENGERS' DNA TO MAKE HIS MUTATES?
IS IT ANY KIND OF SURPRISE THAT ZOLA KNEW THE EXACT MOMENT WHEN STEVE WAS TOO WEAK TO FIGHT BACK?
IS IT ANY KIND OF SURPRISE THAT SHE LET ZOLA GET AWAY?!
SHARON, YOU DON'T UNDERSTAND...THERE HAS TO BE ANOTHER EXPLANATION.

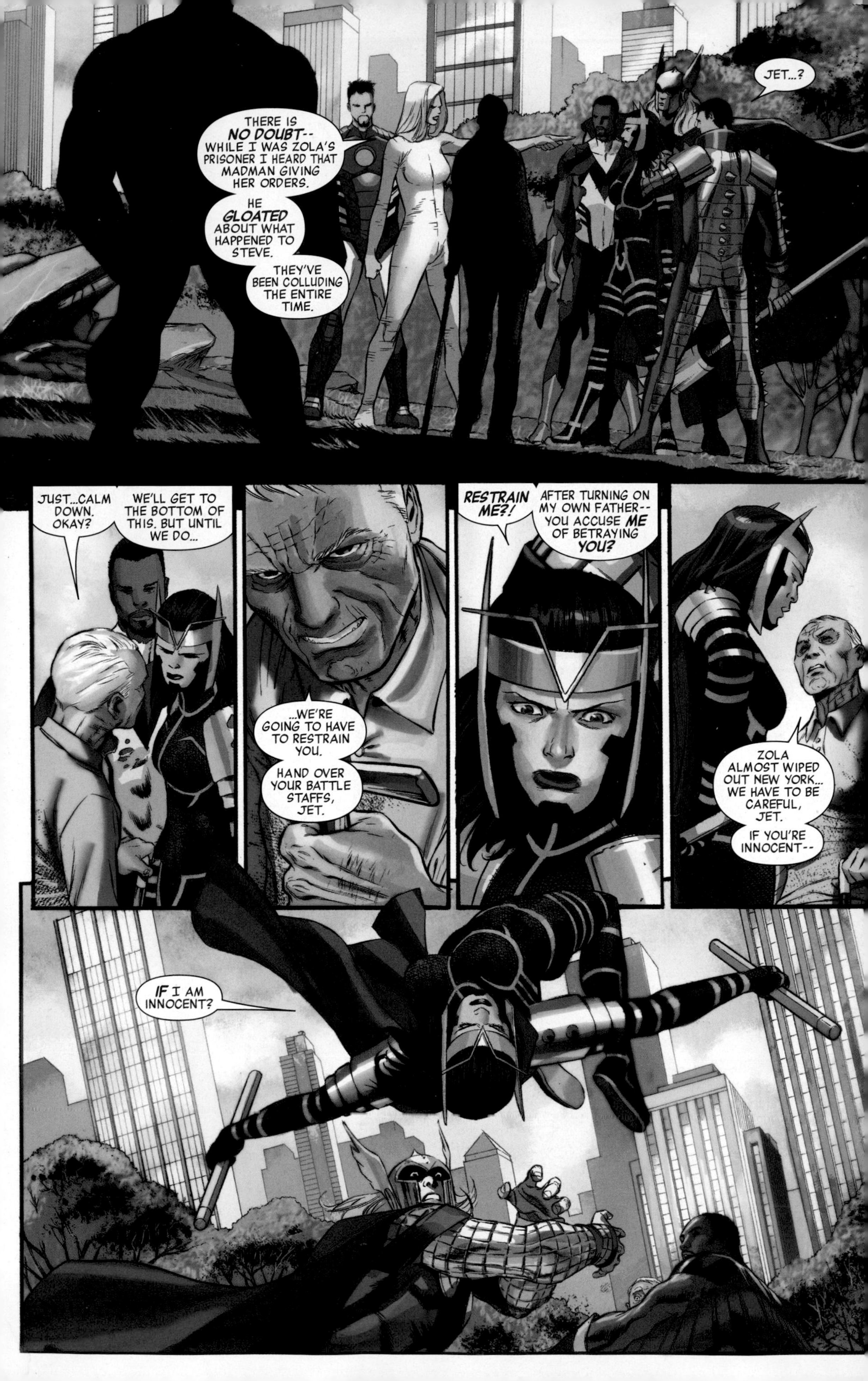
JET...?
THERE IS NO DOUBT-- WHILE I WAS ZOLA'S PRISONER I HEARD THAT MADMAN GIVING HER ORDERS.
HE GLOATED ABOUT WHAT HAPPENED TO STEVE.
THEY'VE BEEN COLLUDING THE ENTIRE TIME.
JUST...CALM DOWN. OKAY?
WE'LL GET TO THE BOTTOM OF THIS. BUT UNTIL WE DO...
...WE'RE GOING TO HAVE TO RESTRAIN YOU.
HAND OVER YOUR BATTLE STAFFS, JET.
RESTRAIN ME?!
AFTER TURNING ON MY OWN FATHER-- YOU ACCUSE ME OF BETRAYING YOU?
ZOLA ALMOST WIPED OUT NEW YORK... WE HAVE TO BE CAREFUL, JET.
IF YOU'RE INNOCENT--
IF I AM INNOCENT?

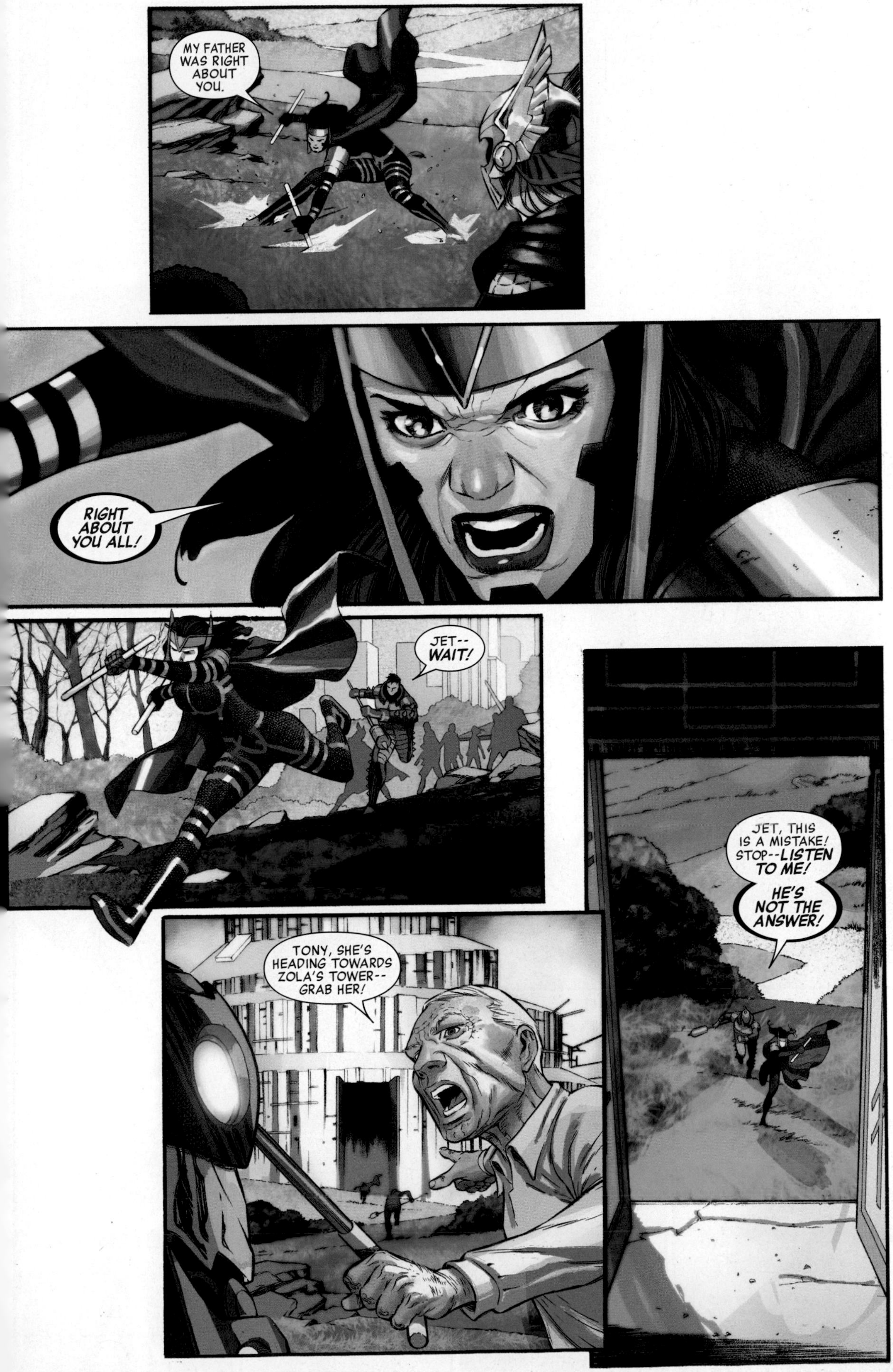
MY FATHER WAS RIGHT ABOUT YOU.
RIGHT ABOUT YOU ALL!
JET-- WAIT!
JET, THIS IS A MISTAKE! STOP--LISTEN TO ME!
HE'S NOT THE ANSWER!
TONY, SHE'S HEADING TOWARDS ZOLA'S TOWER-- GRAB HER!

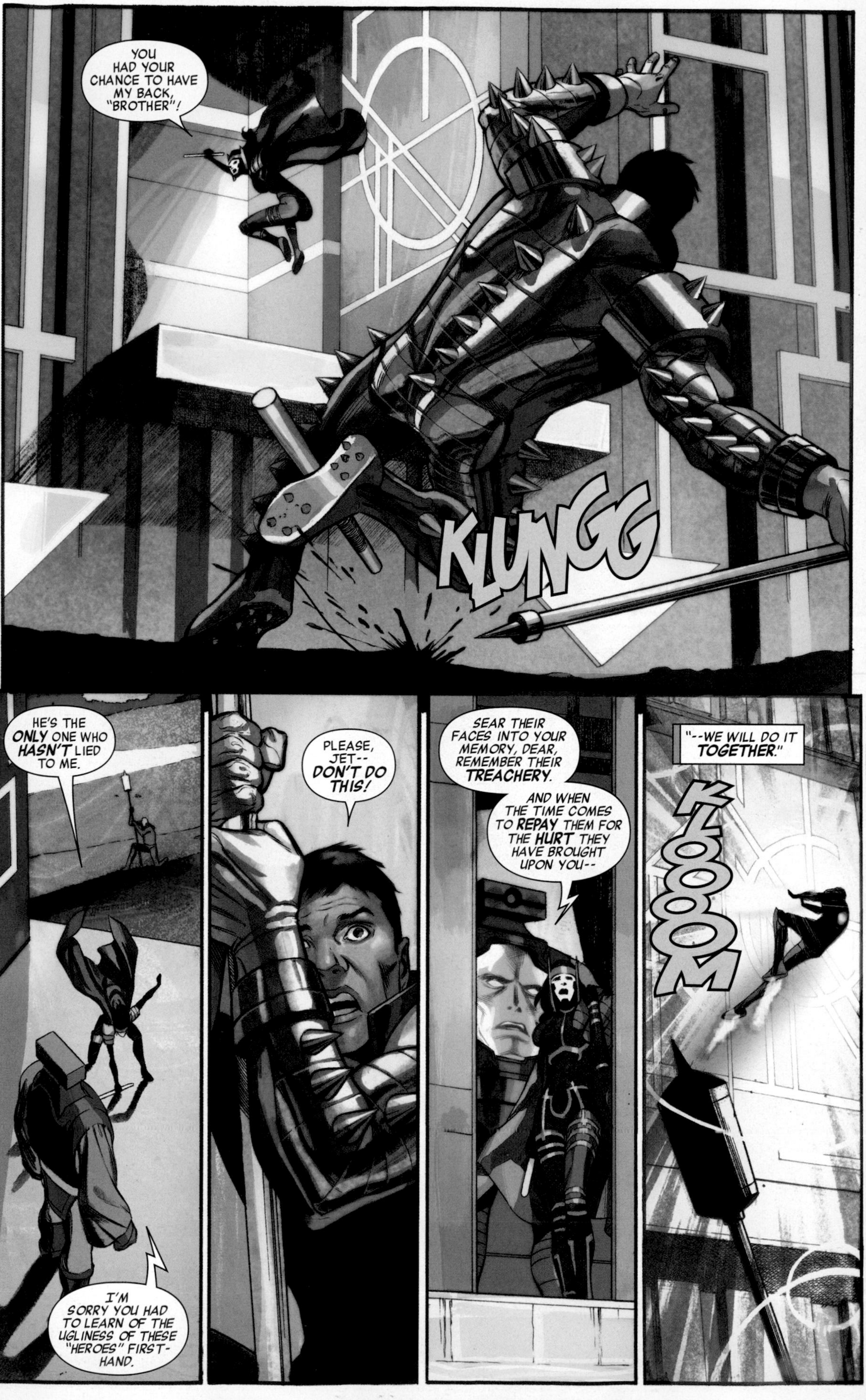
YOU HAD YOUR CHANCE TO HAVE MY BACK, "BROTHER"!
KLUNGG
HE'S THE ONLY ONE WHO HASN'T LIED TO ME.
I'M SORRY YOU HAD TO LEARN OF THE UGLINESS OF THESE "HEROES" FIRST-HAND.
PLEASE, JET-- DON'T DO THIS!
SEAR THEIR FACES INTO YOUR MEMORY, DEAR, REMEMBER THEIR TREACHERY.
AND WHEN THE TIME COMES TO REPAY THEM FOR THE HURT THEY HAVE BROUGHT UPON YOU--
"--WE WILL DO IT TOGETHER."
KLOOOOM

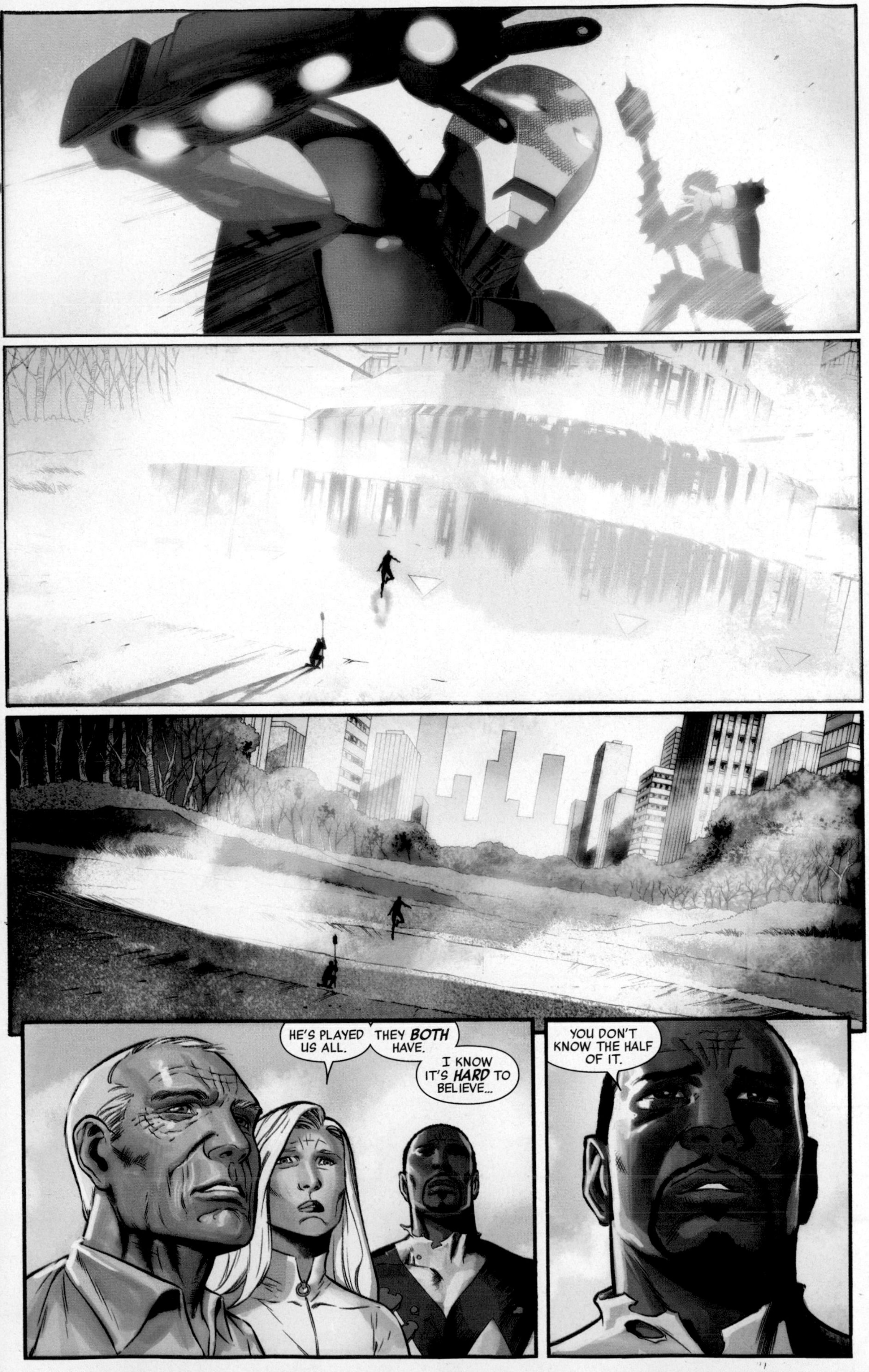
HE'S PLAYED US ALL.
THEY BOTH HAVE.
I KNOW IT'S HARD TO BELIEVE...
YOU DON'T KNOW THE HALF OF IT.

# ONE
# WEEK
# LATER.

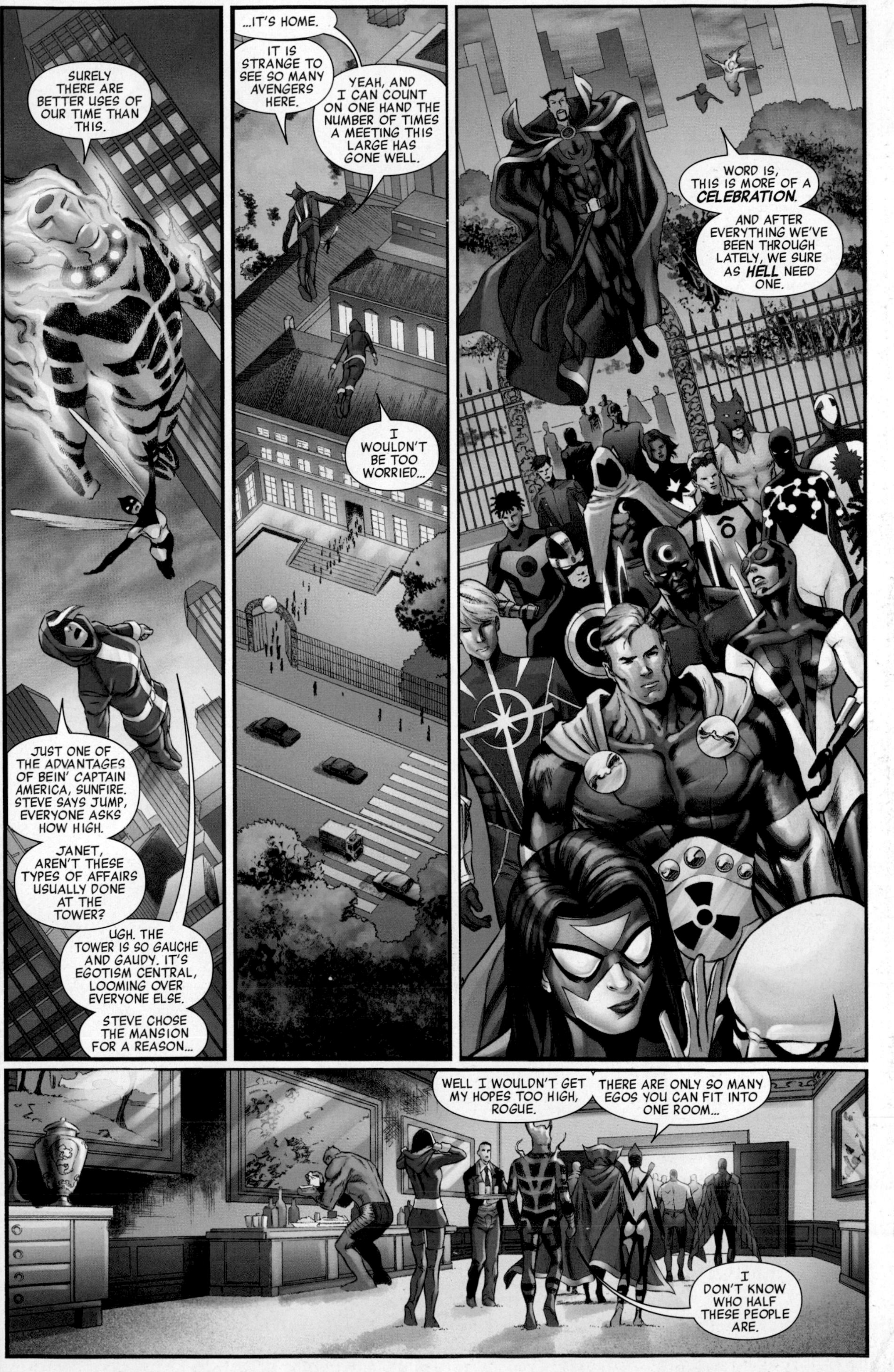
SURELY THERE ARE BETTER USES OF OUR TIME THAN THIS.
JUST ONE OF THE ADVANTAGES OF BEIN' CAPTAIN AMERICA, SUNFIRE. STEVE SAYS JUMP, EVERYONE ASKS HOW HIGH.
JANET, AREN'T THESE TYPES OF AFFAIRS USUALLY DONE AT THE TOWER?
UGH. THE TOWER IS SO GAUCHE AND GAUDY. IT'S EGOTISM CENTRAL, LOOMING OVER EVERYONE ELSE.
STEVE CHOSE THE MANSION FOR A REASON...
...IT'S HOME.
IT IS STRANGE TO SEE SO MANY AVENGERS HERE.
YEAH, AND I CAN COUNT ON ONE HAND THE NUMBER OF TIMES A MEETING THIS LARGE HAS GONE WELL.
I WOULDN'T BE TOO WORRIED...
WORD IS, THIS IS MORE OF A ***CELEBRATION***.
AND AFTER EVERYTHING WE'VE BEEN THROUGH LATELY, WE SURE AS ***HELL*** NEED ONE.
WELL I WOULDN'T GET MY HOPES TOO HIGH, ROGUE.
THERE ARE ONLY SO MANY EGOS YOU CAN FIT INTO ONE ROOM...
I DON'T KNOW WHO HALF THESE PEOPLE ARE.

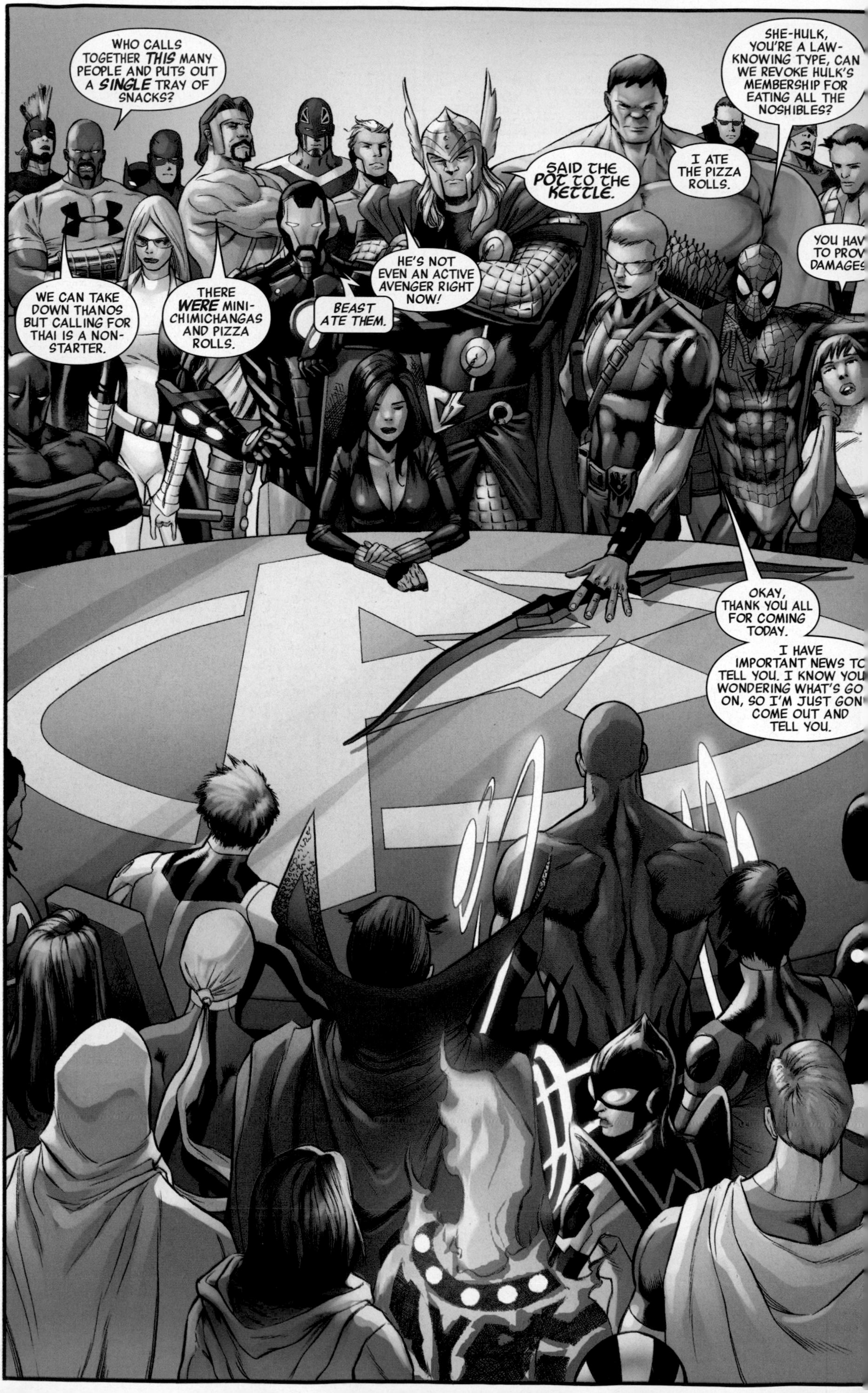
WHO CALLS TOGETHER THIS MANY PEOPLE AND PUTS OUT A SINGLE TRAY OF SNACKS?
WE CAN TAKE DOWN THANOS BUT CALLING FOR THAI IS A NON-STARTER.
THERE WERE MINI-CHIMICHANGAS AND PIZZA ROLLS.
BEAST ATE THEM.
HE'S NOT EVEN AN ACTIVE AVENGER RIGHT NOW!
SAID THE POT TO THE KETTLE.
I ATE THE PIZZA ROLLS.
SHE-HULK, YOU'RE A LAW-KNOWING TYPE, CAN WE REVOKE HULK'S MEMBERSHIP FOR EATING ALL THE NOSHIBLES?
YOU HAV TO PROV DAMAGES
OKAY, THANK YOU ALL FOR COMING TODAY.
I HAVE IMPORTANT NEWS TO TELL YOU. I KNOW YOU WONDERING WHAT'S GO ON, SO I'M JUST GON COME OUT AND TELL YOU.

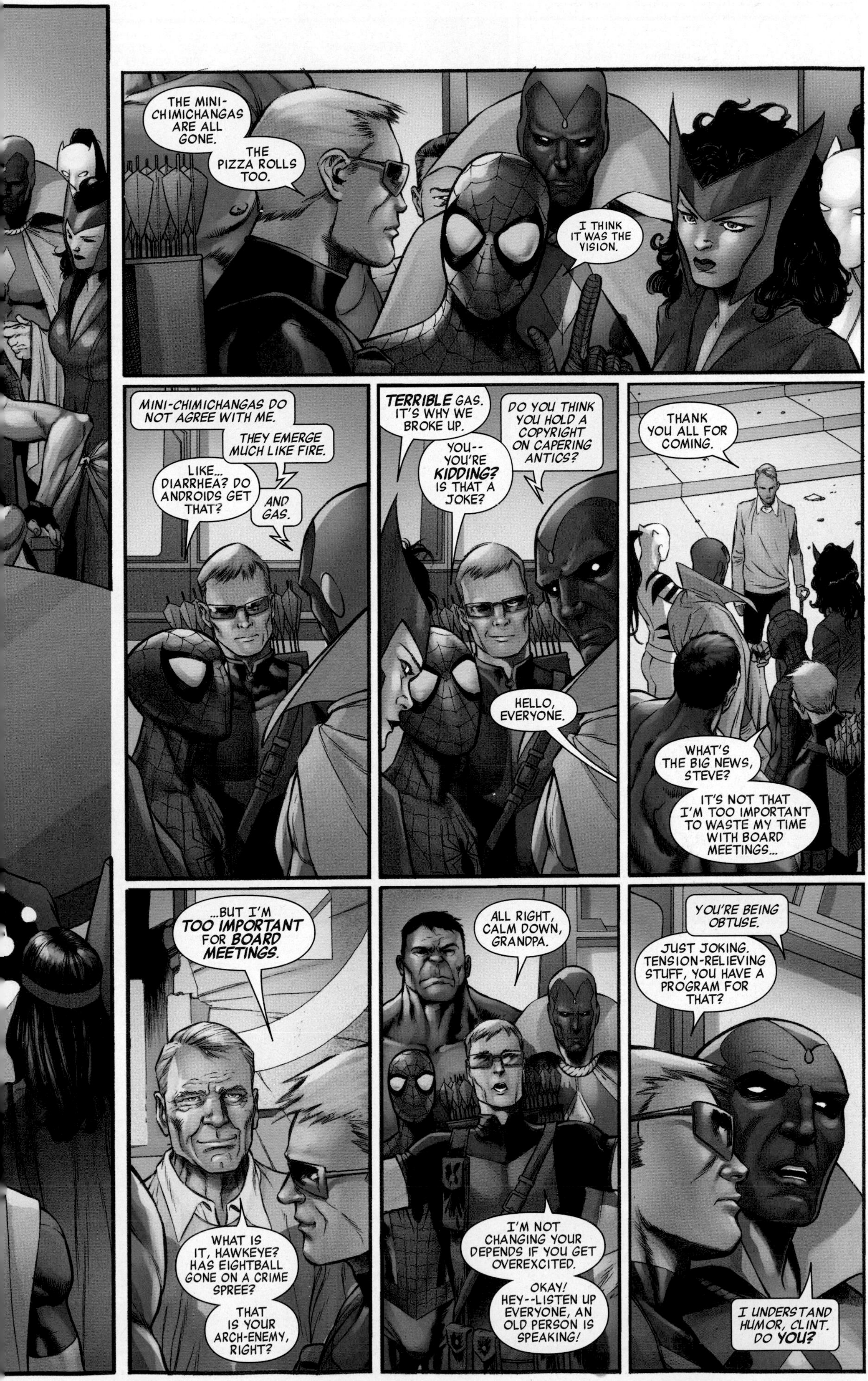
THE MINI-CHIMICHANGAS ARE ALL GONE.
THE PIZZA ROLLS TOO.
I THINK IT WAS THE VISION.
MINI-CHIMICHANGAS DO NOT AGREE WITH ME.
THEY EMERGE MUCH LIKE FIRE.
LIKE... DIARRHEA? DO ANDROIDS GET THAT?
AND GAS.
TERRIBLE GAS. IT'S WHY WE BROKE UP.
YOU-- YOU'RE KIDDING? IS THAT A JOKE?
DO YOU THINK YOU HOLD A COPYRIGHT ON CAPERING ANTICS?
HELLO, EVERYONE.
THANK YOU ALL FOR COMING.
WHAT'S THE BIG NEWS, STEVE?
IT'S NOT THAT I'M TOO IMPORTANT TO WASTE MY TIME WITH BOARD MEETINGS...
...BUT I'M TOO IMPORTANT FOR BOARD MEETINGS.
WHAT IS IT, HAWKEYE? HAS EIGHTBALL GONE ON A CRIME SPREE?
THAT IS YOUR ARCH-ENEMY, RIGHT?
ALL RIGHT, CALM DOWN, GRANDPA.
I'M NOT CHANGING YOUR DEPENDS IF YOU GET OVEREXCITED.
OKAY! HEY--LISTEN UP EVERYONE, AN OLD PERSON IS SPEAKING!
YOU'RE BEING OBTUSE.
JUST JOKING. TENSION-RELIEVING STUFF, YOU HAVE A PROGRAM FOR THAT?
I UNDERSTAND HUMOR, CLINT. DO YOU?

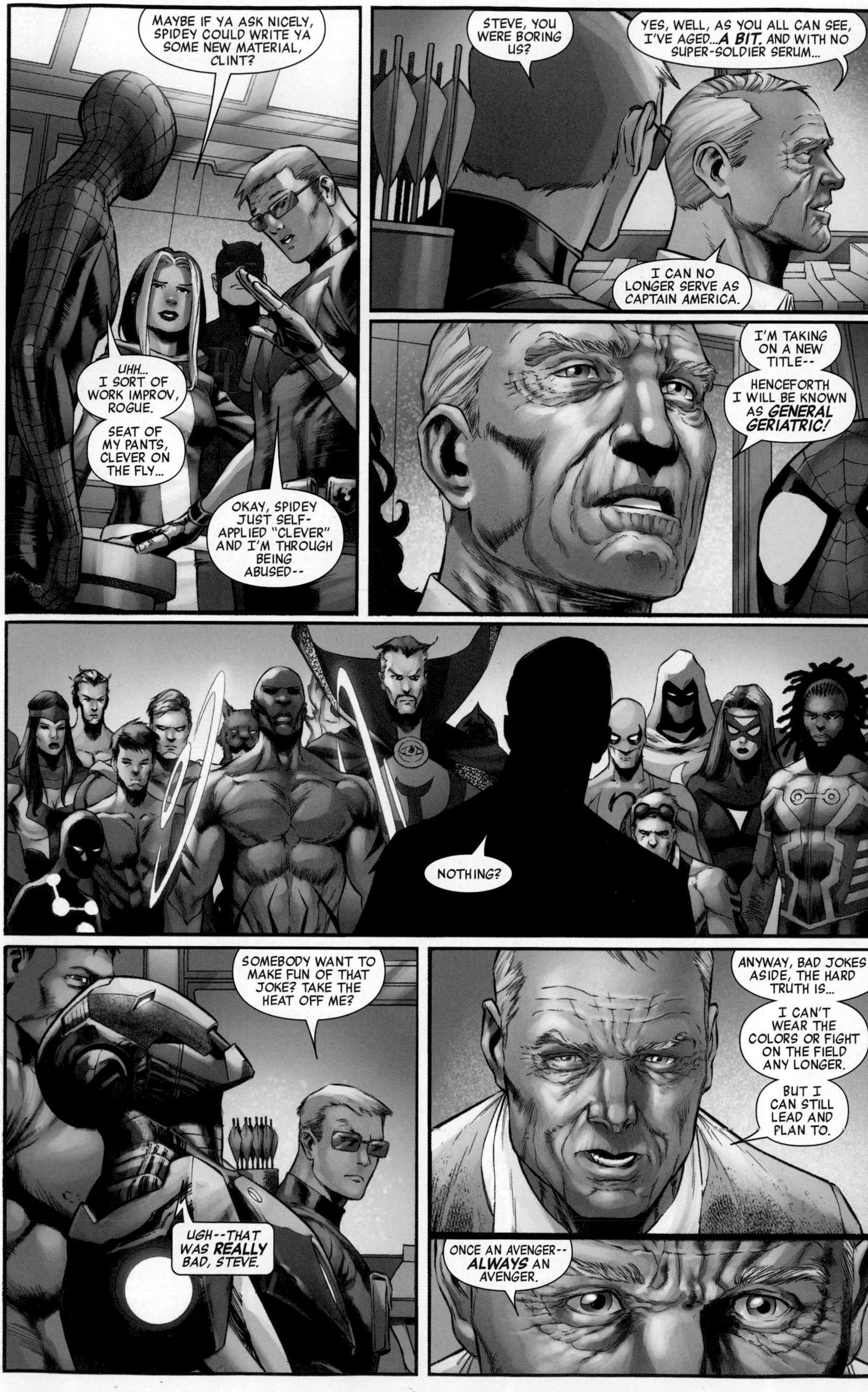

MAYBE IF YA ASK NICELY, SPIDEY COULD WRITE YA SOME NEW MATERIAL, CLINT?
UHH... I SORT OF WORK IMPROV, ROGUE.
SEAT OF MY PANTS, CLEVER ON THE FLY...
OKAY, SPIDEY JUST SELF-APPLIED "CLEVER" AND I'M THROUGH BEING ABUSED--
STEVE, YOU WERE BORING US?
YES, WELL, AS YOU ALL CAN SEE, I'VE AGED...A BIT. AND WITH NO SUPER-SOLDIER SERUM...
I CAN NO LONGER SERVE AS CAPTAIN AMERICA.
I'M TAKING ON A NEW TITLE--
HENCEFORTH I WILL BE KNOWN AS GENERAL GERIATRIC!
NOTHING?
SOMEBODY WANT TO MAKE FUN OF THAT JOKE? TAKE THE HEAT OFF ME?
UGH--THAT WAS REALLY BAD, STEVE.
ANYWAY, BAD JOKES ASIDE, THE HARD TRUTH IS...
I CAN'T WEAR THE COLORS OR FIGHT ON THE FIELD ANY LONGER.
BUT I CAN STILL LEAD AND PLAN TO.
ONCE AN AVENGER--ALWAYS AN AVENGER.

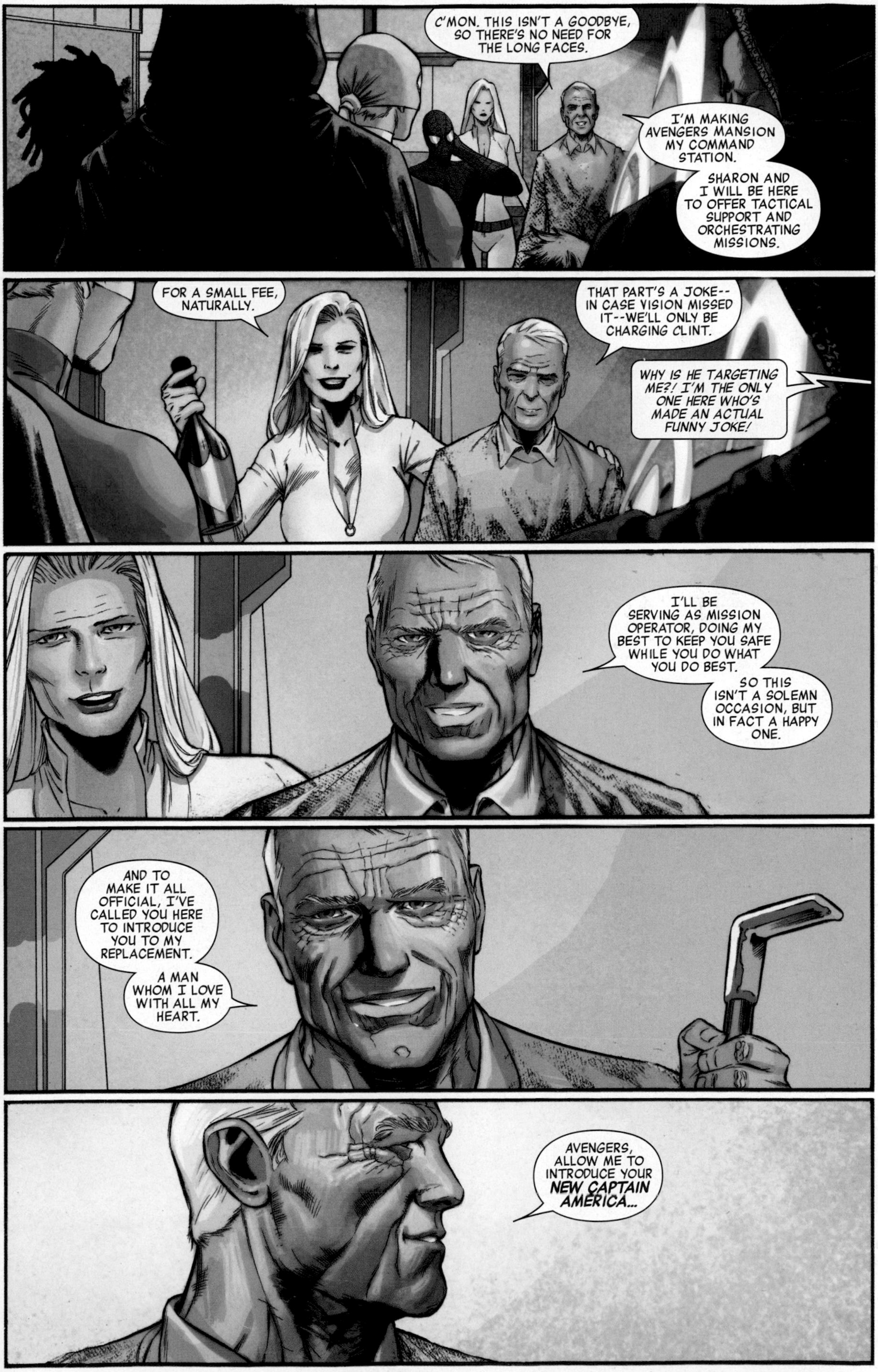
C'MON. THIS ISN'T A GOODBYE, SO THERE'S NO NEED FOR THE LONG FACES.
I'M MAKING AVENGERS MANSION MY COMMAND STATION.
SHARON AND I WILL BE HERE TO OFFER TACTICAL SUPPORT AND ORCHESTRATING MISSIONS.
FOR A SMALL FEE, NATURALLY.
THAT PART'S A JOKE-- IN CASE VISION MISSED IT--WE'LL ONLY BE CHARGING CLINT.
WHY IS HE TARGETING ME?! I'M THE ONLY ONE HERE WHO'S MADE AN ACTUAL FUNNY JOKE!
I'LL BE SERVING AS MISSION OPERATOR, DOING MY BEST TO KEEP YOU SAFE WHILE YOU DO WHAT YOU DO BEST.
SO THIS ISN'T A SOLEMN OCCASION, BUT IN FACT A HAPPY ONE.
AND TO MAKE IT ALL OFFICIAL, I'VE CALLED YOU HERE TO INTRODUCE YOU TO MY REPLACEMENT.
A MAN WHOM I LOVE WITH ALL MY HEART.
AVENGERS, ALLOW ME TO INTRODUCE YOUR NEW CAPTAIN AMERICA...

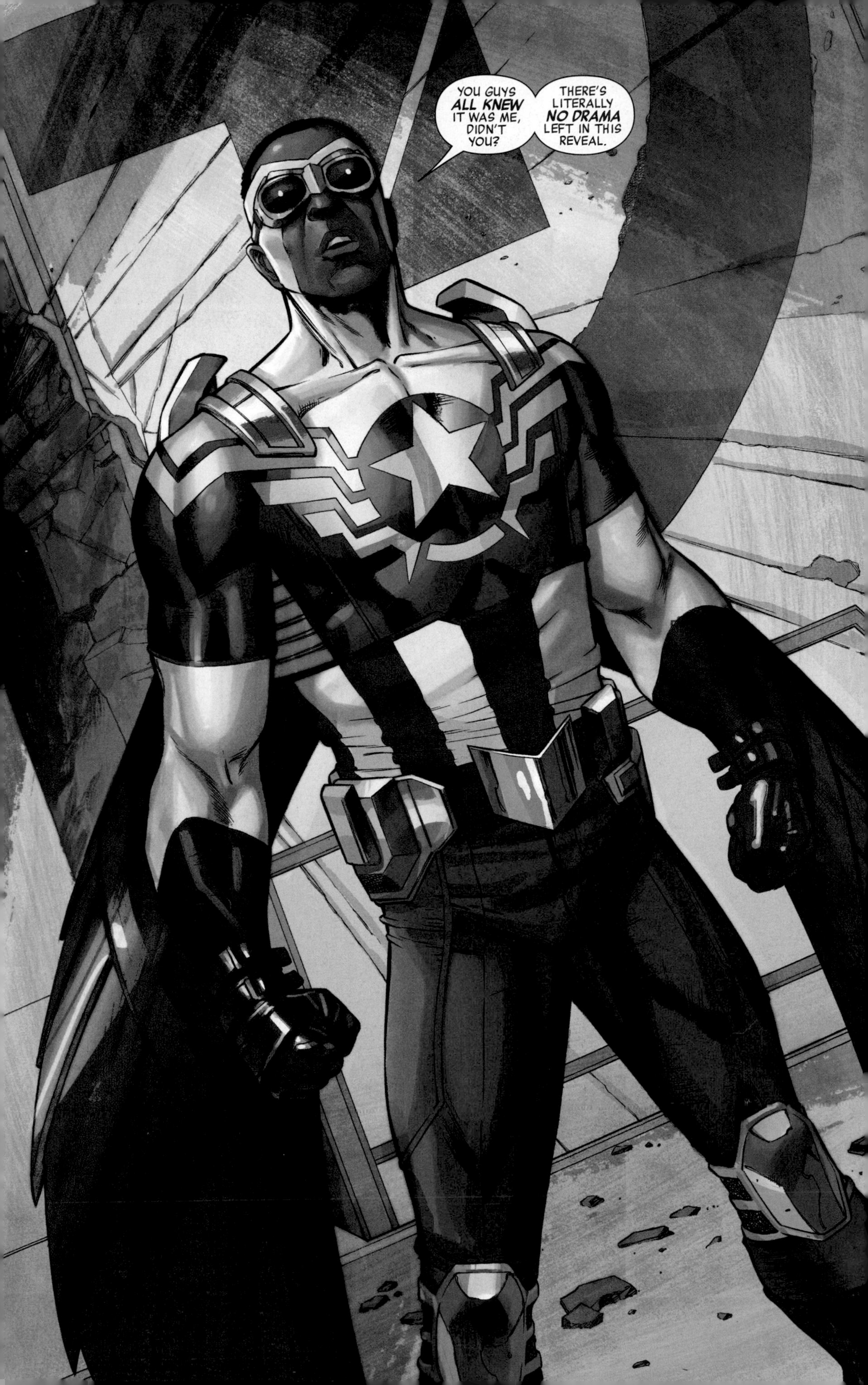
YOU GUYS ALL KNEW IT WAS ME, DIDN'T YOU?
THERE'S LITERALLY NO DRAMA LEFT IN THIS REVEAL.

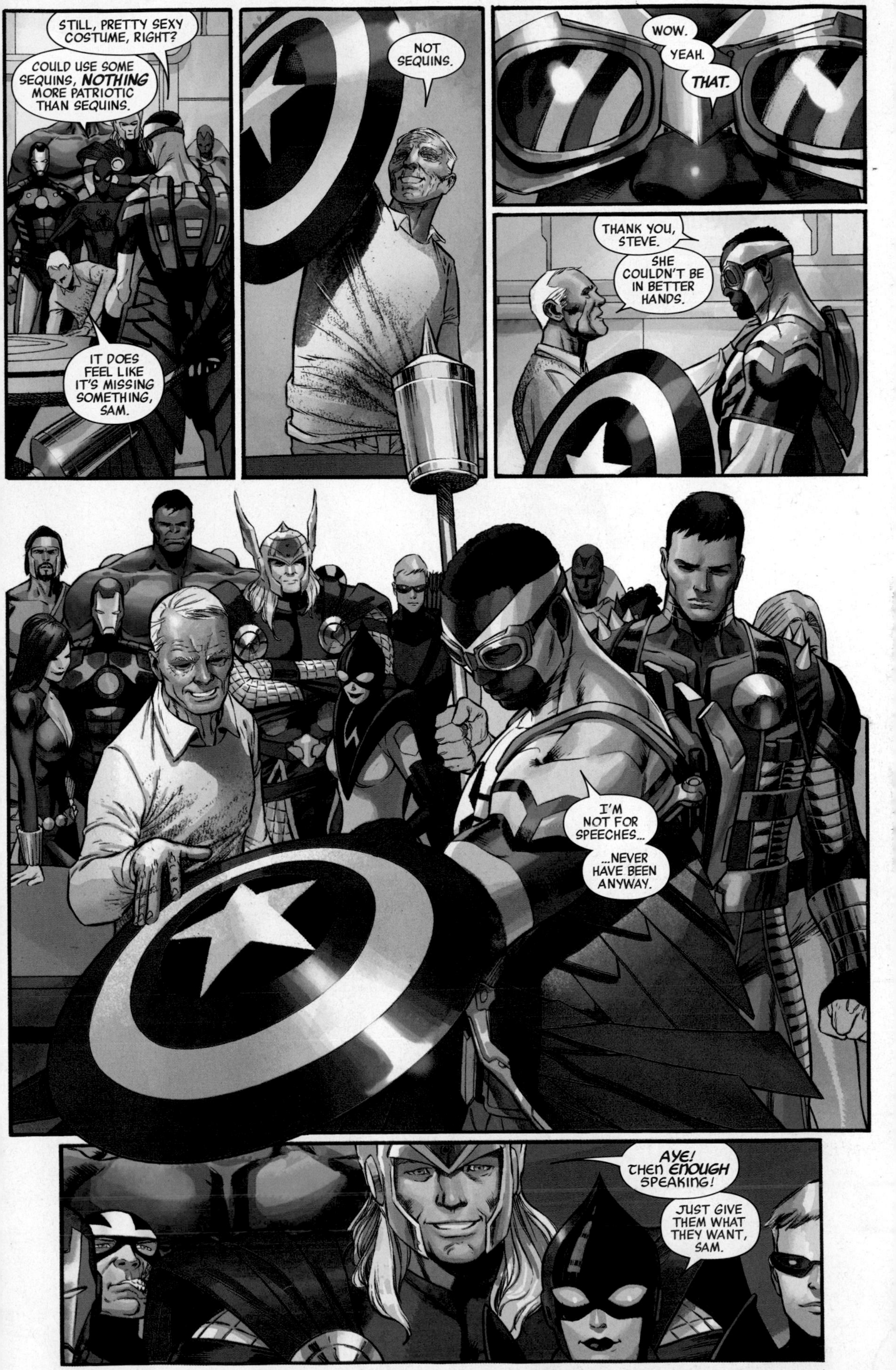
STILL, PRETTY SEXY COSTUME, RIGHT?
COULD USE SOME SEQUINS, NOTHING MORE PATRIOTIC THAN SEQUINS.
IT DOES FEEL LIKE IT'S MISSING SOMETHING, SAM.
NOT SEQUINS.
WOW.
YEAH.
THAT.
THANK YOU, STEVE.
SHE COULDN'T BE IN BETTER HANDS.
I'M NOT FOR SPEECHES...
...NEVER HAVE BEEN ANYWAY.
AYE! THEN ENOUGH SPEAKING!
JUST GIVE THEM WHAT THEY WANT, SAM.

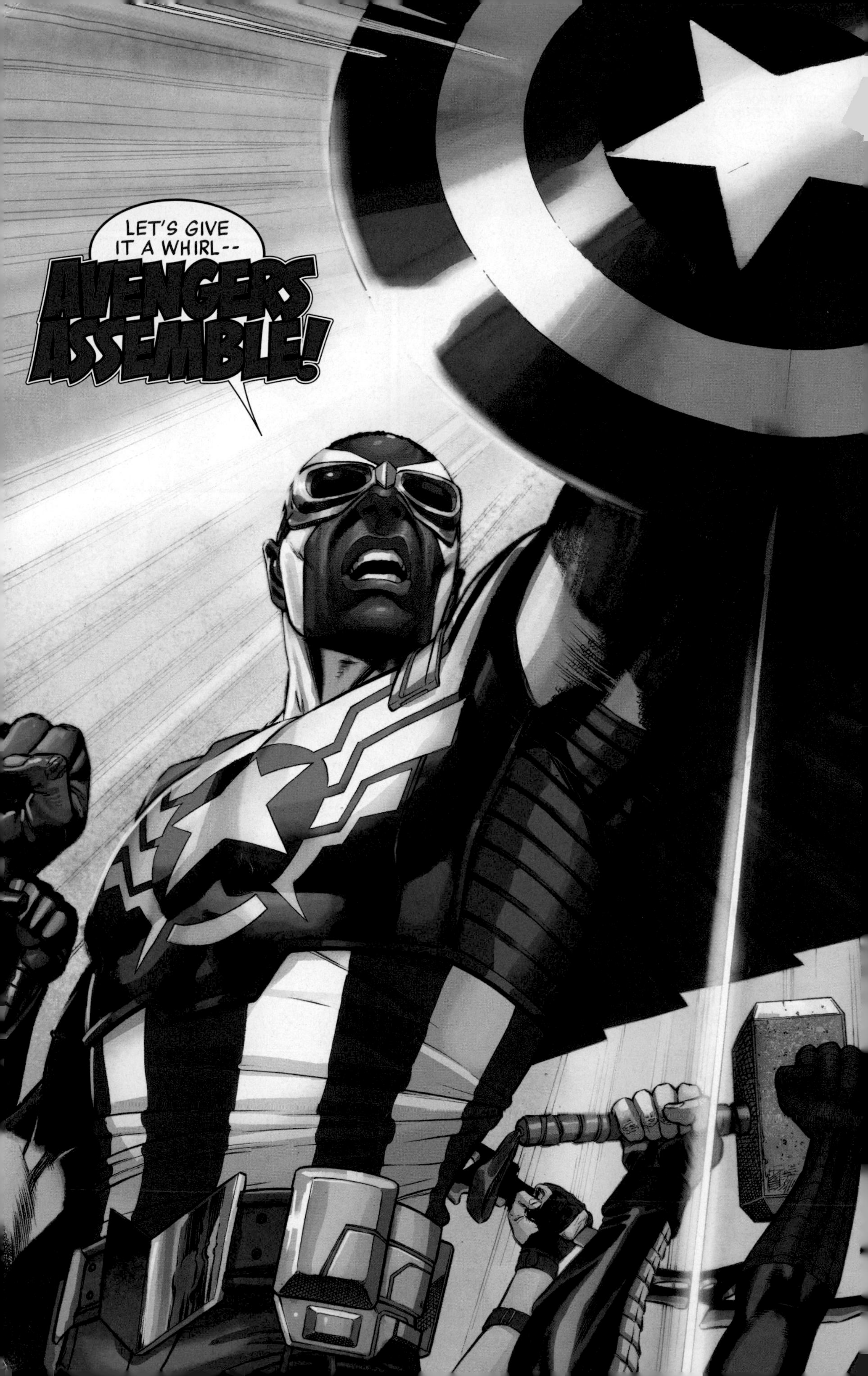
LET'S GIVE IT A WHIRL-- AVENGERS ASSEMBLE!

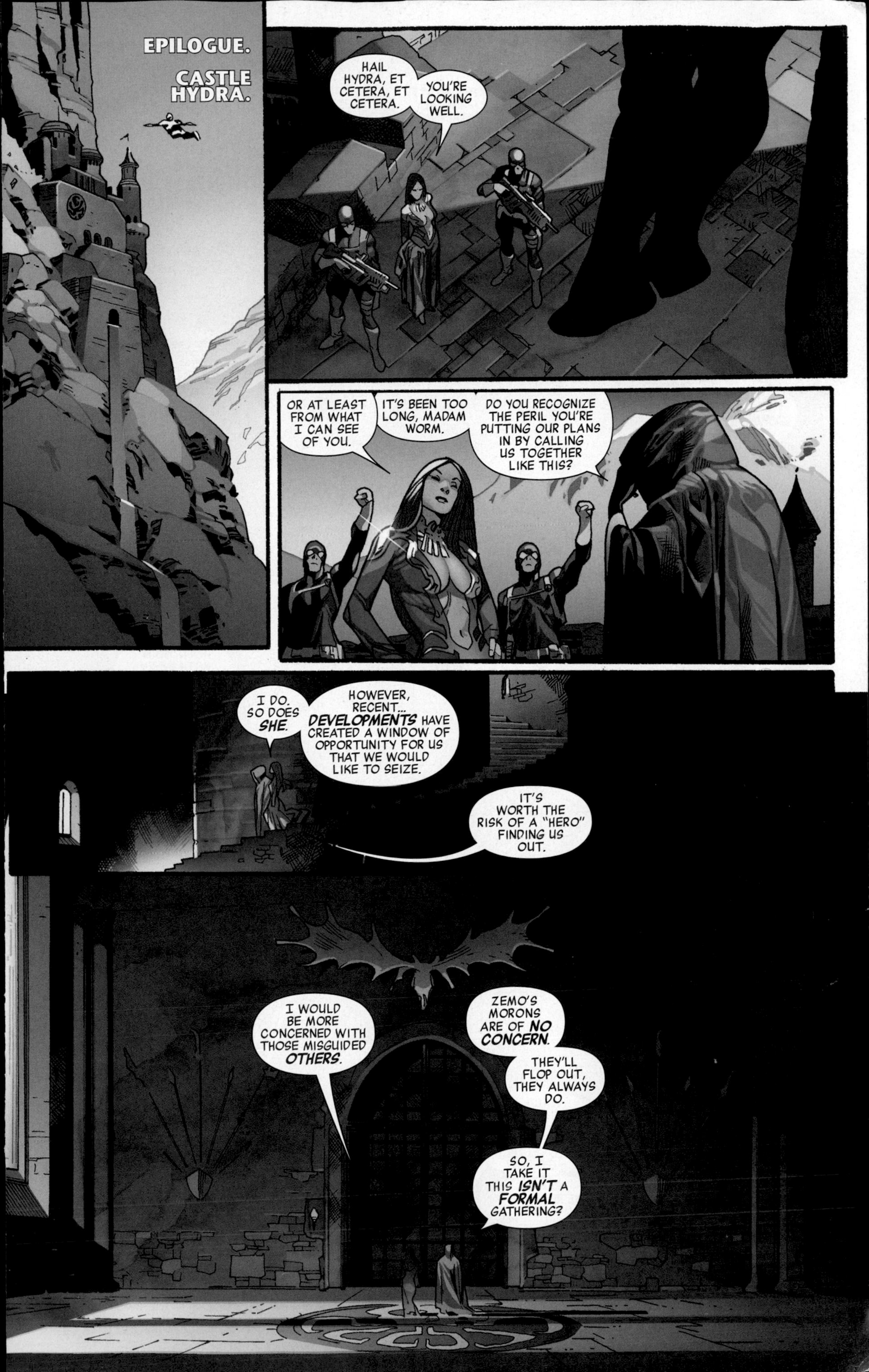
EPILOGUE.
CASTLE HYDRA.
HAIL HYDRA, ET CETERA, ET CETERA.
YOU'RE LOOKING WELL.
OR AT LEAST FROM WHAT I CAN SEE OF YOU.
IT'S BEEN TOO LONG, MADAM WORM.
DO YOU RECOGNIZE THE PERIL YOU'RE PUTTING OUR PLANS IN BY CALLING US TOGETHER LIKE THIS?
I DO. SO DOES SHE.
HOWEVER, RECENT... DEVELOPMENTS HAVE CREATED A WINDOW OF OPPORTUNITY FOR US THAT WE WOULD LIKE TO SEIZE.
IT'S WORTH THE RISK OF A "HERO" FINDING US OUT.
I WOULD BE MORE CONCERNED WITH THOSE MISGUIDED OTHERS.
ZEMO'S MORONS ARE OF NO CONCERN.
THEY'LL FLOP OUT, THEY ALWAYS DO.
SO, I TAKE IT THIS ISN'T A FORMAL GATHERING?

IT IS THE MOST FORMAL GATHERING...
...WHENEVER THE UNKNOWN COUNCIL COMES TOGETHER.
AH, HERE HE IS NOW, RIGHT FROM THE CHRISTENING OF THE NEW CAPTAIN AMERICA.
SUCH A GALA EVENT.
HOBNOBBIN' WITH EVERY AVENGER. MUST'VE PAINED YA TO LEAVE EARLY.
WHICH IS PRECISELY WHY CALLING THIS MEETING IS SO INCREDIBLY STUPID.
RELAX. WE'RE IN NO DANGER.
THEY'D NEVER SUSPECT YOU.
UNLESS YOU HAVE REASON TO BELIEVE THEY'RE SUSPICIOUS OF YOU?
THEY ARE NOT.

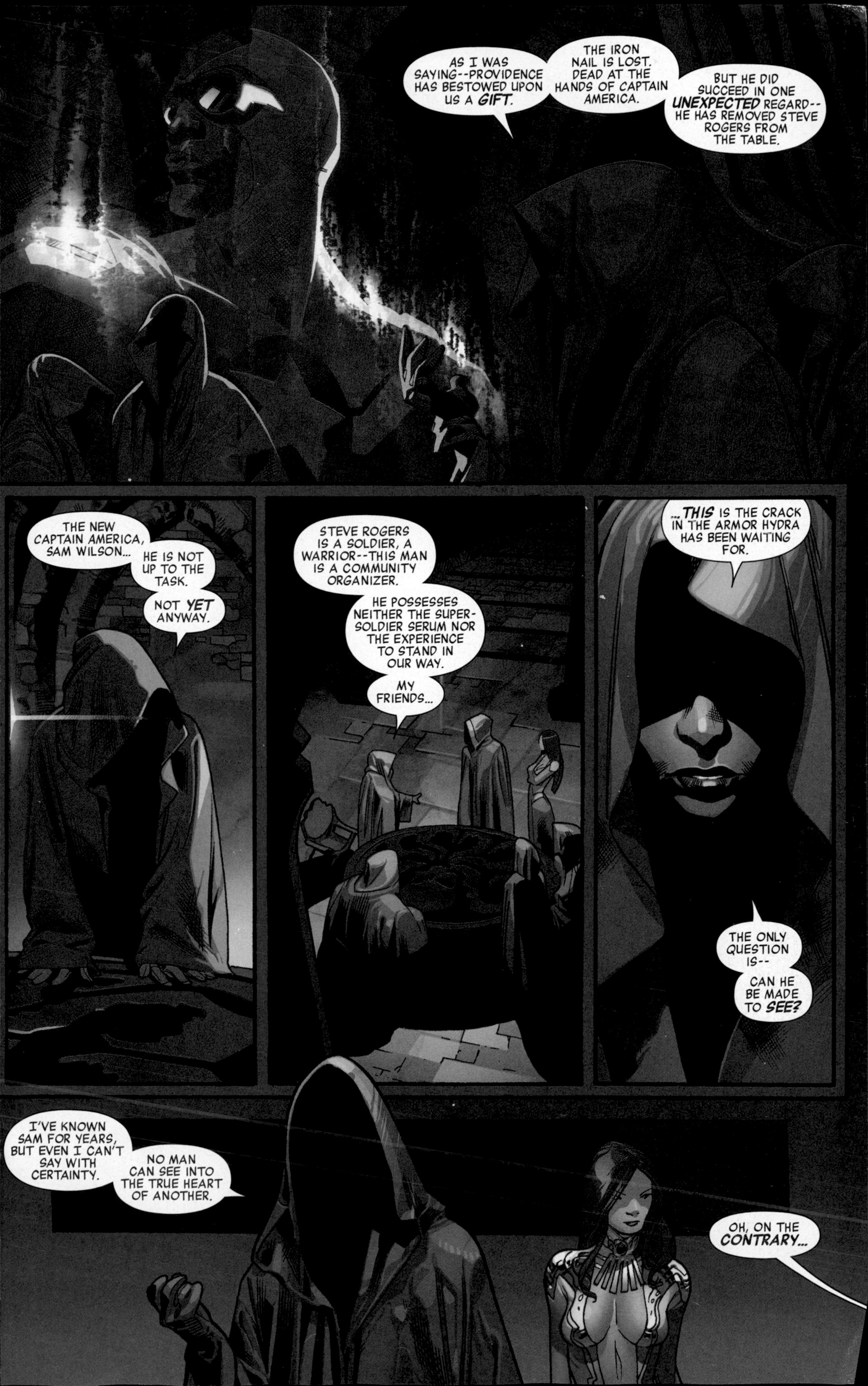
AS I WAS SAYING--PROVIDENCE HAS BESTOWED UPON US A GIFT.
THE IRON NAIL IS LOST. DEAD AT THE HANDS OF CAPTAIN AMERICA.
BUT HE DID SUCCEED IN ONE UNEXPECTED REGARD-- HE HAS REMOVED STEVE ROGERS FROM THE TABLE.
THE NEW CAPTAIN AMERICA, SAM WILSON...
HE IS NOT UP TO THE TASK.
NOT YET ANYWAY.
STEVE ROGERS IS A SOLDIER, A WARRIOR--THIS MAN IS A COMMUNITY ORGANIZER.
HE POSSESSES NEITHER THE SUPER-SOLDIER SERUM NOR THE EXPERIENCE TO STAND IN OUR WAY.
MY FRIENDS...
...THIS IS THE CRACK IN THE ARMOR HYDRA HAS BEEN WAITING FOR.
THE ONLY QUESTION IS--
CAN HE BE MADE TO SEE?
I'VE KNOWN SAM FOR YEARS, BUT EVEN I CAN'T SAY WITH CERTAINTY.
NO MAN CAN SEE INTO THE TRUE HEART OF ANOTHER.
OH, ON THE CONTRARY...

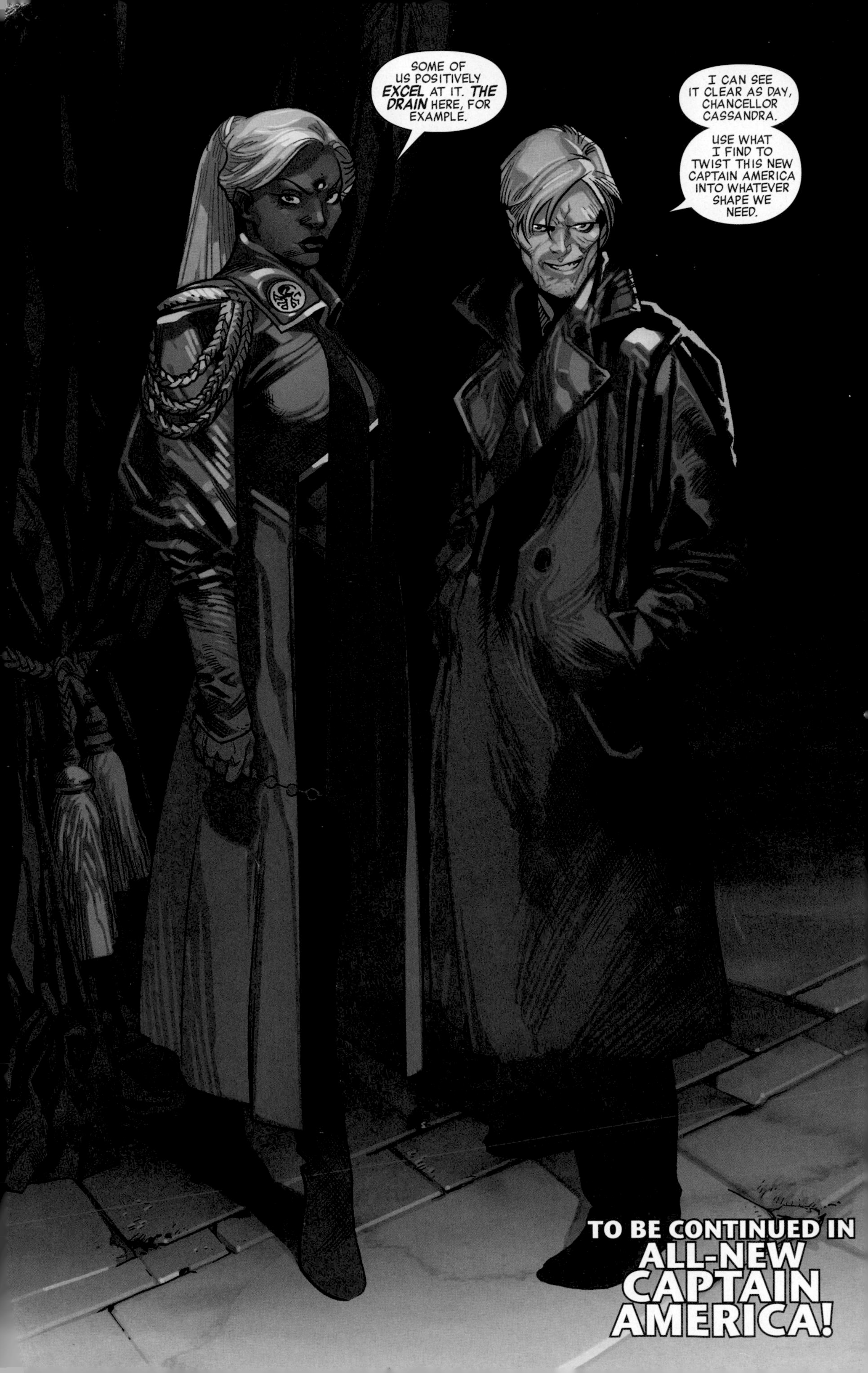
SOME OF US POSITIVELY EXCEL AT IT. THE DRAIN HERE, FOR EXAMPLE.
I CAN SEE IT CLEAR AS DAY, CHANCELLOR CASSANDRA.
USE WHAT I FIND TO TWIST THIS NEW CAPTAIN AMERICA INTO WHATEVER SHAPE WE NEED.
TO BE CONTINUED IN ALL-NEW CAPTAIN AMERICA!

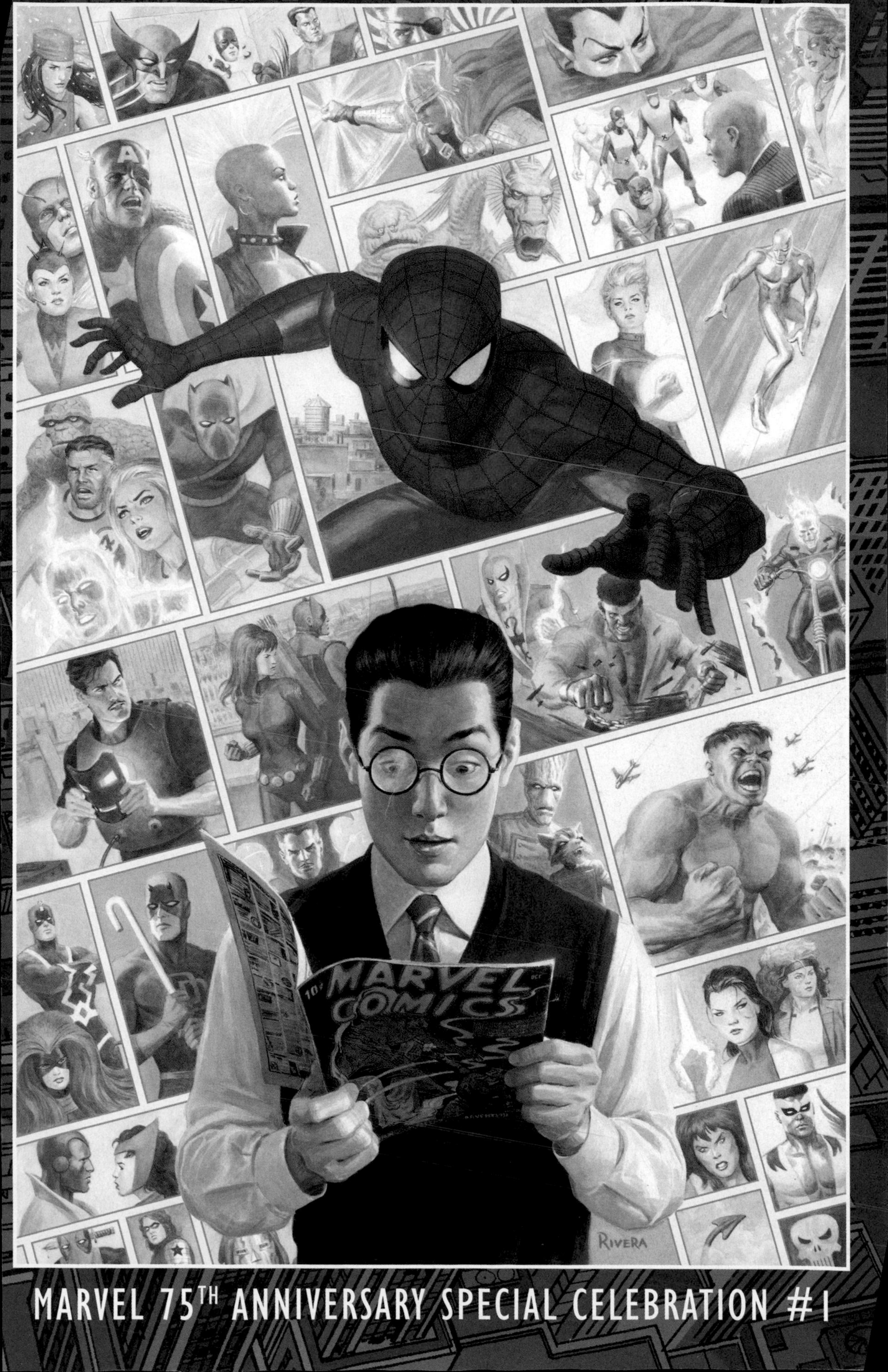
10¢
MARVEL COMICS
RIVERA

MARVEL 75TH ANNIVERSARY SPECIAL CELEBRATION #1

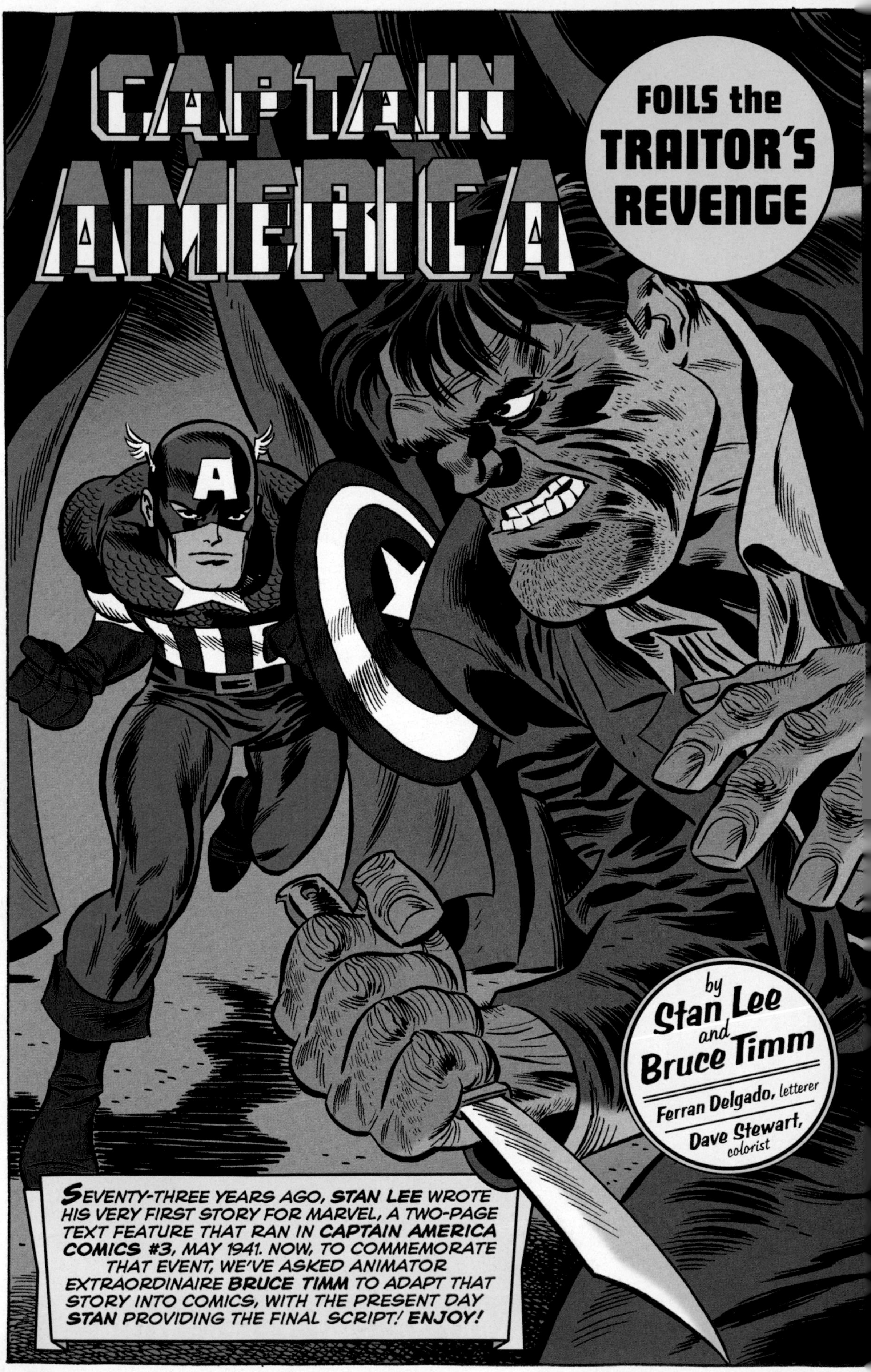
CAPTAIN AMERICA
FOILS the TRAITOR'S REVENGE
by Stan Lee and Bruce Timm
Ferran Delgado, letterer
Dave Stewart, colorist
SEVENTY-THREE YEARS AGO, STAN LEE WROTE HIS VERY FIRST STORY FOR MARVEL, A TWO-PAGE TEXT FEATURE THAT RAN IN CAPTAIN AMERICA COMICS #3, MAY 1941. NOW, TO COMMEMORATE THAT EVENT, WE'VE ASKED ANIMATOR EXTRAORDINAIRE BRUCE TIMM TO ADAPT THAT STORY INTO COMICS, WITH THE PRESENT DAY STAN PROVIDING THE FINAL SCRIPT! ENJOY!

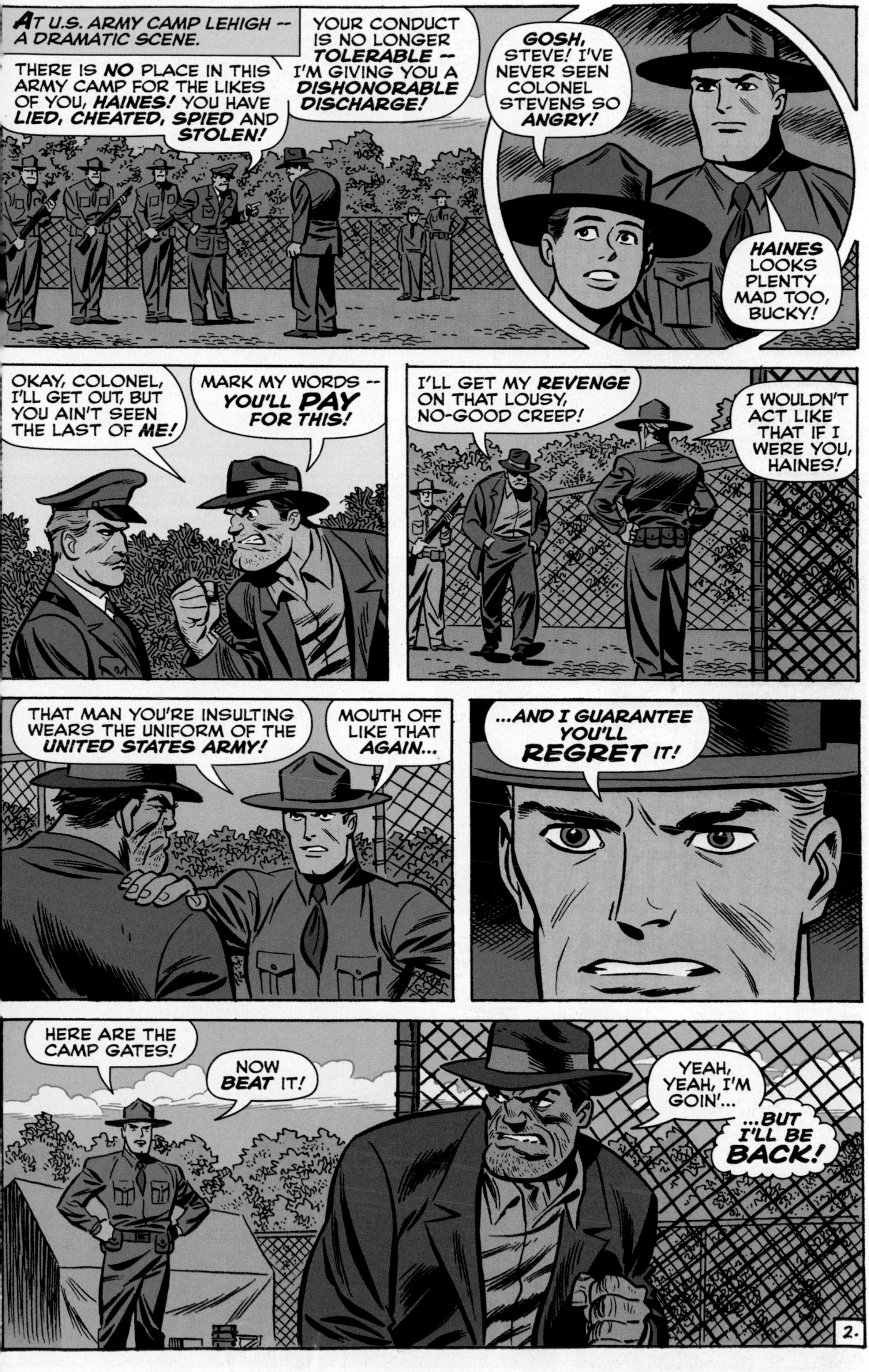

AT U.S. ARMY CAMP LEHIGH -- A DRAMATIC SCENE.
THERE IS NO PLACE IN THIS ARMY CAMP FOR THE LIKES OF YOU, HAINES! YOU HAVE LIED, CHEATED, SPIED AND STOLEN!
YOUR CONDUCT IS NO LONGER TOLERABLE -- I'M GIVING YOU A DISHONORABLE DISCHARGE!
GOSH, STEVE! I'VE NEVER SEEN COLONEL STEVENS SO ANGRY!
HAINES LOOKS PLENTY MAD TOO, BUCKY!
OKAY, COLONEL, I'LL GET OUT, BUT YOU AIN'T SEEN THE LAST OF ME!
MARK MY WORDS -- YOU'LL PAY FOR THIS!
I'LL GET MY REVENGE ON THAT LOUSY, NO-GOOD CREEP!
I WOULDN'T ACT LIKE THAT IF I WERE YOU, HAINES!
THAT MAN YOU'RE INSULTING WEARS THE UNIFORM OF THE UNITED STATES ARMY!
MOUTH OFF LIKE THAT AGAIN...
...AND I GUARANTEE YOU'LL REGRET IT!
HERE ARE THE CAMP GATES!
NOW BEAT IT!
YEAH, YEAH, I'M GOIN'...
...BUT I'LL BE BACK!
2.

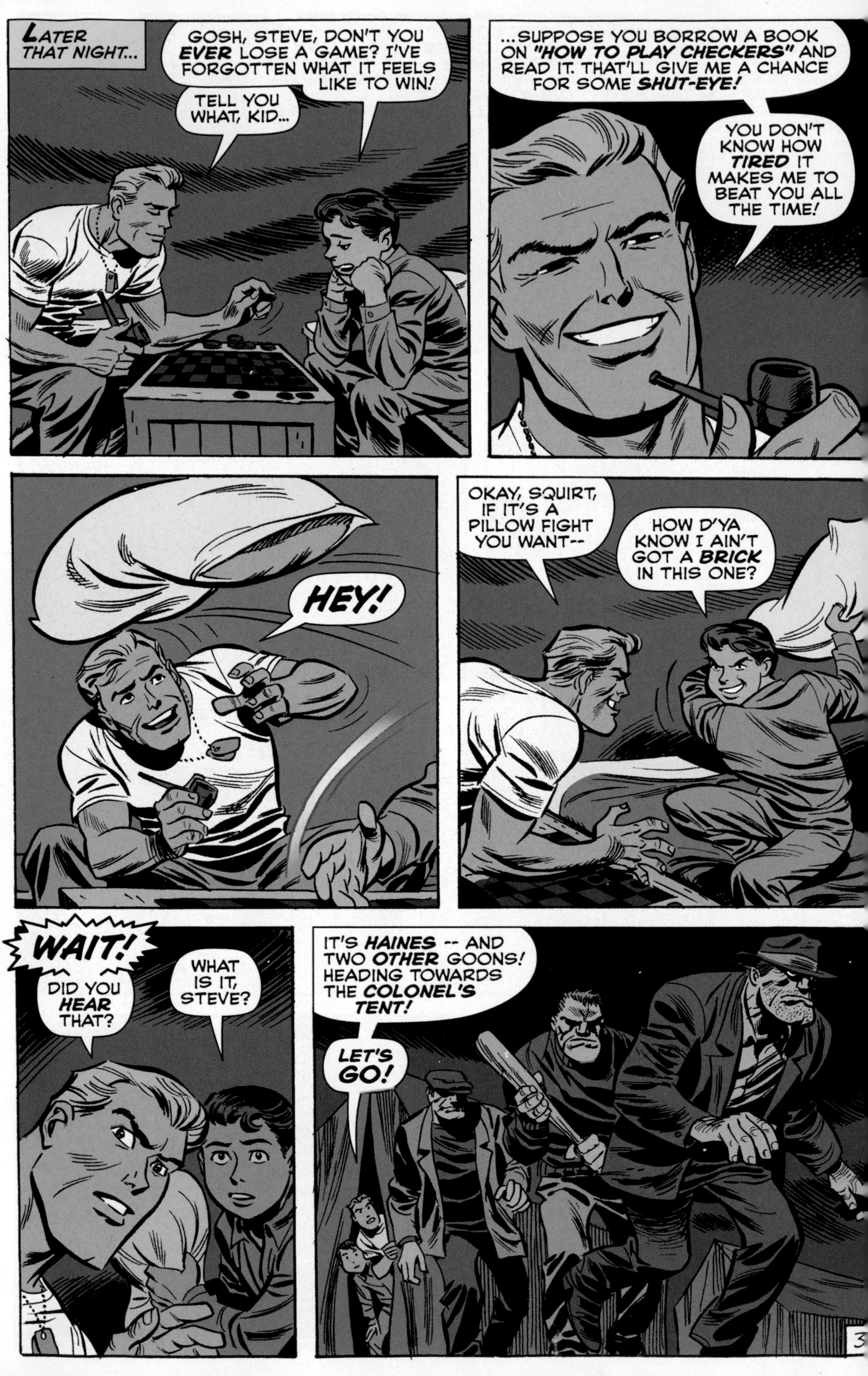
LATER THAT NIGHT...
GOSH, STEVE, DON'T YOU EVER LOSE A GAME? I'VE FORGOTTEN WHAT IT FEELS LIKE TO WIN!
TELL YOU WHAT, KID...
...SUPPOSE YOU BORROW A BOOK ON "HOW TO PLAY CHECKERS" AND READ IT. THAT'LL GIVE ME A CHANCE FOR SOME SHUT-EYE!
YOU DON'T KNOW HOW TIRED IT MAKES ME TO BEAT YOU ALL THE TIME!
HEY!
OKAY, SQUIRT, IF IT'S A PILLOW FIGHT YOU WANT--
HOW D'YA KNOW I AIN'T GOT A BRICK IN THIS ONE?
WAIT!
DID YOU HEAR THAT?
WHAT IS IT, STEVE?
IT'S HAINES -- AND TWO OTHER GOONS! HEADING TOWARDS THE COLONEL'S TENT!
LET'S GO!
3

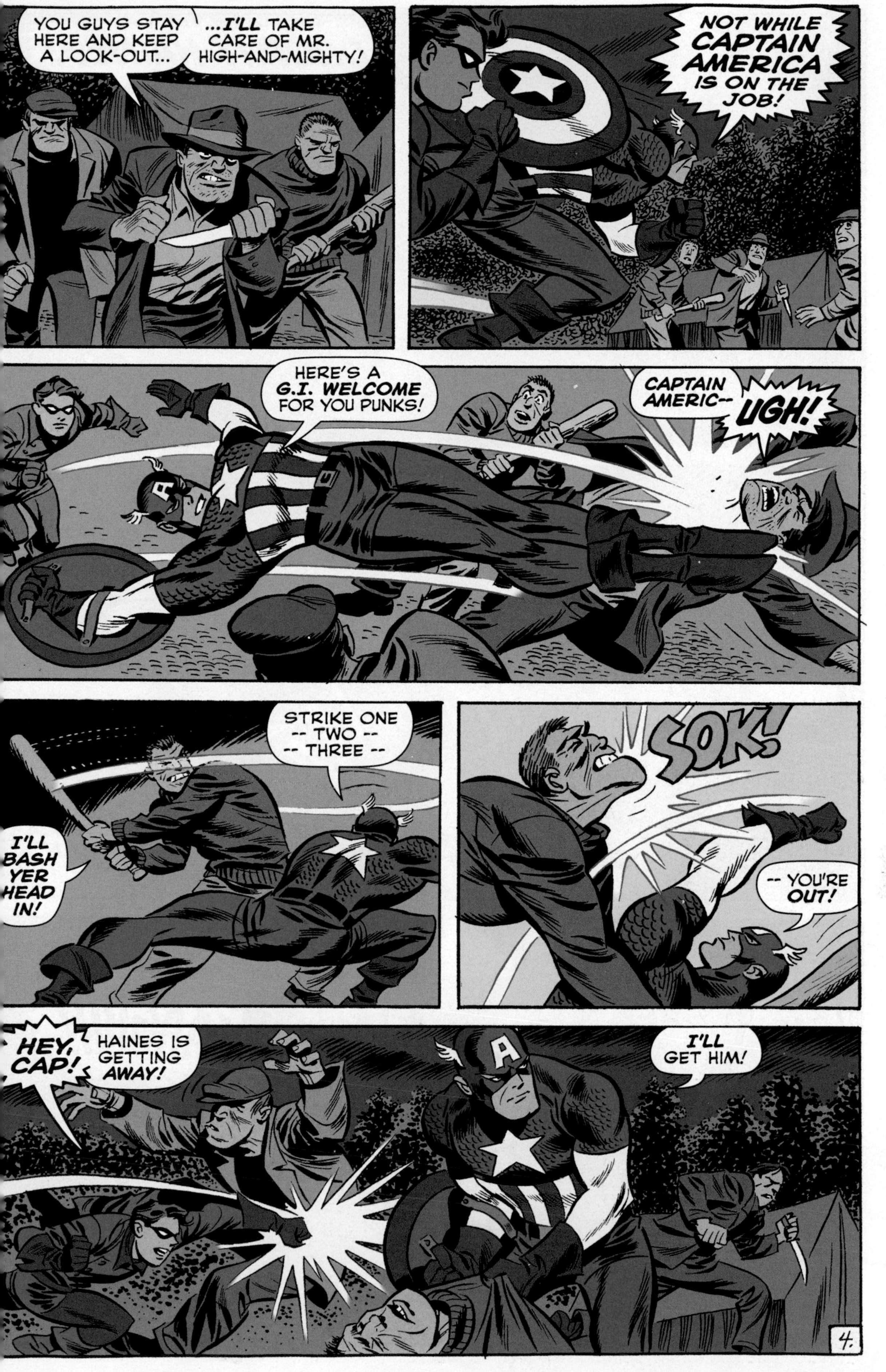
YOU GUYS STAY HERE AND KEEP A LOOK-OUT...
...I'LL TAKE CARE OF MR. HIGH-AND-MIGHTY!
NOT WHILE CAPTAIN AMERICA IS ON THE JOB!
HERE'S A G.I. WELCOME FOR YOU PUNKS!
CAPTAIN AMERIC--
UGH!
STRIKE ONE -- TWO -- -- THREE --
I'LL BASH YER HEAD IN!
SOK!
-- YOU'RE OUT!
HEY, CAP!
HAINES IS GETTING AWAY!
I'LL GET HIM!
4.

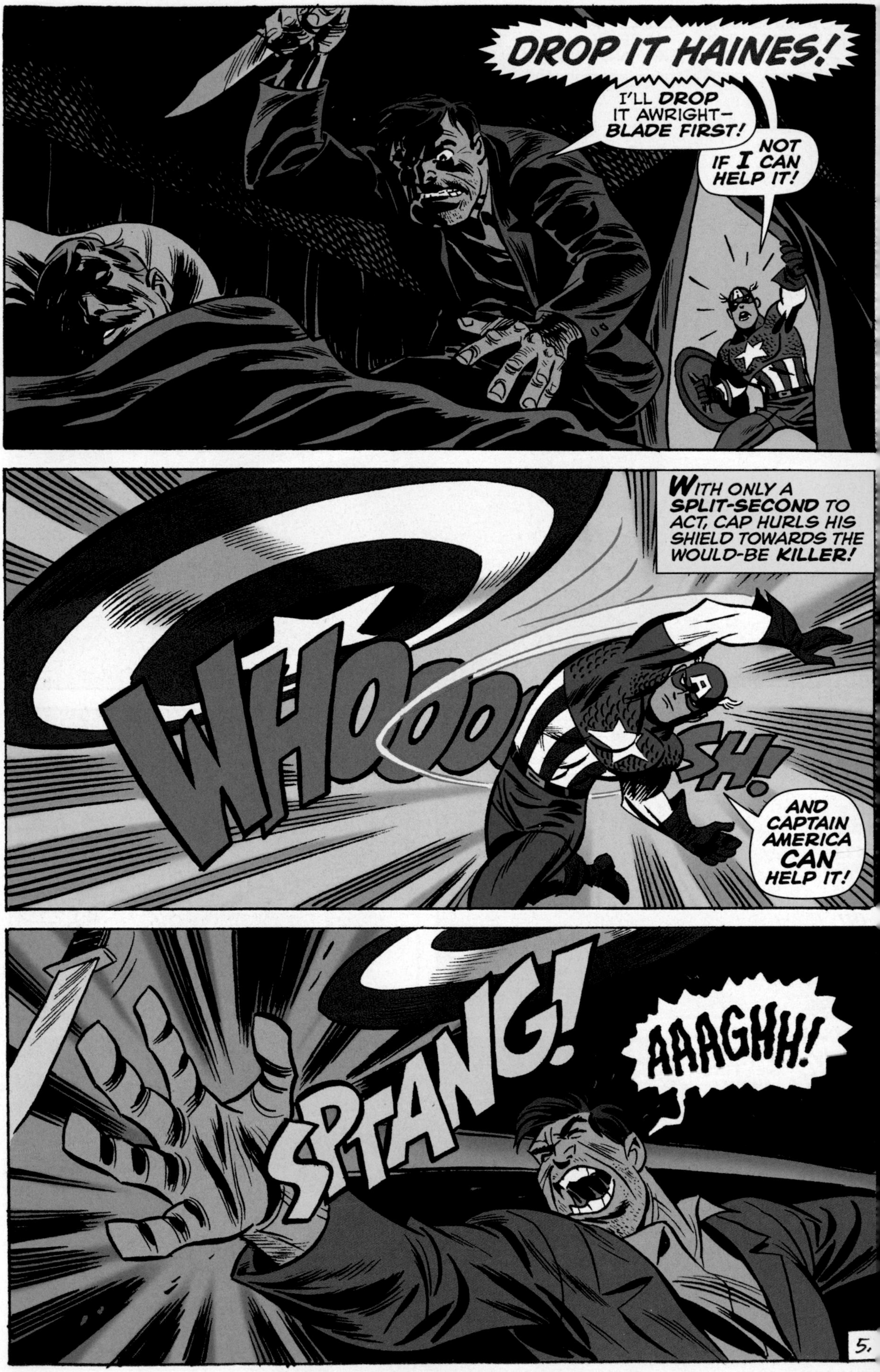
DROP IT HAINES!
I'LL DROP IT AWRIGHT— BLADE FIRST!
NOT IF I CAN HELP IT!
WITH ONLY A SPLIT-SECOND TO ACT, CAP HURLS HIS SHIELD TOWARDS THE WOULD-BE KILLER!
WHOOOOOSH!
AND CAPTAIN AMERICA CAN HELP IT!
SPTANG!
AAAGHH!

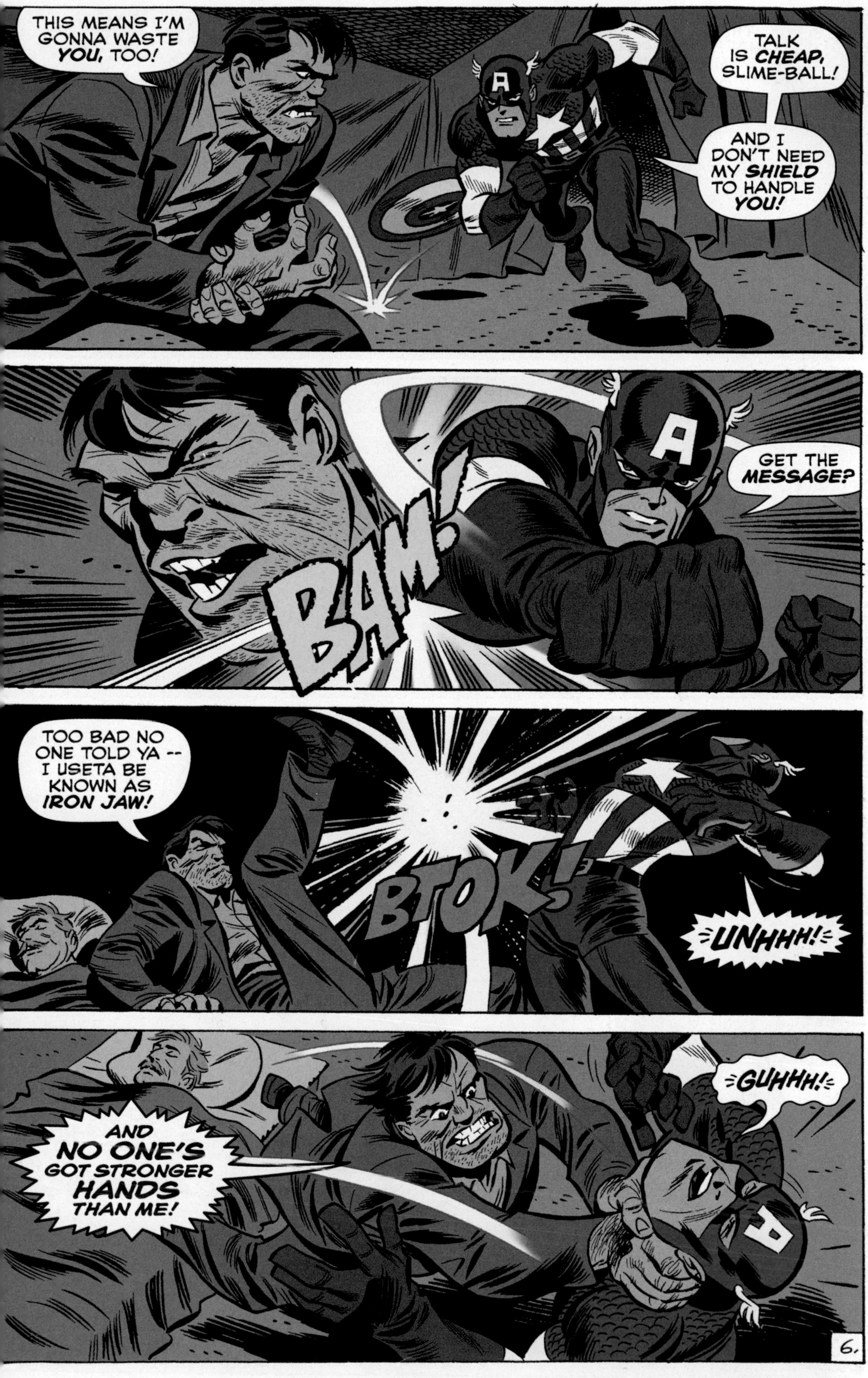
THIS MEANS I'M GONNA WASTE YOU, TOO!
TALK IS CHEAP, SLIME-BALL!
AND I DON'T NEED MY SHIELD TO HANDLE YOU!
BAM!
GET THE MESSAGE?
TOO BAD NO ONE TOLD YA -- I USETA BE KNOWN AS IRON JAW!
BTOK!
UNHHH!
GUHHH!
AND NO ONE'S GOT STRONGER HANDS THAN ME!

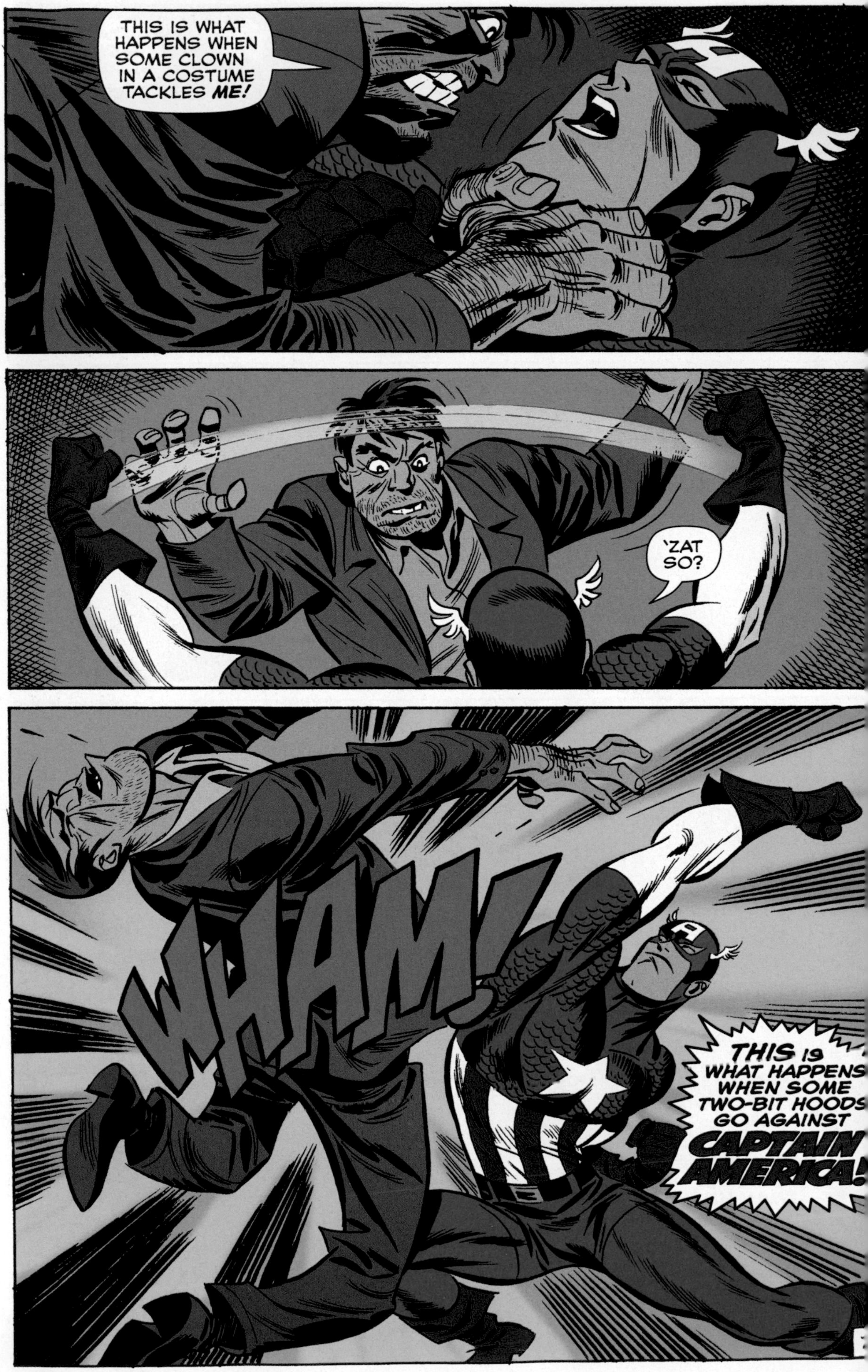
THIS IS WHAT HAPPENS WHEN SOME CLOWN IN A COSTUME TACKLES ME!
'ZAT SO?
WHAM!
THIS IS WHAT HAPPENS WHEN SOME TWO-BIT HOODS GO AGAINST CAPTAIN AMERICA!

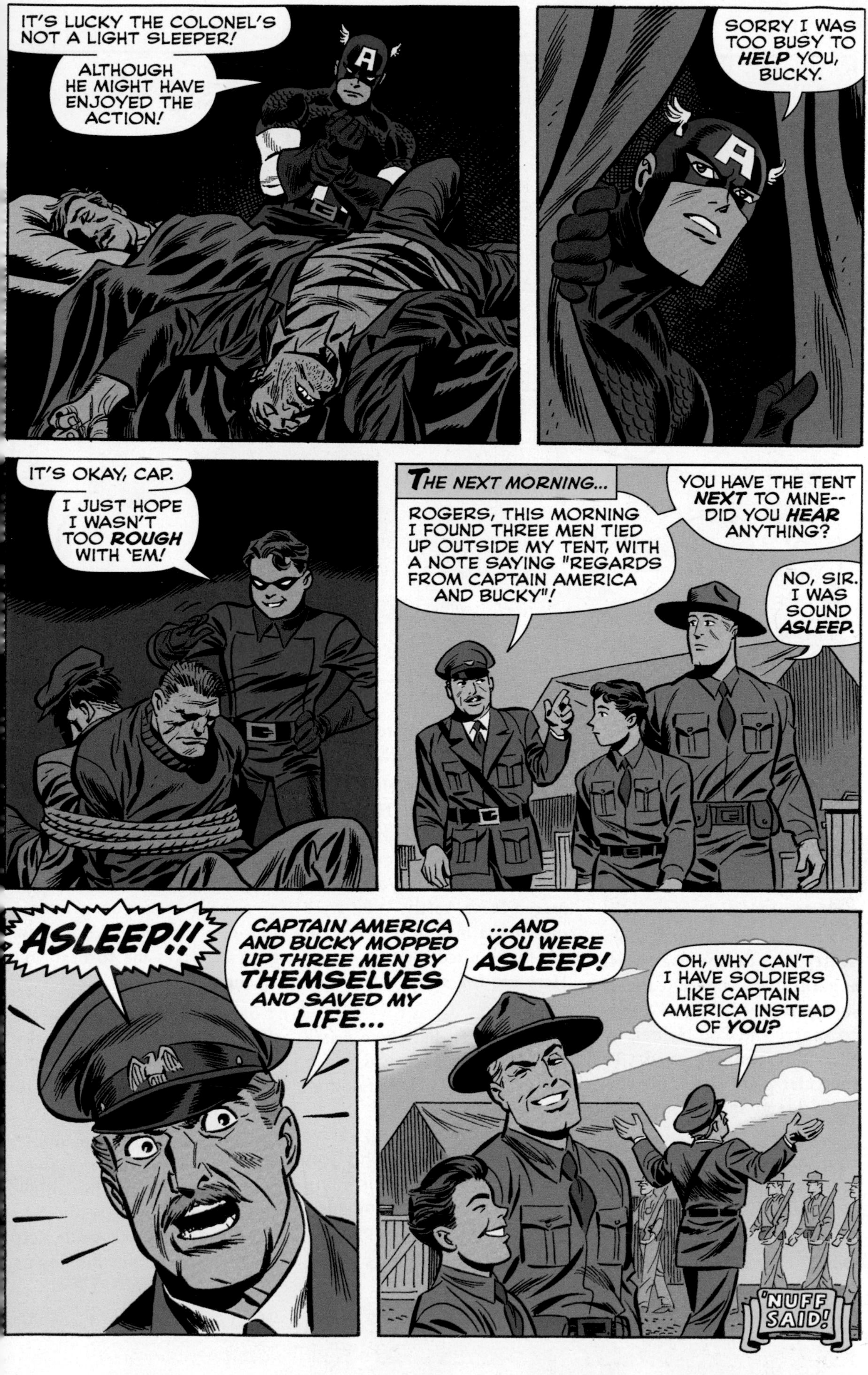
IT'S LUCKY THE COLONEL'S NOT A LIGHT SLEEPER!
ALTHOUGH HE MIGHT HAVE ENJOYED THE ACTION!
SORRY I WAS TOO BUSY TO HELP YOU, BUCKY.
IT'S OKAY, CAP.
I JUST HOPE I WASN'T TOO ROUGH WITH 'EM!
THE NEXT MORNING...
ROGERS, THIS MORNING I FOUND THREE MEN TIED UP OUTSIDE MY TENT, WITH A NOTE SAYING "REGARDS FROM CAPTAIN AMERICA AND BUCKY"!
YOU HAVE THE TENT NEXT TO MINE--DID YOU HEAR ANYTHING?
NO, SIR. I WAS SOUND ASLEEP.
ASLEEP!!
CAPTAIN AMERICA AND BUCKY MOPPED UP THREE MEN BY THEMSELVES AND SAVED MY LIFE...
...AND YOU WERE ASLEEP!
OH, WHY CAN'T I HAVE SOLDIERS LIKE CAPTAIN AMERICA INSTEAD OF YOU?
'NUFF SAID!

# CAPTAIN AMERICA FOILS the TRAITOR'S REVENGE

## By Stan Lee

"I'm sorry, Haines, but there is no place in this army camp for the likes of you. You have lied, cheated, spied, and stolen. Your conduct is no longer tolerable and I'm giving you a dishonorable discharge. Now get out!"

Private Steve Rogers, doing sentry duty nearby, was watching the scene interestedly. He had never seen Colonel Stevens so angry; and Lou Haines, too, was threateningly mad. The muscular giant shook his enormous fist at the Colonel.

"O.K. Colonel," snarled Lou, "I'll get out. But let me warn you now, you ain't seen the last of me! I'll get even somehow. Mark my words, you'll pay for this!" Haines walked toward the camp gates, muttering insults under his breath.

Suddenly Haines felt a strong hand grasp his arm. He looked around into the flashing eyes of Steve Rogers! "I wouldn't act like that if I were you," murmured Steve, softly, "you were insulting a man in the uniform of the United States Army! Here are the camp gates; now beat it!"

Haines left, but there was a look of hate in his eyes which Steve could not help but notice!

* * * * *

Later that evening, Steve Rogers was sitting in his tent playing checkers with his young side-kick, Bucky, the camp mascot. Bucky looked disappointed.

"Gosh, Steve," wailed Bucky, "don't you EVER lose a game? I've forgotten what it feels like to win."

Steve smiled cheerfully. "I'll tell you what, kid: suppose you borrow a book on 'how to play checkers' and read it. That'll give me a chance to get some shut-eye. You don't know how tired it makes me to beat you all the time!"

Steve ducked just in time to dodge the pillow that Bucky threw at him. "Why, you little squirt," he grinned, "I ought to put you over my knee!"

"Oh yeah, you big palooka? You and what other army?" Bucky picked up another pillow and was holding it ready

Suddenly Steve's smile left his face and he put his fingers

to his lips "Listen," he whispered.

Bucky put down the pillow and was silent. He knew that Steve's sensitive hearing must have detected something important! Then Steve spoke:

"There it is again, Bucky. Three pairs of footsteps outside Colonel Stevens' tent. We'd better look into this!"

In an instant, both Steve and Bucky peeled off their outer uniforms, and seconds later they stood revealed as CAPTAIN AMERICA and BUCKY, Sentinals Of Our Shores! "Let's go!" cried CAPTAIN AMERICA!

The two trouble hunters stole from their tent and noiselessly trod to Colonel Stevens' quarters. Outside his tent were three tough-looking thugs!

"Will we all rush him at once?" asked the first. Captain America saw that the man he was talking to was Lou Haines! "Naw," sneered Haines, "you guys stay here and keep 'chickee'. I'll go in and tend to him myself!" Then Captain America noticed that Haines was holding a wicked-looking knife in his hand!

"Not a second to lose!" cried the Red White and Blue Knight as he raced toward the three assassins like an avenging hurricane.

Lou Haines was the first to see the twin-tornadoes rushing at him. "Take care of these two fancy-pants," he ordered his men, "I'll attend to the Colonel in a second!"

Haines' two accomplices grinned as they watched Captain America and Bucky speeding toward them. They took out their revolvers and prepared to fire But Captain America suddenly picked up Bucky by his arms and swung him right into the two thugs, knocking their guns out of reach. "All right, Bucky, m'lad," he cried, "see how brave they are without their toys!" Then he dashed into the tent.

Inside the tent, the American Avenger saw Lou Haines about to plunge his knife into the sleeping Colonel's heart! There wasn't time for Captain America to reach Haines before the evil deed could be done. But with the speed of thought, he sent his shield spinning through the air to the other end of the tent where it smacked the knife out of Haines' hand!

Then the mighty crime-fighter leaped at Haines and landed a blow at his head. But the traitorous ex-soldier seemed to just shake off the blow and he grabbed Captain America by the throat with his tremendous fingers. As Haines forced more and more pressure into his grip, Captain America began to get weaker and weaker. His eyes grew dim and it became difficult for him to breathe. But he managed to summon all his remaining strength into one last effort, and brought his right fist up under Haines' jaw with enough force to fell an ox. No human being could have stood that blow, and Haines instantly relaxed his grip and sank to the floor — unconscious!

Outside the tent, Captain America found the other two crooks tied back-to-back, and Bucky was standing over them, patting their heads! "I do hope I wasn't too rough with them, Cap," said the gallant lad.

\* \* \* \* \*

The next morning Colonel Stevens was talking with Private Rogers. "Rogers," he said, "this morning I found three men tied outside my tent with a note pinned on them, reading: 'Regards from Captain America and Bucky'. Now you have the tent next to mine; did you hear anything last night?"

"No, Sir," answered Steve, "I was sound asleep."

"Asleep!" roared the Colonel, "Captain America and Bucky mopped up three armed men by themselves and saved my life – and YOU were asleep! Oh, why can't I have some soldiers like Captain America in this army – instead of YOU!"

But Colonel Stevens didn't notice the grin on Private Rogers' face as he left the tent!

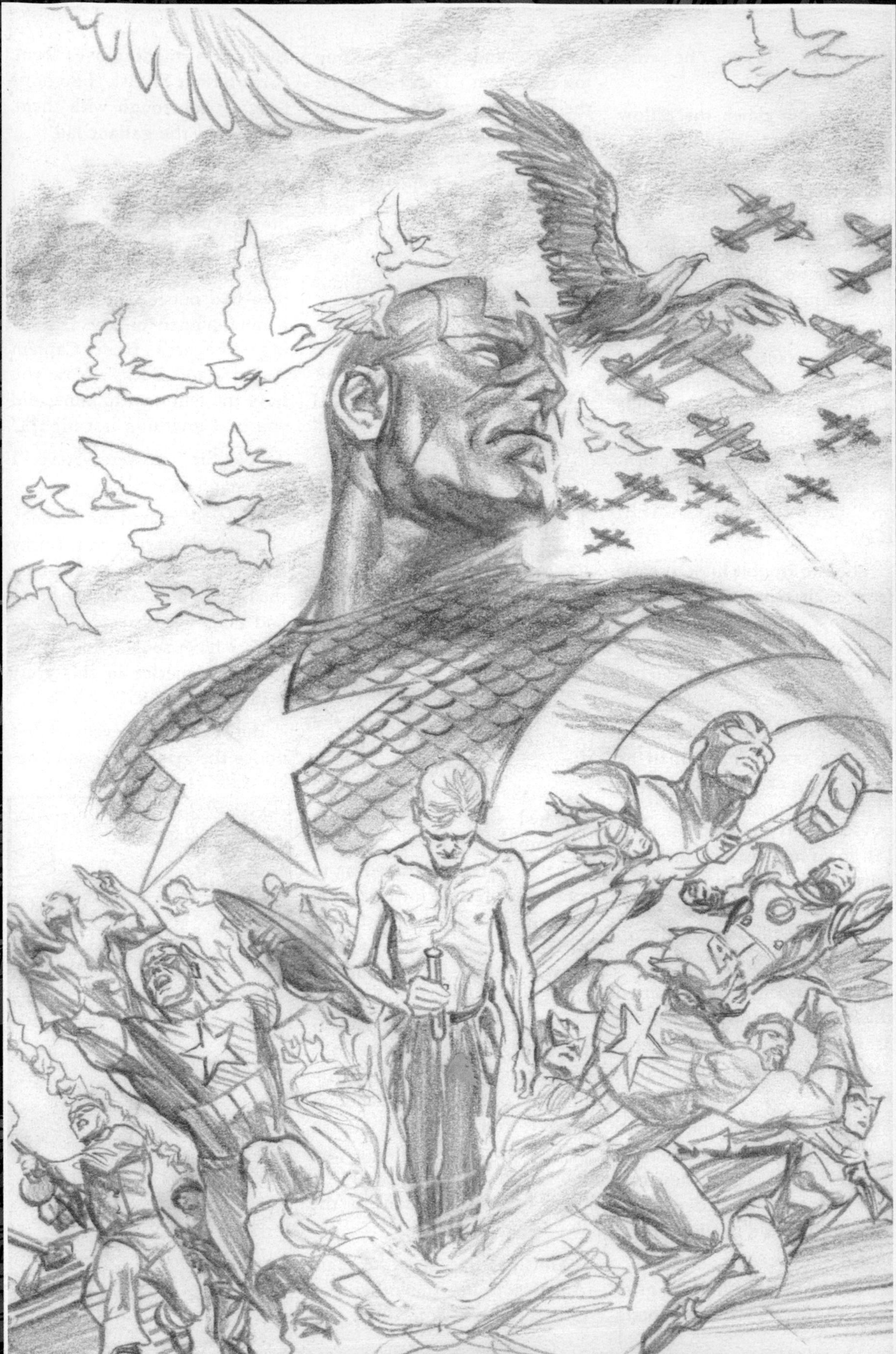

#22 75TH ANNIVERSARY SKETCH VARIANT BY ALEX ROSS

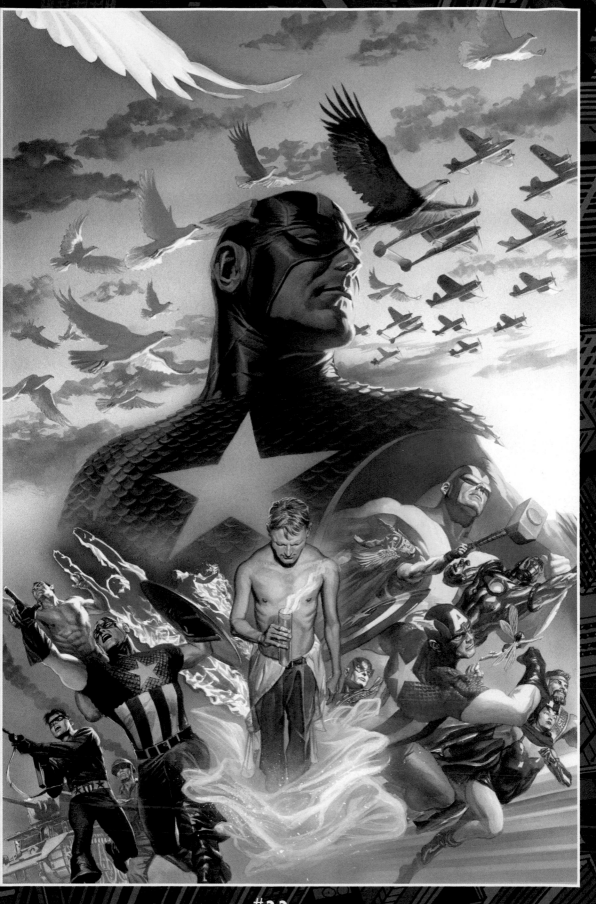

#22 75TH ANNIVERSARY VARIANT BY ALEX ROSS

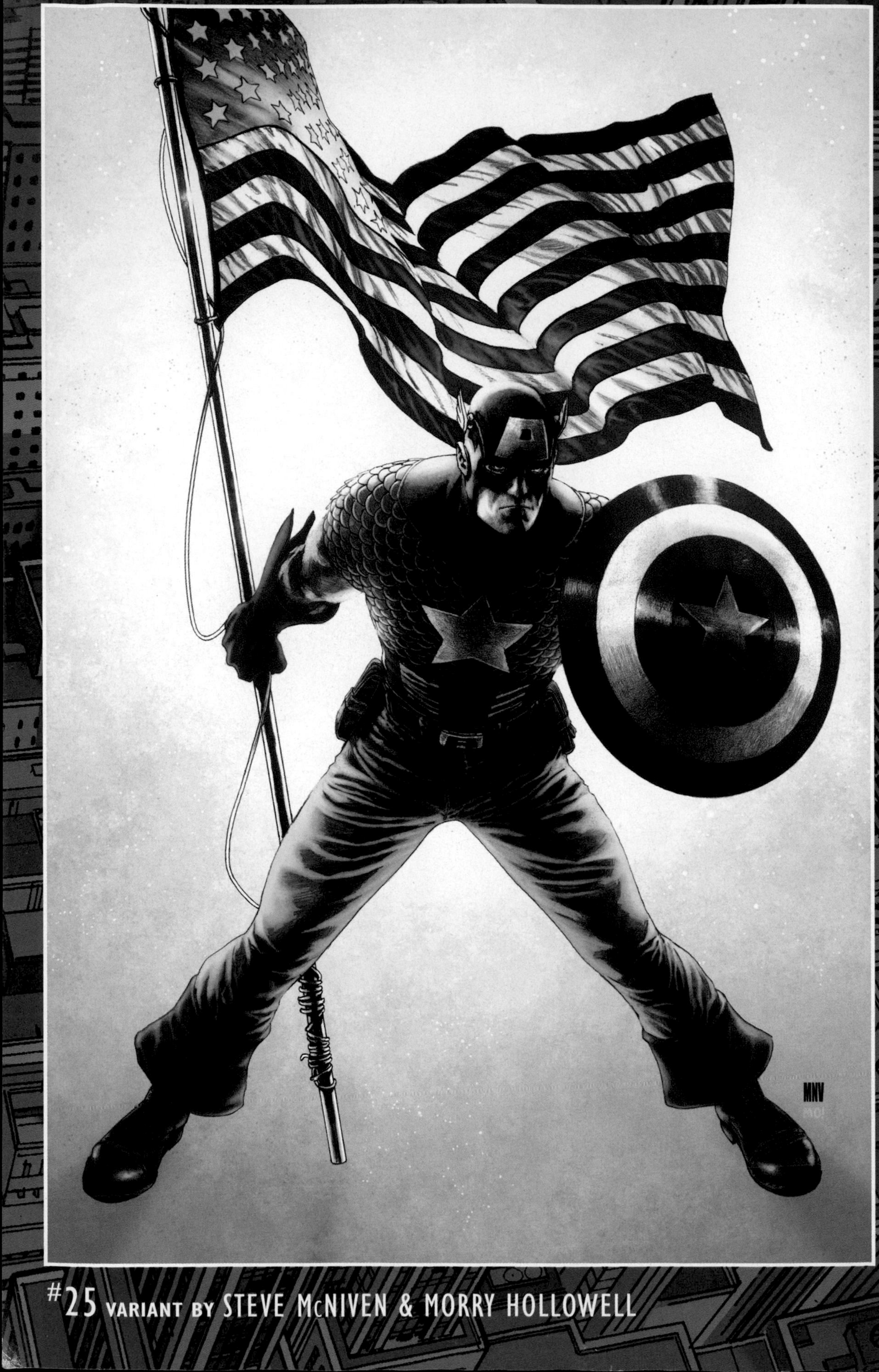
MNV

#25 VARIANT BY STEVE McNIVEN & MORRY HOLLOWELL

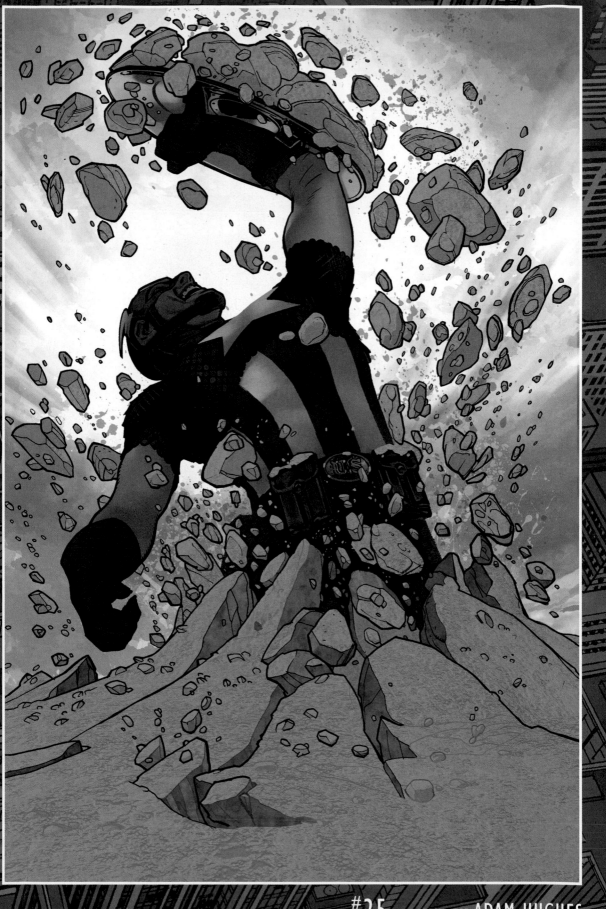

#25 VARIANT BY ADAM HUGHES

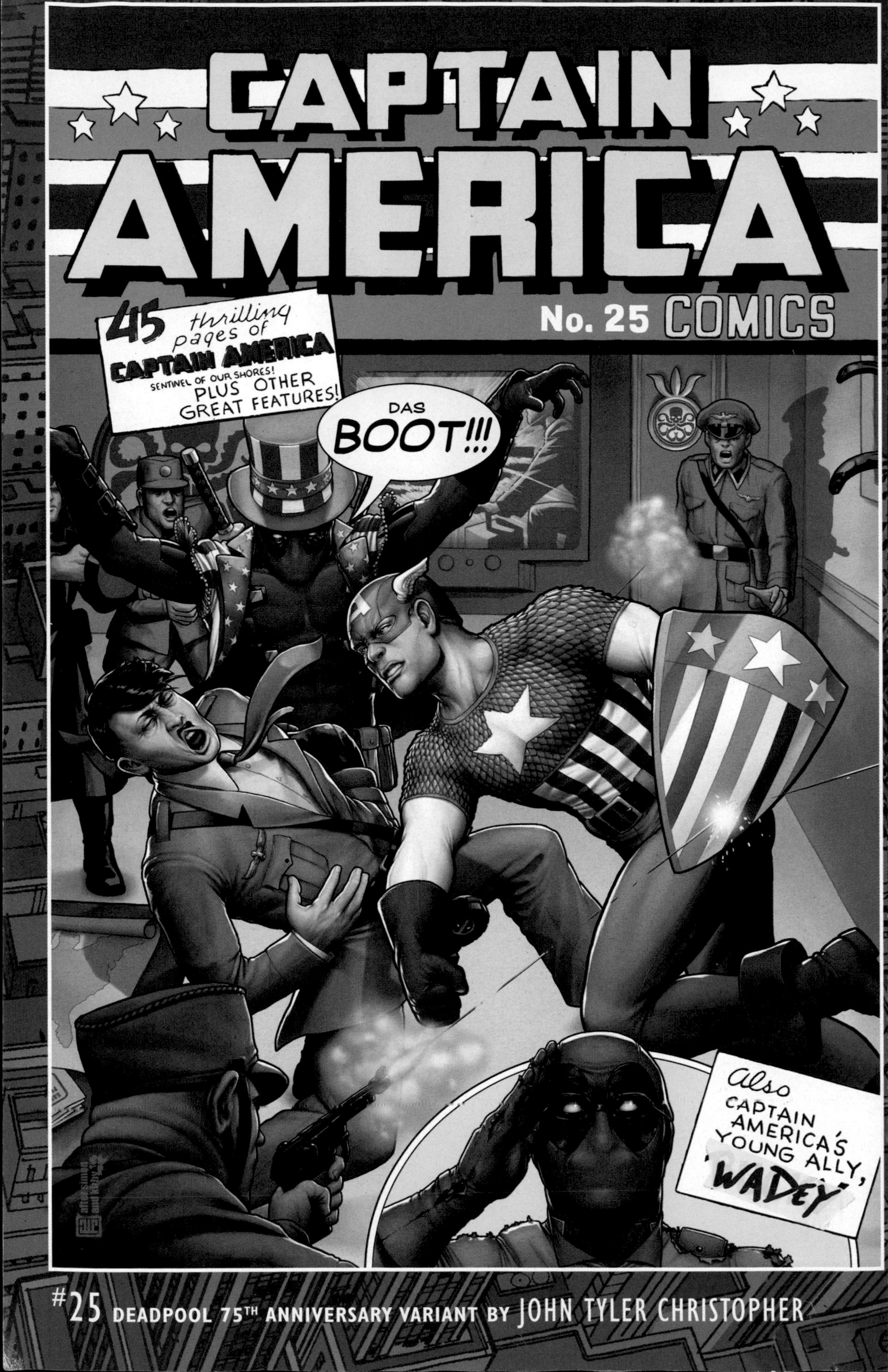
CAPTAIN AMERICA
No. 25 COMICS
45 thrilling pages of CAPTAIN AMERICA SENTINEL OF OUR SHORES! PLUS OTHER GREAT FEATURES!
DAS BOOT!!!
Also CAPTAIN AMERICA'S YOUNG ALLY, 'WADEY'

#25 DEADPOOL 75TH ANNIVERSARY VARIANT BY JOHN TYLER CHRISTOPHER

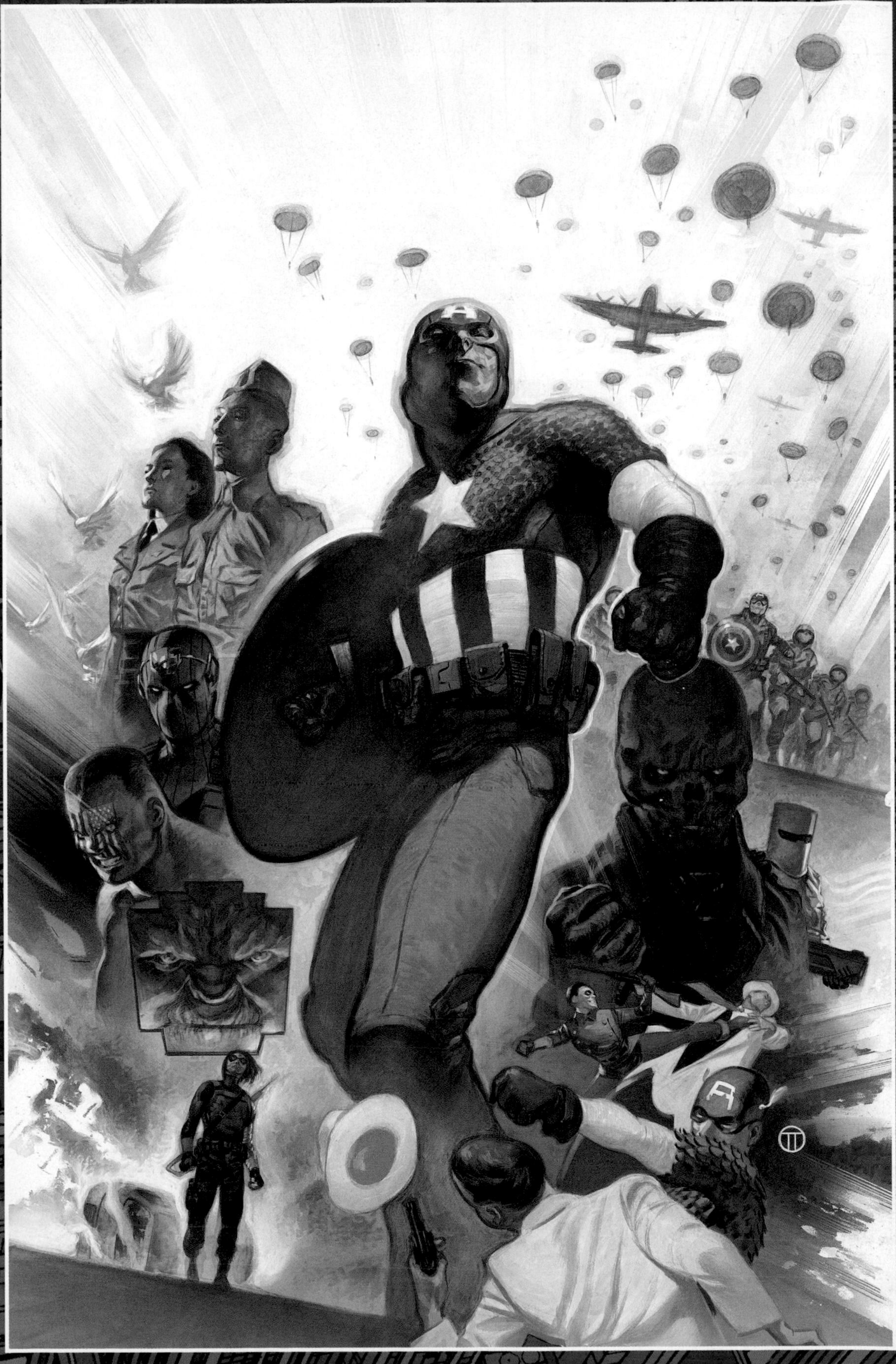

#25 WIZARD WORLD AUSTIN VARIANT BY JULIAN TOTINO TEDESCO

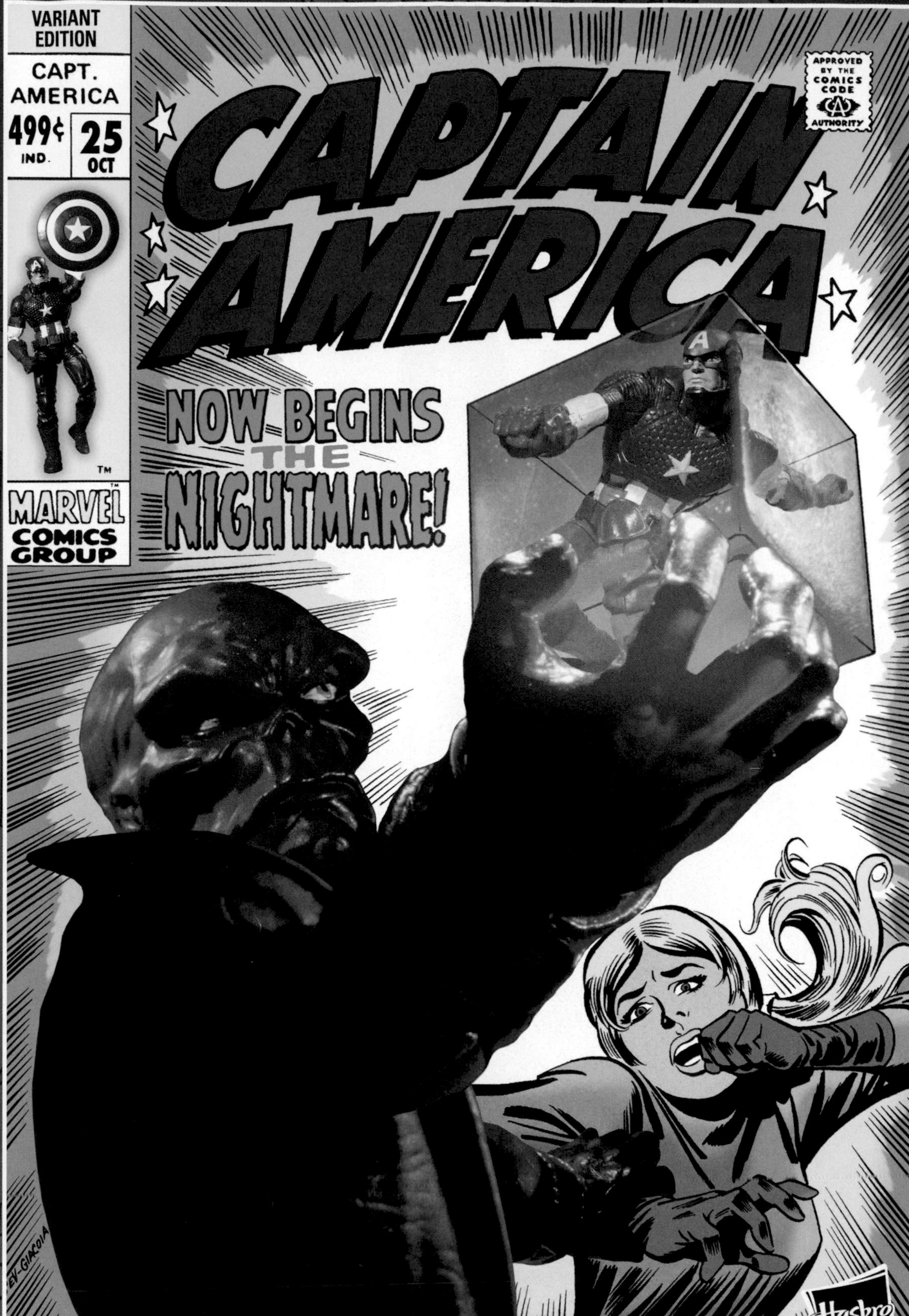


#25 HASBRO VARIANT

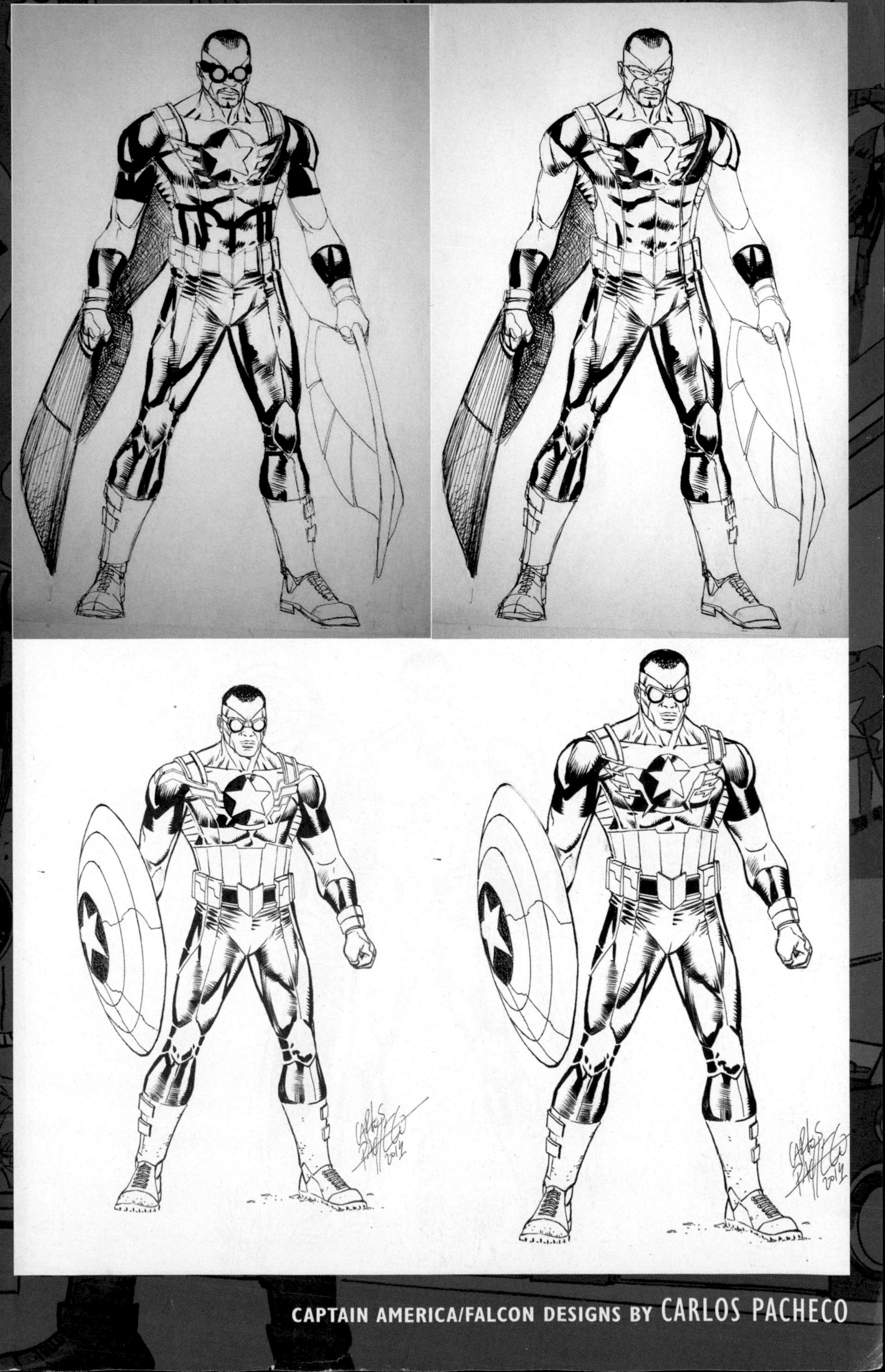

CAPTAIN AMERICA/FALCON DESIGNS BY CARLOS PACHECO

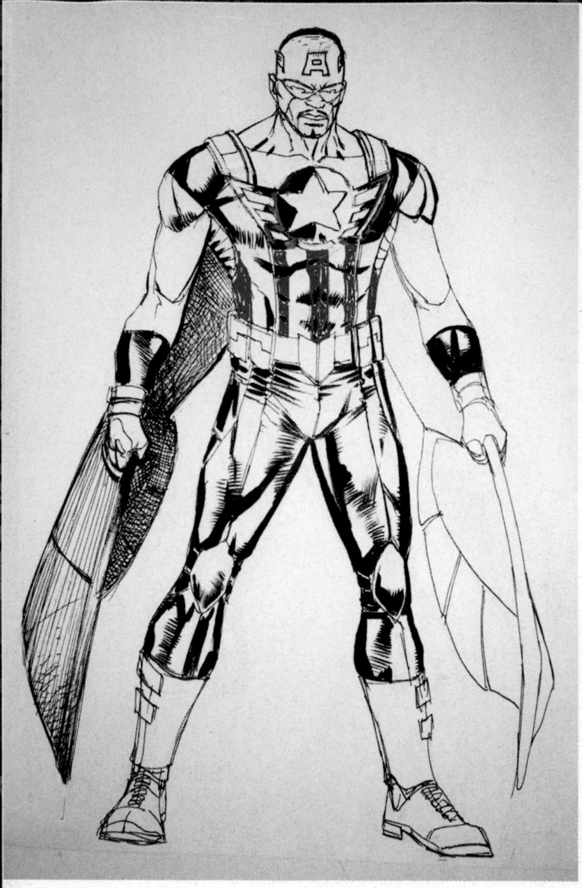

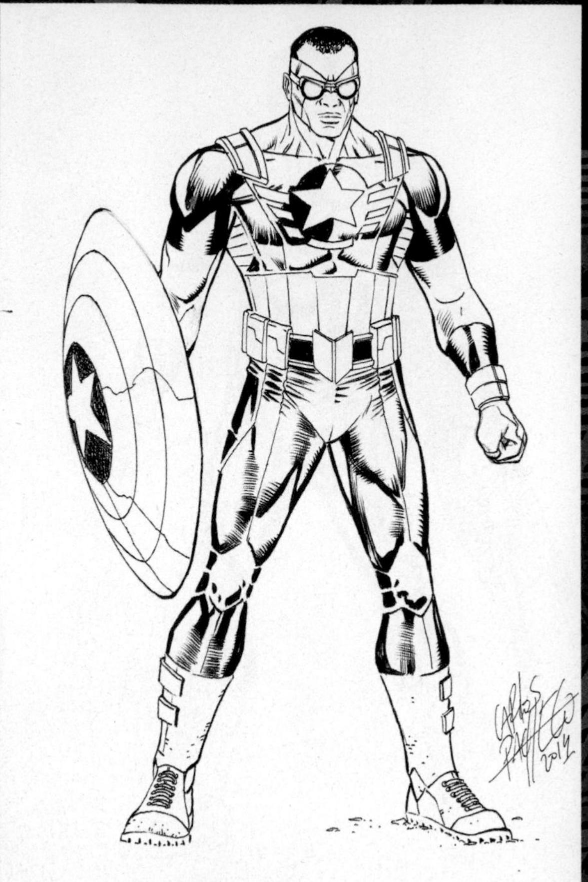

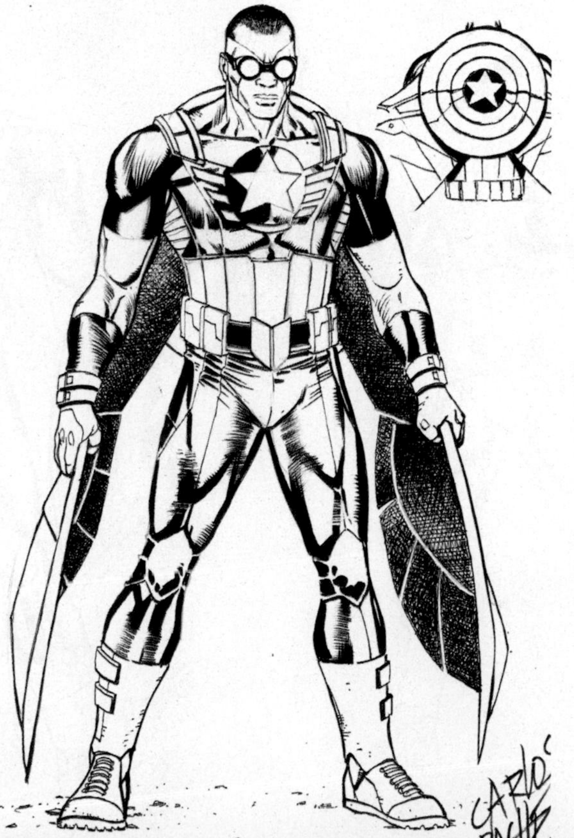

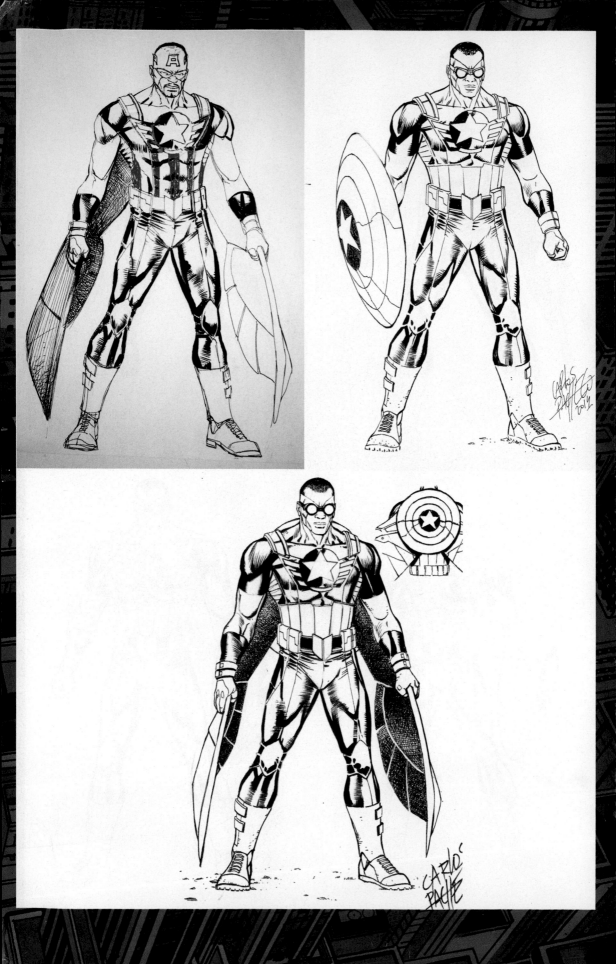

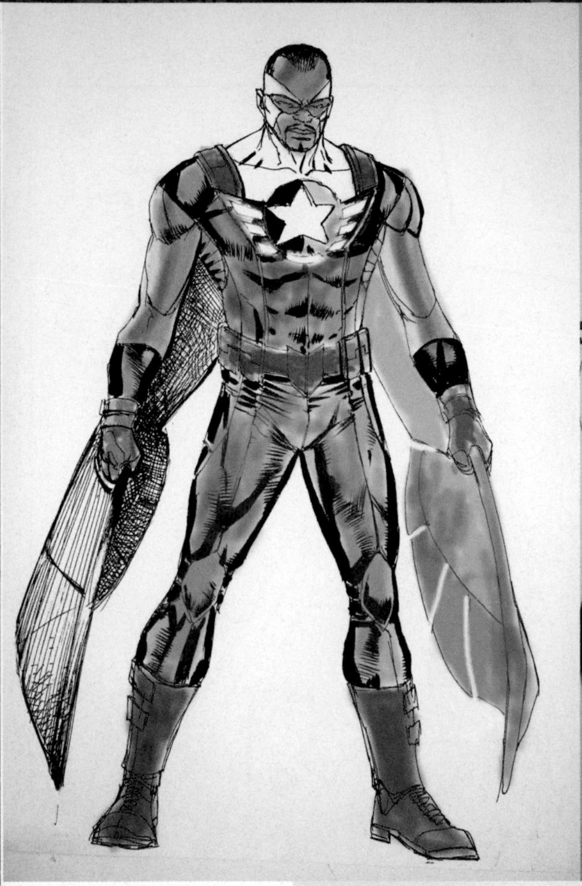

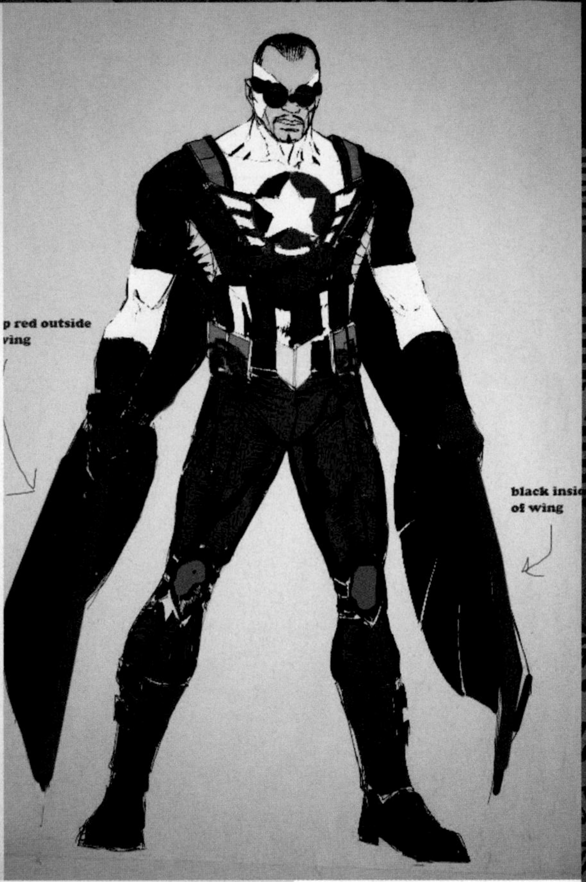
p red outside
ving
black insi
of wing

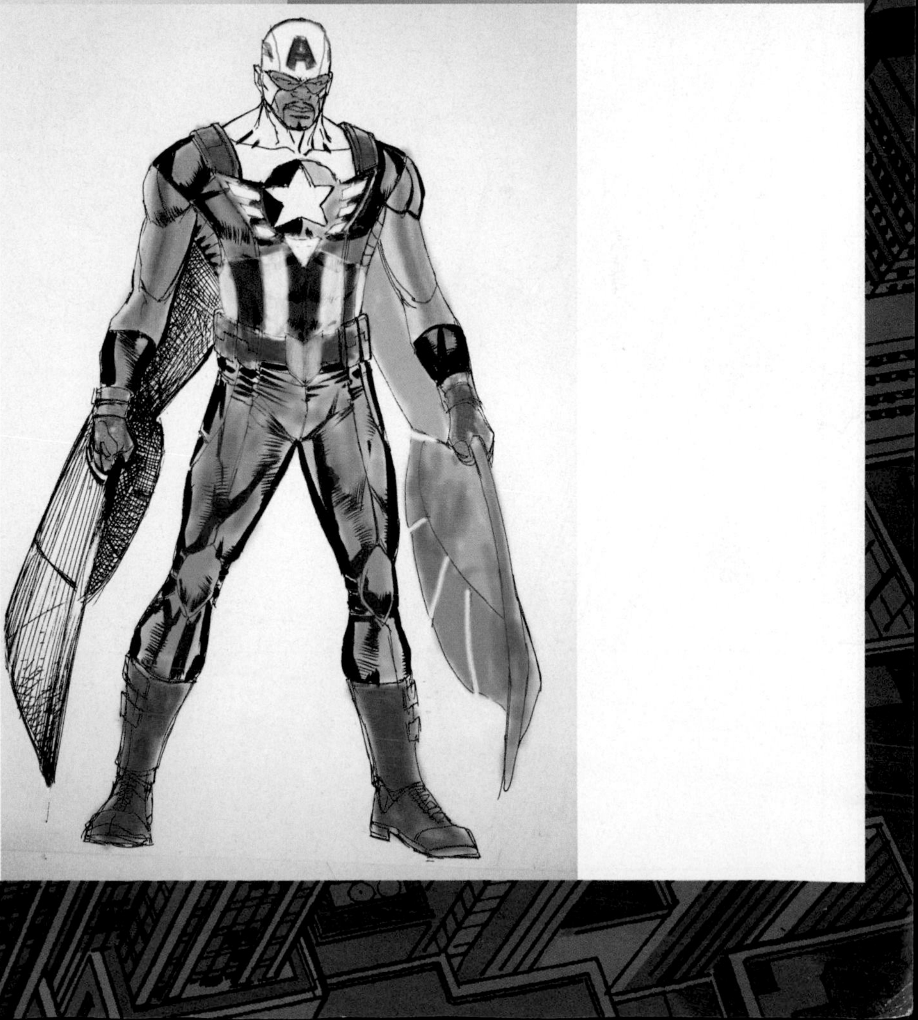

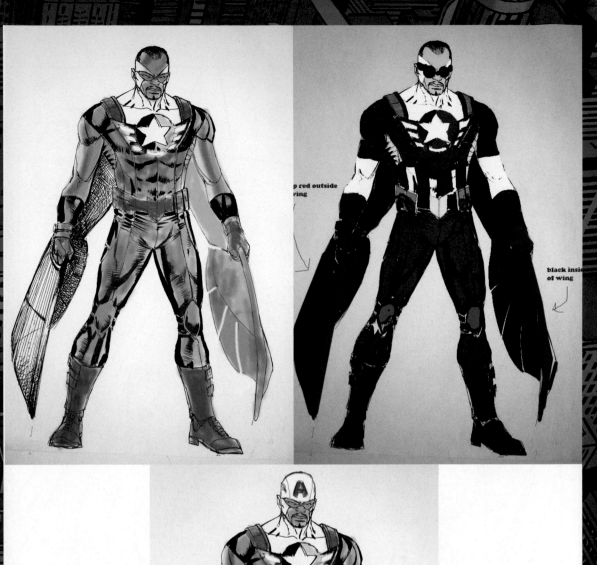

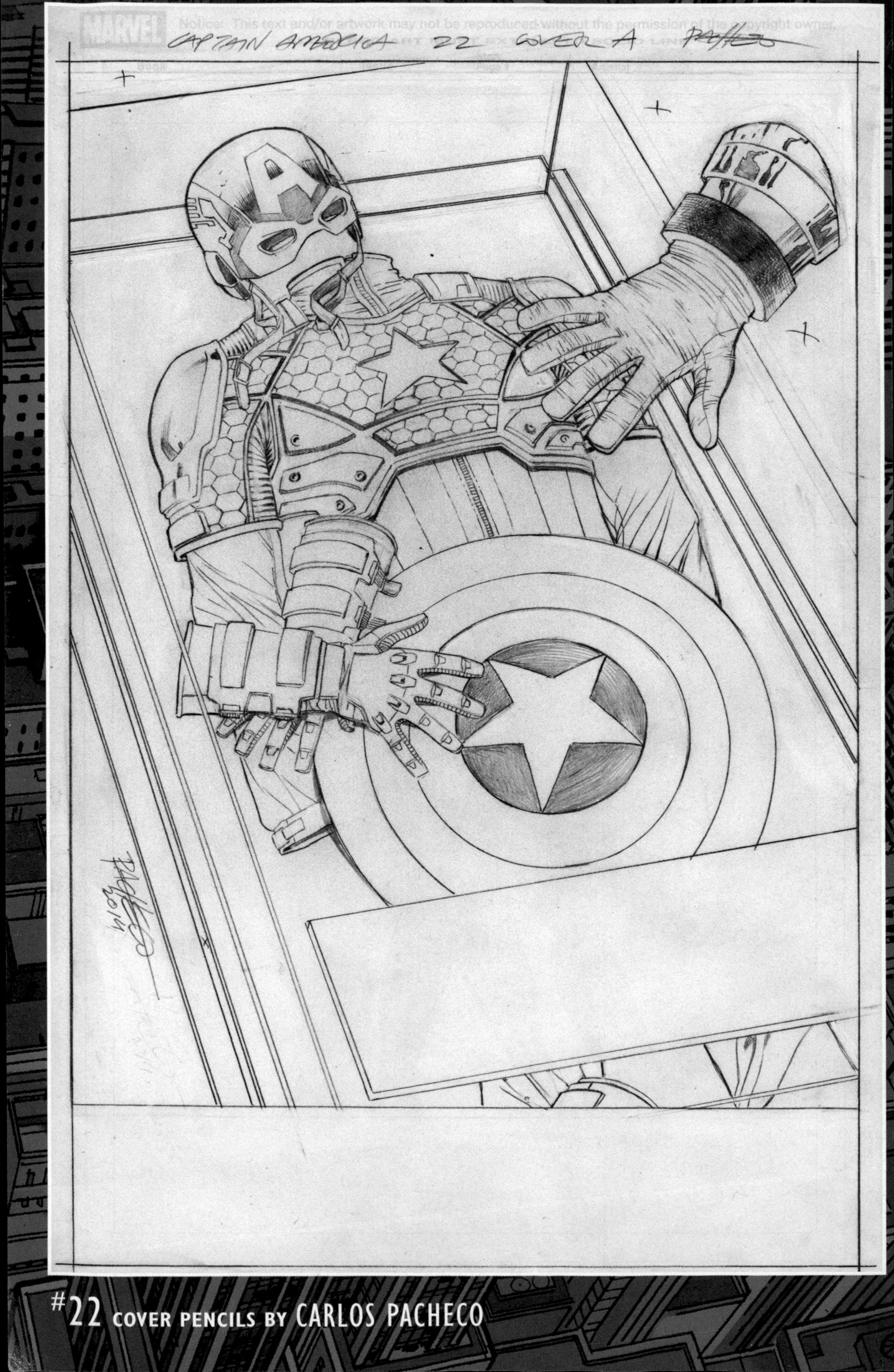
Notice: This text and/or artwork may not be reproduced without the permission of the copyright owner.
CAPTAIN AMERICA 22 COVER A

#22 COVER PENCILS BY CARLOS PACHECO

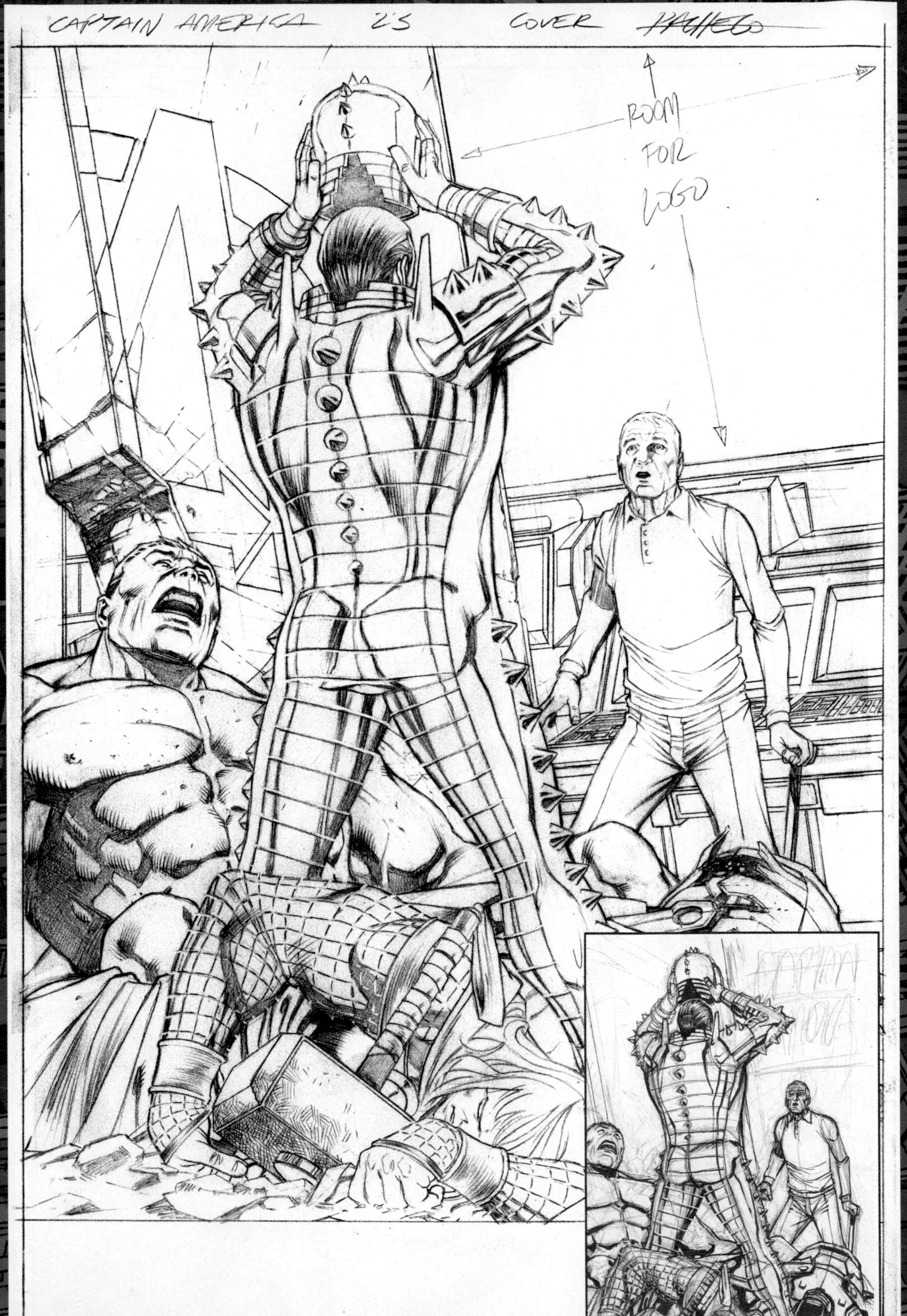
CAPTAIN AMERICA 23 COVER
ROOM FOR LOGO

#23 COVER SKETCH & PENCILS BY CARLOS PACHECO

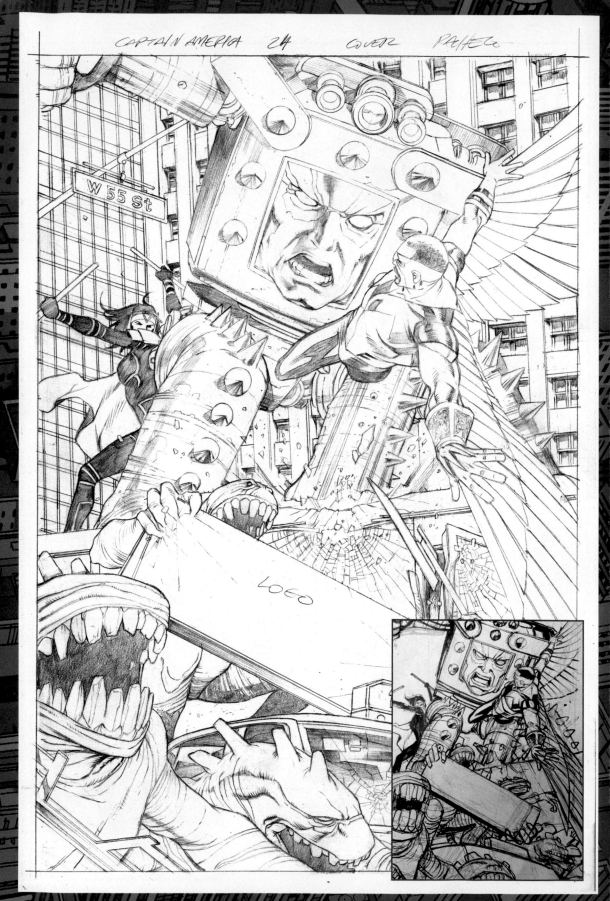

CAPTAIN AMERICA 24 COVER PACHECO

#24 COVER SKETCH & PENCILS BY CARLOS PACHECO

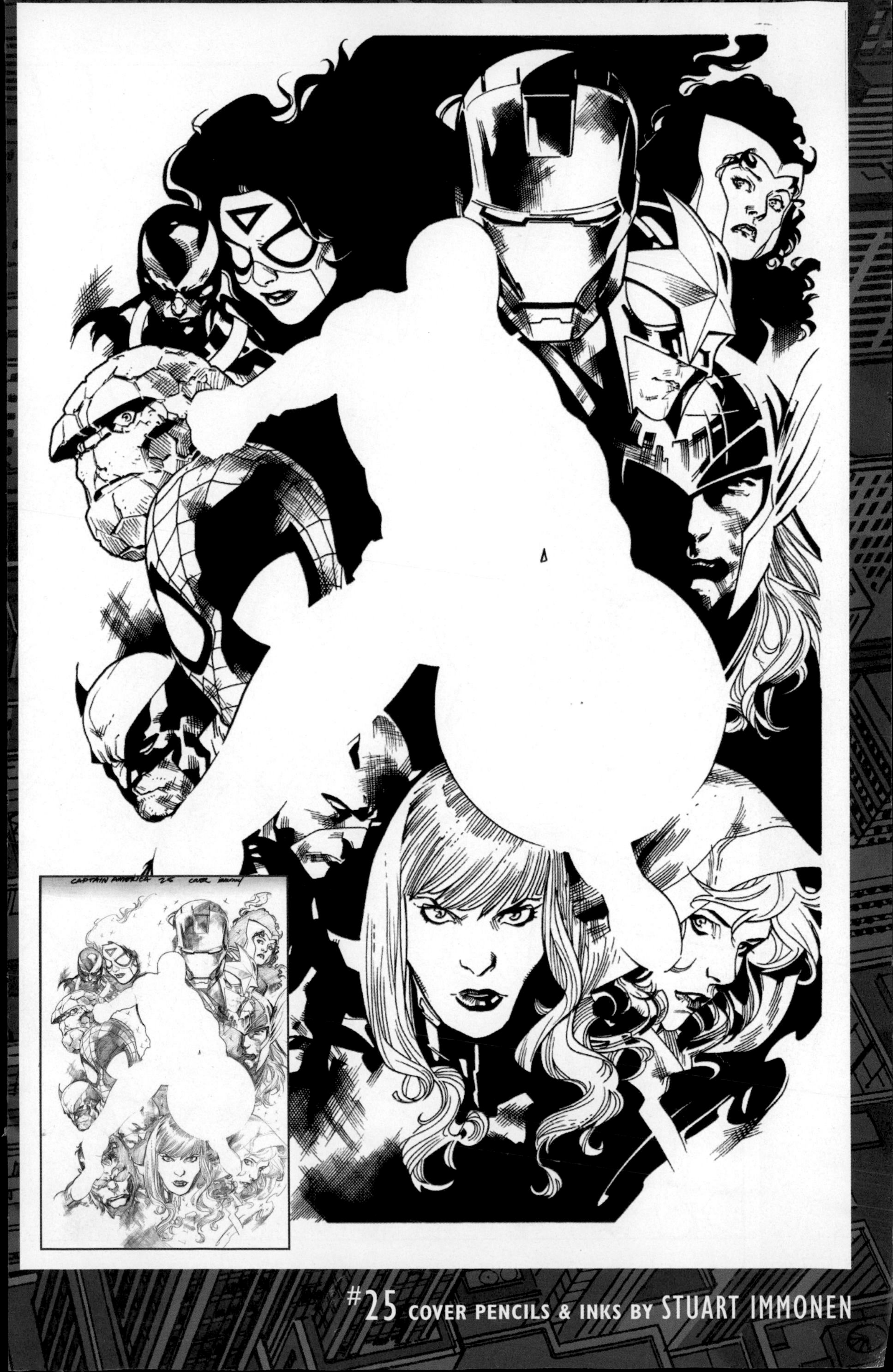

#25 COVER PENCILS & INKS BY STUART IMMONEN

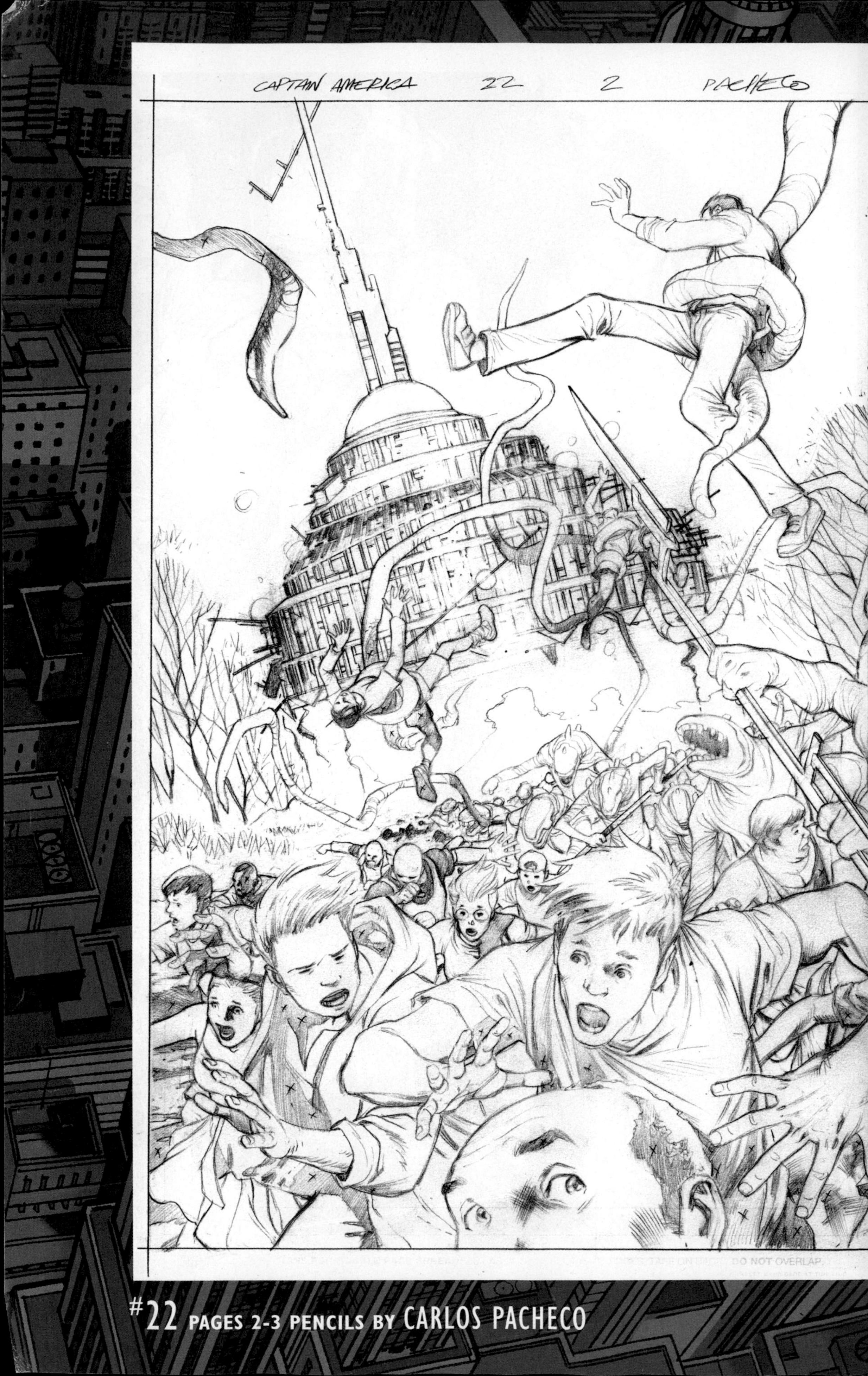
CAPTAIN AMERICA 22 2 PACHECO
DO NOT OVERLAP

#22 PAGES 2-3 PENCILS BY CARLOS PACHECO

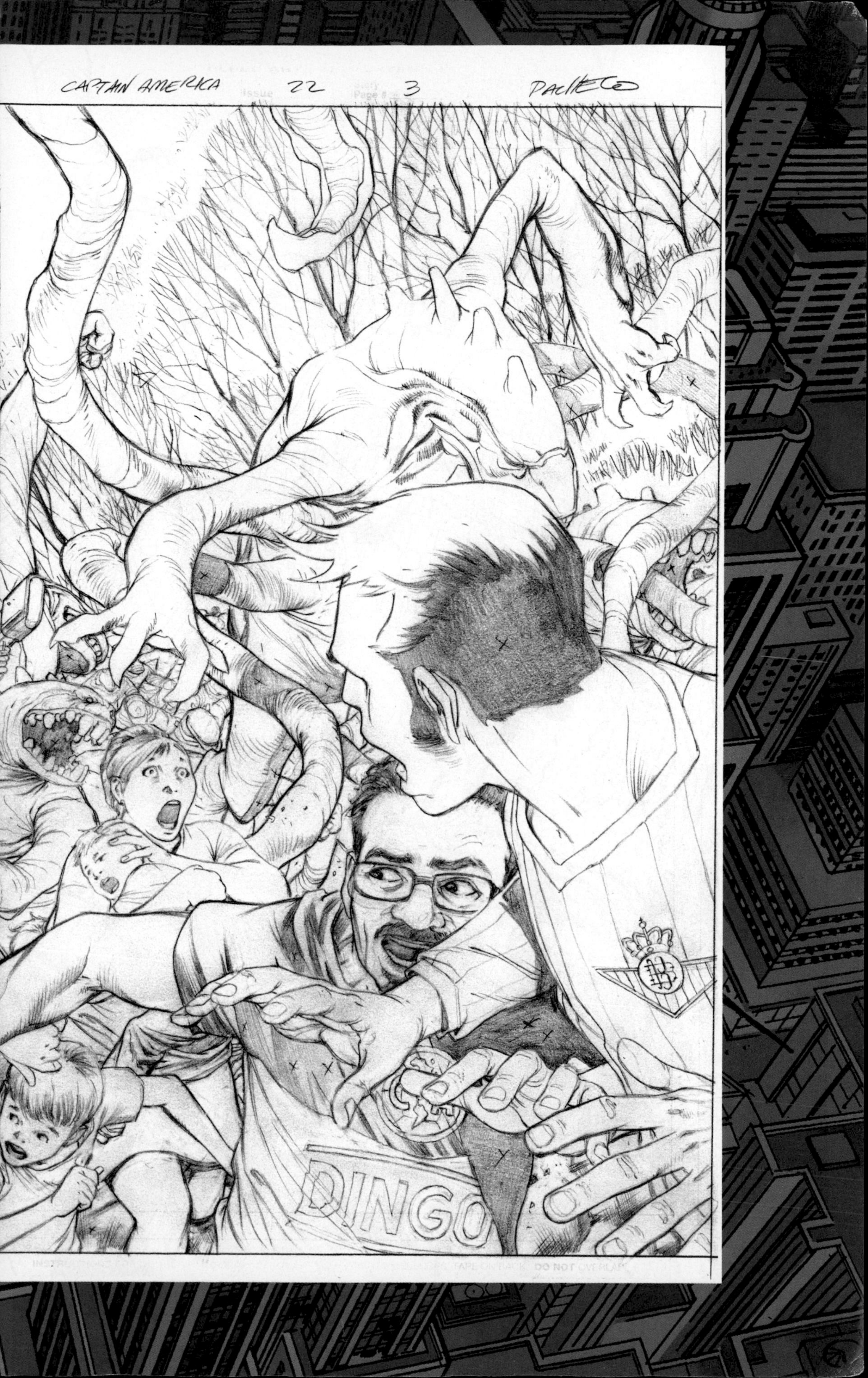
CAPTAIN AMERICA 22 3 PACHECO
DINGO
TAPE ON BACK DO NOT OVERLAP

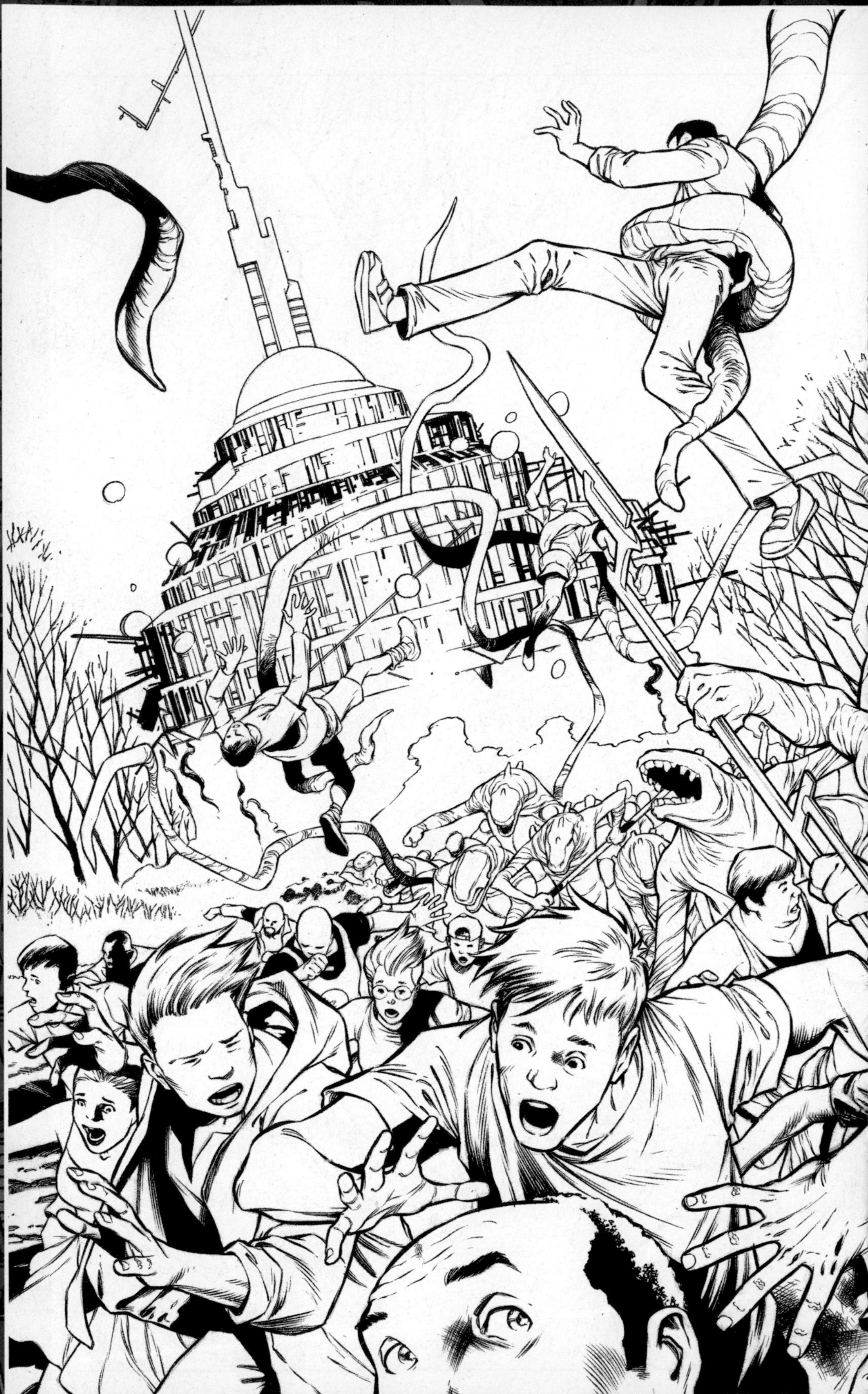

#22 PAGES 2-3 INKS BY MARIANO TAIBO

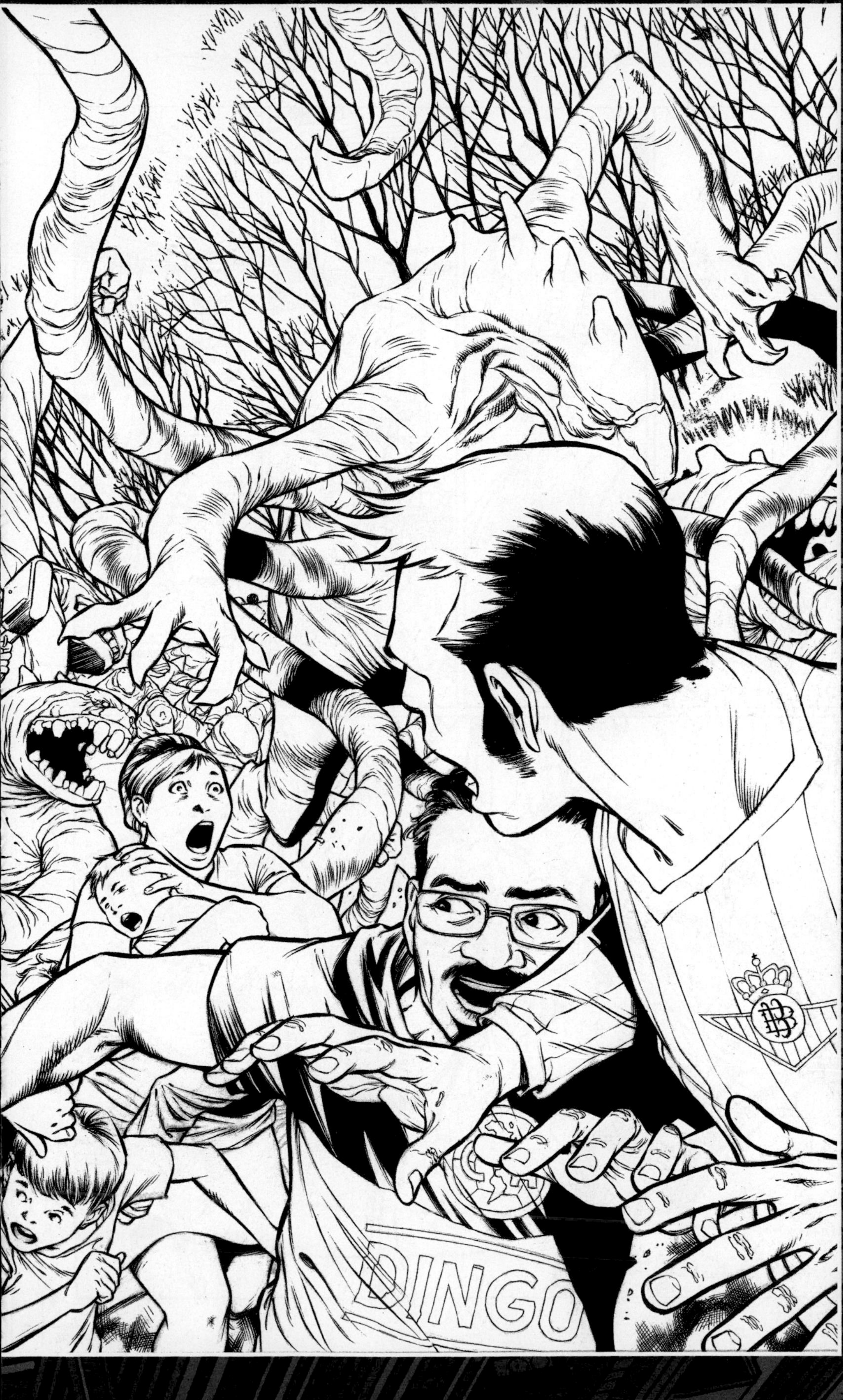
DINGO

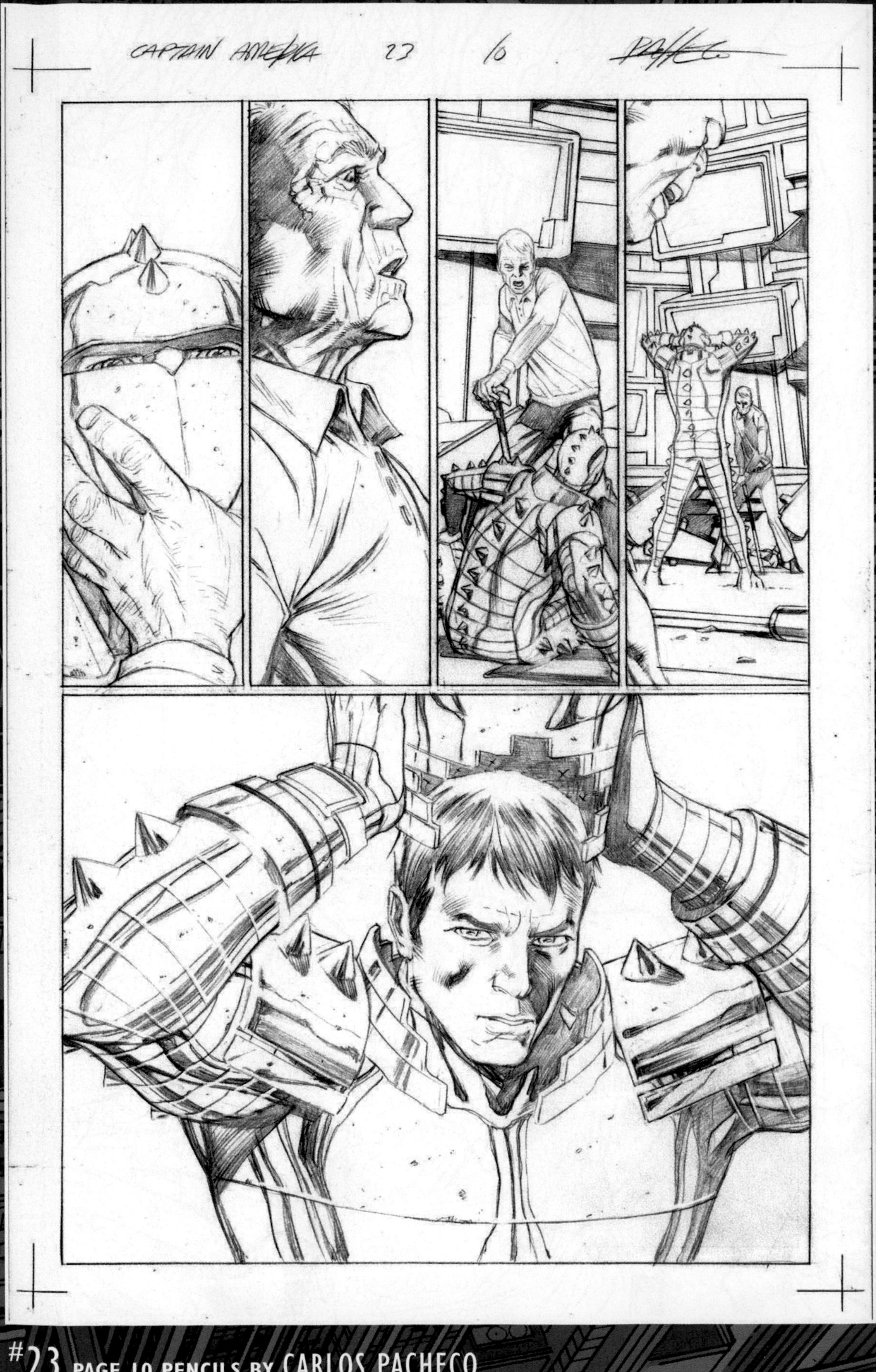
CAPTAIN AMERICA 23 10

#23 PAGE 10 PENCILS BY CARLOS PACHECO

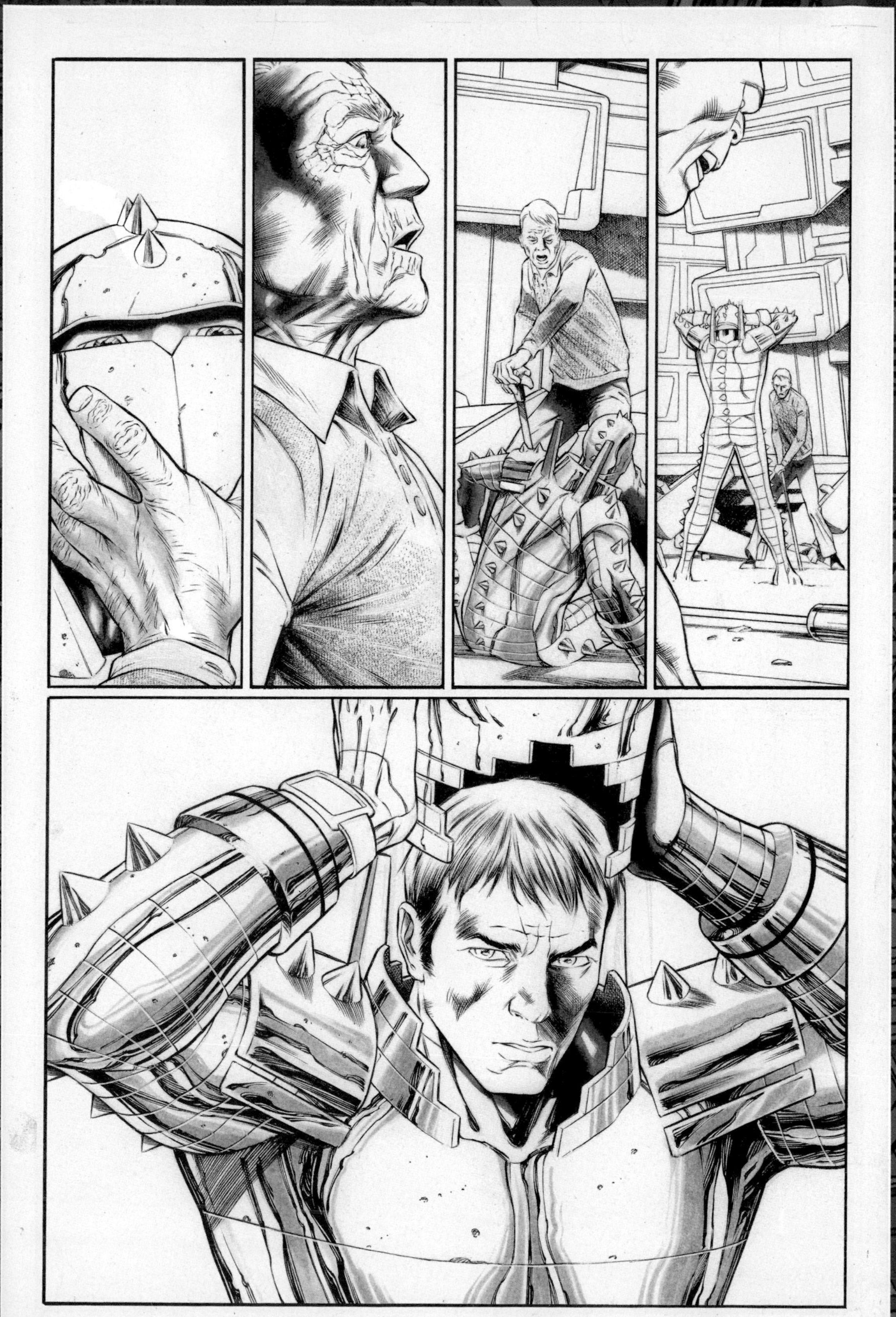

#23 PAGE 10 INKS BY MARIANO TAIBO

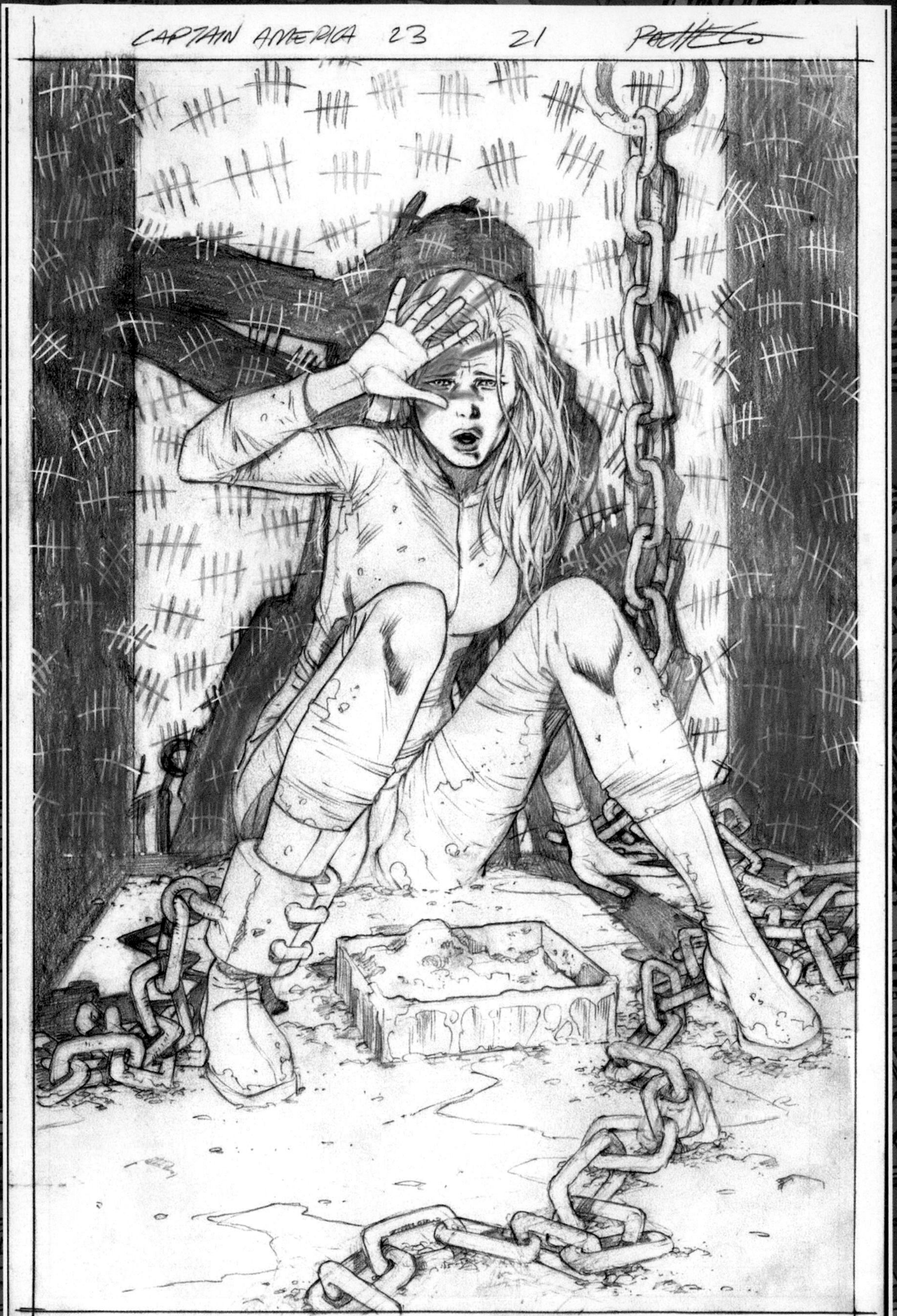
CAPTAIN AMERICA 23
21
PACHECO

#23 PAGE 20 PENCILS BY CARLOS PACHECO

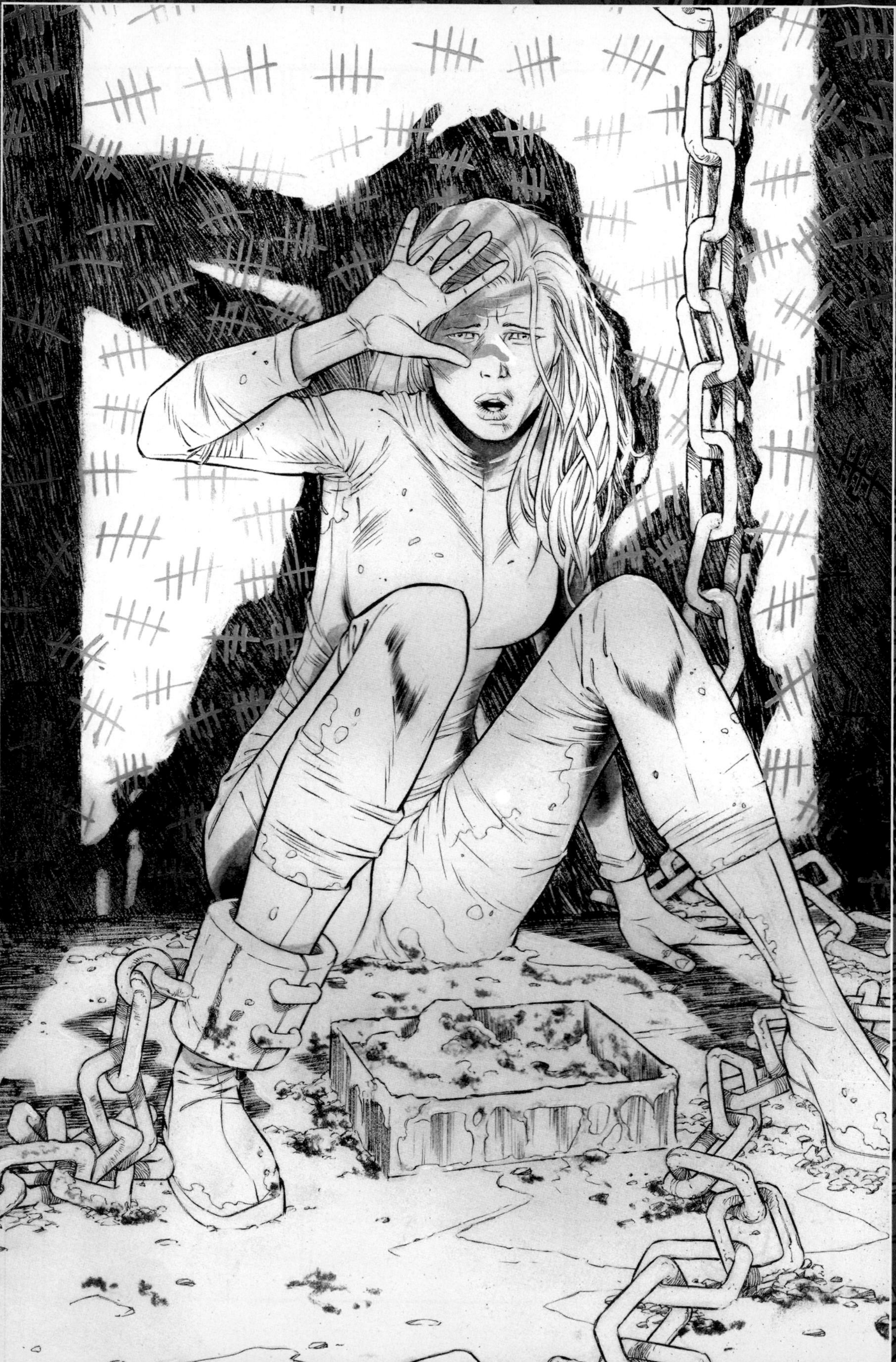

#23 PAGE 20 INKS BY MARIANO TAIBO

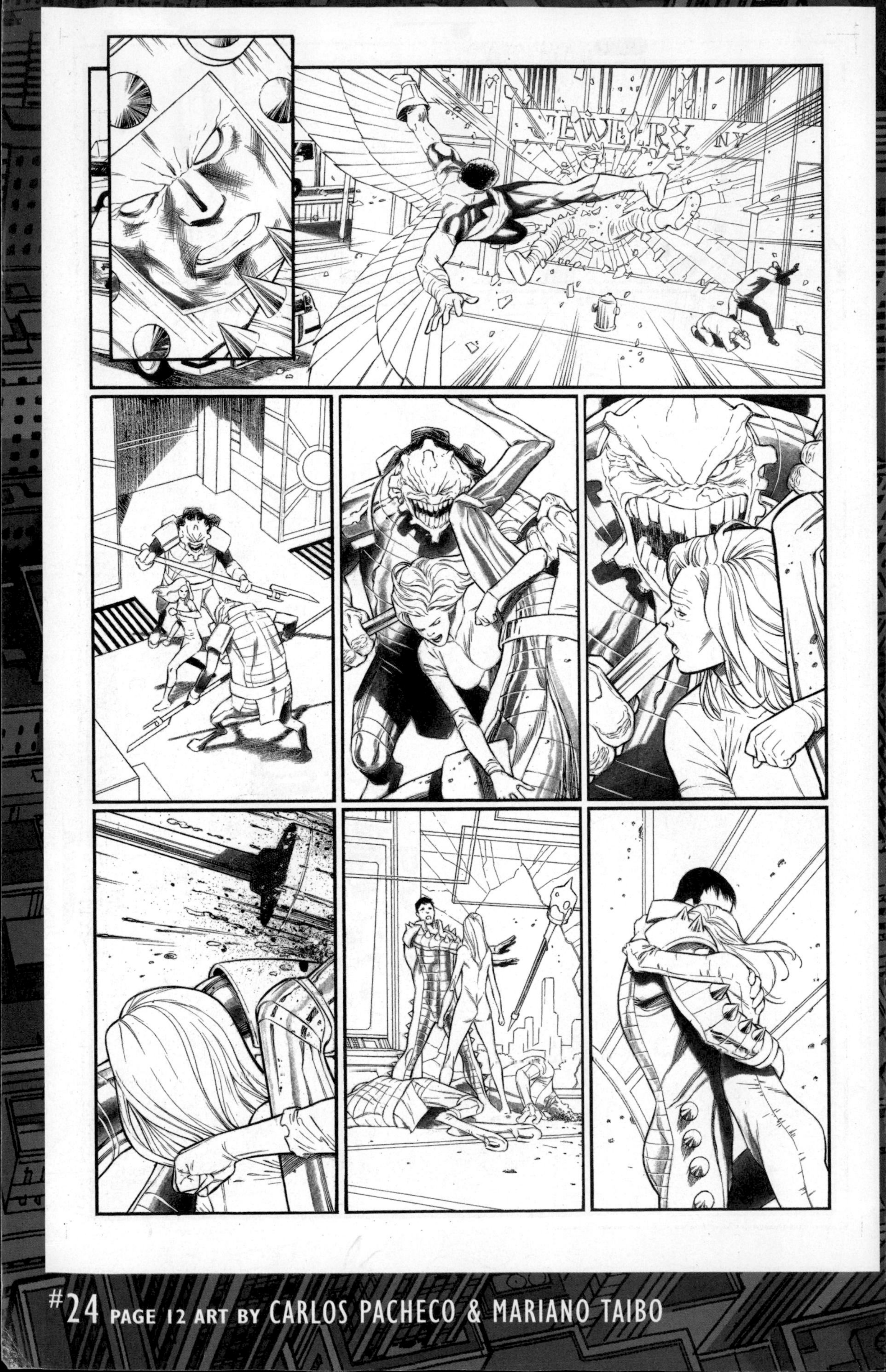
JEWELRY
NY

#24 PAGE 12 ART BY CARLOS PACHECO & MARIANO TAIBO

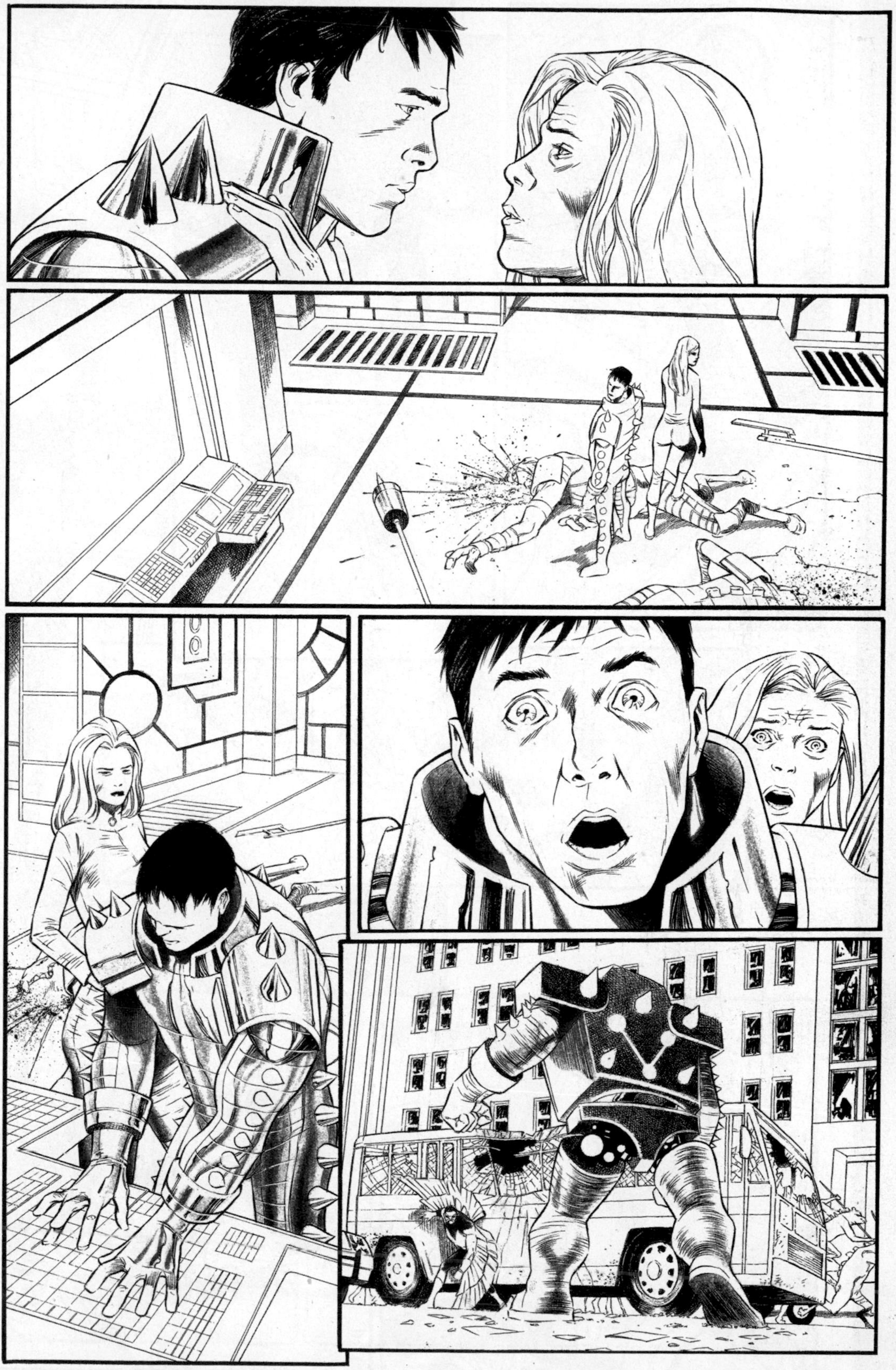

#24 PAGE 13 ART BY CARLOS PACHECO & MARIANO TAIBO

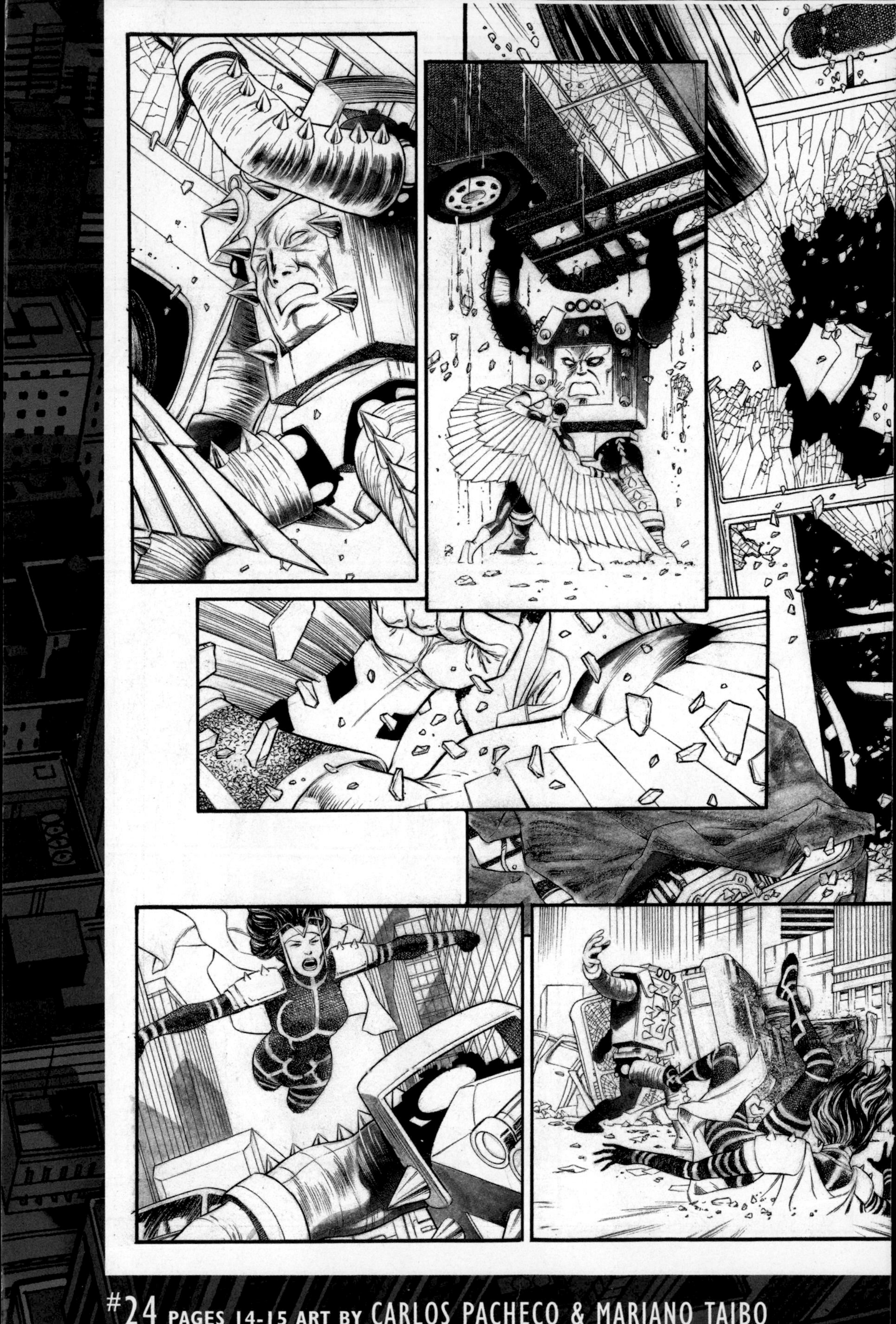

#24 PAGES 14-15 ART BY CARLOS PACHECO & MARIANO TAIBO

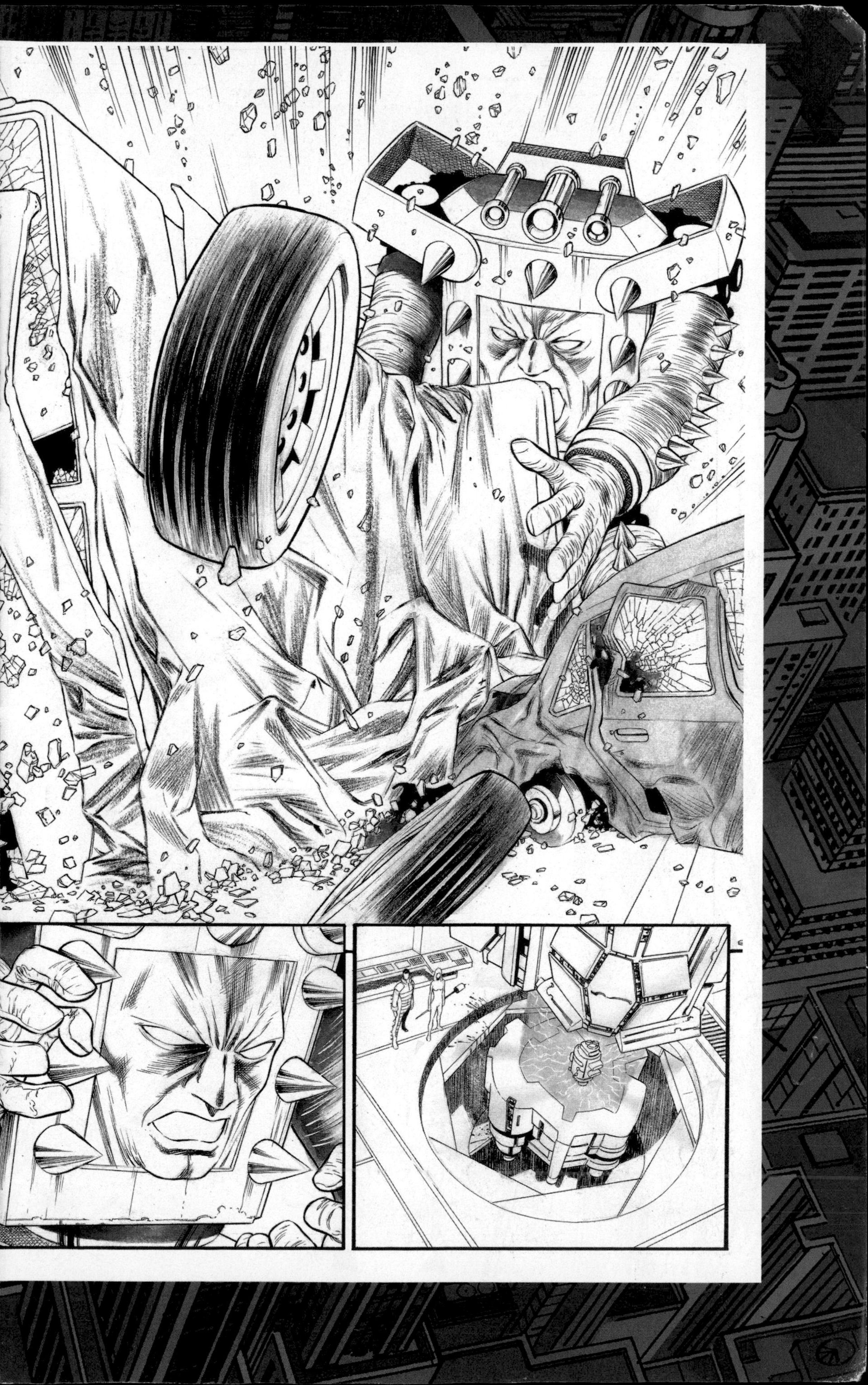

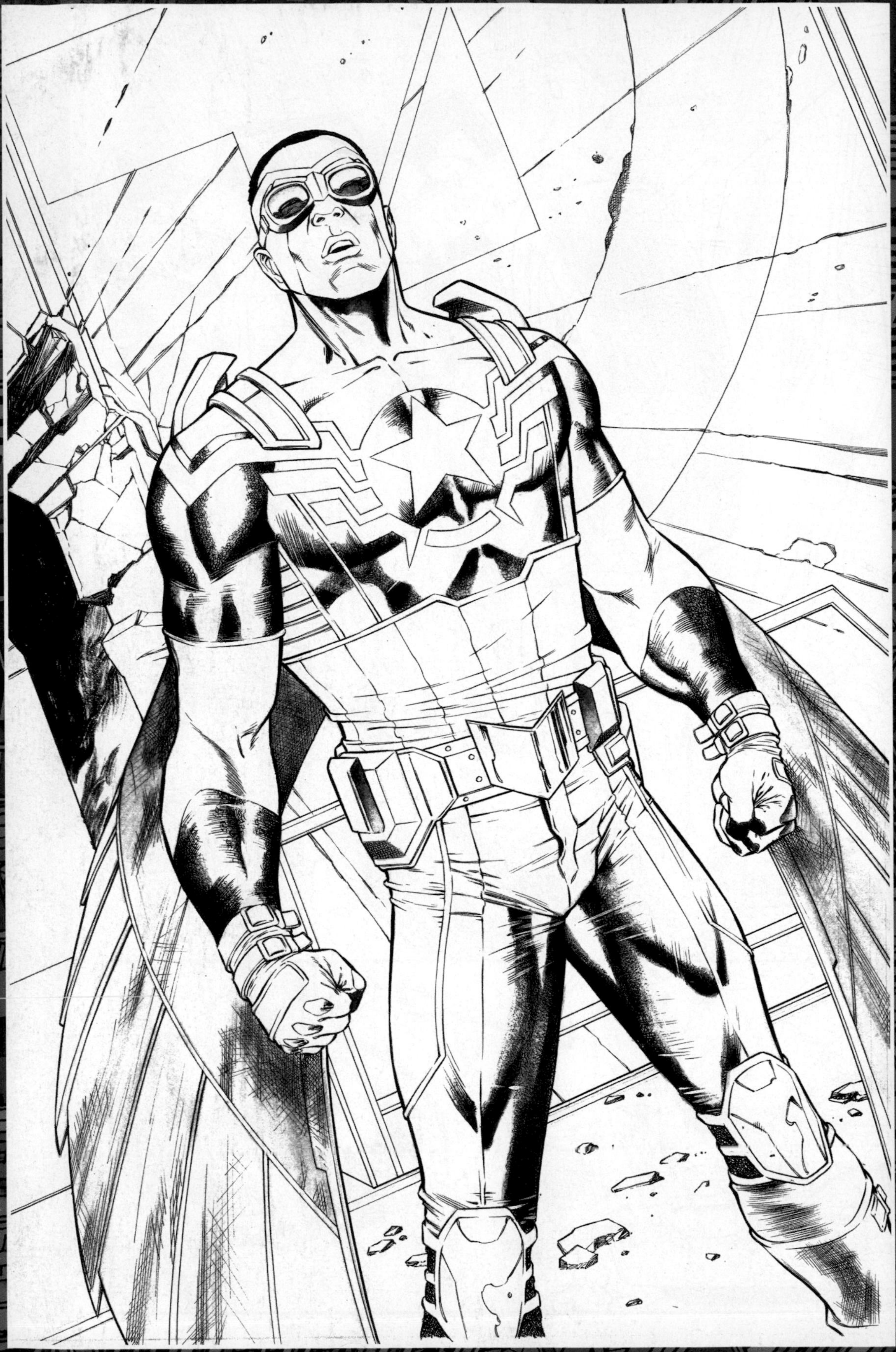

#25 PAGE 20 ART BY CARLOS PACHECO & MARIANO TAIBO

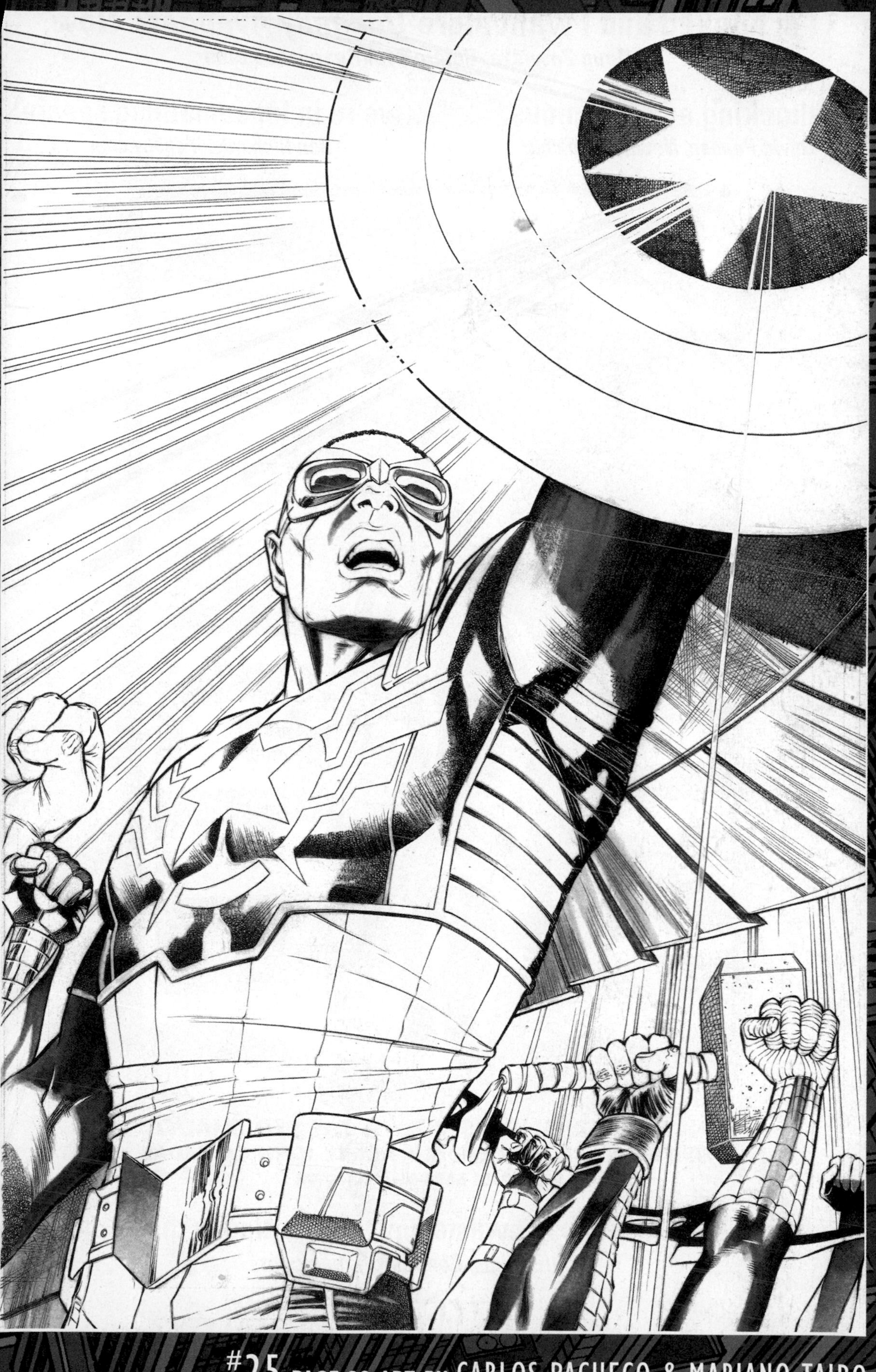

#25 PAGE 22 ART BY CARLOS PACHECO & MARIANO TAIBO

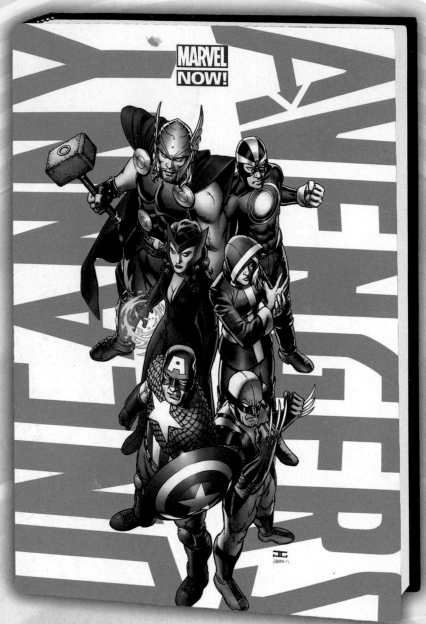